LIFE
IS NOT A
Rehearsal

ROSS HARTSHORN

DEDICATION

In memory of my wonderful sister Avron
who always told me that *Life is not rehearsal*,
and also, Mr Anthony O'Shea MC BA, a wonderful man
and a gifted headmaster of St Marks RC School, Harlow.
I will treasure memories of him and his family forever.

AUTHOR'S NOTE

This is my story, told from my point of view, about just some of the events that have happened to me. As with all things, I may not be 100% accurate but this book conveys what I remember as best as I can. Many of the names and settings have been changed in order to maintain the anonymity of the people concerned.

ACKNOWLEDGEMENTS

My most sincere thanks also go to:

Ron and Milly Bright
Diamonds set in 24 carat gold. Wonderful supporters.

John and Jane Lloyd
A window onto what true friendship is all about.

John Williams
My rock of support.

John Costello
My gift from Ireland, steadfast and true.

Frank Quarrell
*An extraordinary nonagenarian, as well as
being the best neighbour & friend.*

Tony Carter
*A man who arrived from nowhere and steered me away
from the gates of hell. We wouldn't have made it without you.*

Alan Moore
*The brilliant owner of Medlock Electrical Distributors Ltd. You changed
my life for so much the better – not once, not twice but three times.*

Susan Cohen (The Wee Book Company)
*Your words on the Magellan were inspirational
to me "Only you can write your Story".*

Mary Turner Thomson (Author of The Bigamist & The Psychopath)
*How lucky was I that Susan Cohen put me in touch
with this amazing editor and mentor.*

Karen Graham
*A partner of incredible patience and understanding, a very special lady
for whom I have nothing but the greatest love and admiration.*

PROLOGUE

It was the May Bank Holiday, 2014. The sun was shining brightly, and the garden looked beautiful. However, ominous storm clouds were not only gathering but had already arrived, delivering, without mercy, untold misery and devastation. Karen, my long-suffering partner, and I were sitting on the tree seat which encircled the willow at the bottom of our garden, each of us trying to enjoy a soothing cornetto.

As we sat there in a seemingly trancelike state, over and over again we tried to make sense of our seemingly hopeless and rapidly worsening situation. Our business was gone, we had a hefty mortgage that would be beyond us, meaning that we would forfeit our house. Neither of us had a job and our only income was my £600 per month pension. I was 67 and Karen was 61. The only guidance on offer from Citizens Advice and the DWP was that we should seek a privately rented room which, with zero financial assistance available to us, we could probably afford with my pension, although food might be a problem. Our beloved cats would, of course, have to go!

How had our situation spiralled into that abyss? What had I got so terribly wrong to cause that disaster? Could I have done things differently and avoided that dreadful end result? Or was it the end result that just had to be accepted and endured?

This is the story of the long journey which got me to that May Bank Holiday in 2014 and, indeed, the events that have followed on from that fateful ice cream in the garden until the present day.

CHAPTER 1

GRANDPARENTS

My father's parents owned their own house in Brynmawr, South Wales in the early 1900s. My father Ronald was born in 1914 and even then, his father Theophilus was a man of some importance in the St John's ambulance organisation and it was probably through this position that he became friends with James Grimston, the fourth Earl of Verulam. The First World War would have impacted upon my father's early life and as he entered his teens the great depression was about to engulf Great Britain and was to bring South Wales to its knees.

In 1919, 25 miles away in the village of Treherbert, in Brook Street, my mother Avice was born, the second youngest of seven children. My mother's mother died and her father re-married, a wife much younger than himself, a lady who turned out to be the stepmother from hell, according to my mother.

During the years of the great depression, from 1926 onwards, times were extremely challenging in South Wales with little in the way of support for anybody. Because my father's parents owned their own property and were considered well off, I remember my dad telling me that they were told to "eat your bricks and mortar".

So it was that at the age of 14 my dad left home to become a pageboy in a hotel in Worthing. We have a picture of him in his uniform and it is the archetypal picture of a pageboy in those times, in that he was very small in stature, barely 5 foot six when he was fully grown and not one bean over eight stone in weight. However, being from the valleys of South Wales, he was as hard as nails, a great gymnast, swimmer and boxer.

Whilst he was working in Worthing, he received news from his father, Theophilus, that James Grimston, the Earl of Verulam, had asked if he would be prepared to go to England and join the workforce of his newly founded company Enfield Cables, later to become Enfield Rolling Mills. So it was that in 1931 Ronnie joined that prestigious firm where he was to stay until his death in 1977.

My father was a very clever and skilled engineer and the most practical man you could ever wish to meet. He would be able to repair absolutely anything and, for his size, was an incredibly strong man. He was, like his father extremely altruistic and would do whatever he could for anybody who needed assistance. To that end he managed to get jobs at Enfield Cables for two boys from Brynmawr, Trevor Price and Arthur Flight, the latter being a foundling who was to go on to become my sisters godfather and marry his wife Alice, who made a name for herself in tailoring, rising to become a gown maker for the Queen.

At a similar time, around 1932, times were hard in my mother's household and the children were sent away to find work. Avice, my mother, arrived in Finsbury Park, London where she was to go into service for an orthodox Jewish family, Finsbury Park, then, as it is now, being a well-known area for the orthodox Jewish community. Here she was paid the good wage of two shillings a week (10p) which, of course, she had to send home.

In the middle 1930s there was a lot of unrest in London and it was a very tough area.

Money was tight and had to be earned any way it could. I remember my dad telling me how, when he and Arthur were in pubs, they used to goad the locals with the challenge "Us two will take you five on for a shilling". More often than not they would get hammered but, by the same token, they would win a hell of a lot of fights and take the money.

"Always get your retaliation in first," was my father's great advice to me – advice which was useful to me on more than one occasion in my life. Once, he told me, he was dared to jump off the roof of the house for a half a crown bet. He duly did it but smashed up both of his ankles at the same time - but he got the half crown.

I think it was written in the stars that my parents should meet and it was uncanny that they did so in Tottenham, when they were born only 25 miles apart in South Wales. They met in 1934 when my dad was 20 and my mum was 15. Four years later on April 9, 1938 they were married at Tottenham registry office and returned home to a brand-new third floor council flat in Ladysmith Road, barely a quarter of a mile away from the Spurs ground at White Hart Lane. They gave this flat the name Penbryn, welsh for "top of the hill". The date of the ninth was significant in my father's life because he was born on the 9th, married on the 9th and was later to pass away on the 9th of December 1977.

As I mentioned earlier, Ronald could turn his hand to anything and used his carpentry skills to make most of the furniture in the new flat. While working at Enfield Cables during the day, he would do shopfitting at night, working and saving hard to build a good and better life. Avice became "a nippy" in the famous Lyons corner house In the West End of London and she always told us how, even from the age of 12 when she first arrived at Finsbury Park, Londoners had always been hostile to her – "go home you bloody foreigner," was the stock remark, probably because the depression was deep and Londoners did not want people coming from Wales to take their jobs. Consequently, even in 1938, respect was not in great supply for a waitress coming from the valleys.

Her most amusing story arising from working in the corner house was that, on one occasion, when she was serving poached egg on toast to a table next to one where an obnoxious customer was continually demanding his bill in a very unpleasant manner, she lost her temper, tipped the egg over the man's face and then hit him on the head with her tray. Incredibly she was not sacked for this offence but was demoted to the wall station, which I think was pretty good management, especially in those times. It was after three years of marriage, in 1941, that my sister was born, and was ingenuously named Avron, half of Avice and half of Ronald. This name maintained its curiosity factor for all of her 79 years.

During the war years, 1939 to 1945, my father was in a reserved occupation, his company now designated to make shell cases for the military. This work involved actively dealing with the industrial grease remover trichlorethylene, exposure to which would have far reaching consequences for his health in later years. Desperate to do his bit for the war effort, he became an aircraft spotter and was stationed on top of the roof of the flats in Ladysmith Road, Tottenham where he watched for planes and doodlebugs. Residents would go to the underground air raid shelter in the park where, as my sister remembers, they would sing songs like "roll out the barrel". There were three new blocks of flats in Ladysmith Road, a road that runs parallel to the famous Tottenham High Road 50 yards away, and dad would tell of the night that a Luftwaffe plane flew down the line of the high road dropping its three bombs, my dad looking up from the rooftop while my mum was in the stairwell at the bottom of the flats with my sister in her arms. The first bomb missed the first block of flats where we lived, the second bomb destroyed the middle ones, while the third missed the last block - quite an experience!

Sadness was to follow in the last days of the war, however, during a time when my sister, who often spent time in Brynmawr with nanna and grandad in order to get away from the London bombing, was staying there. In 1944 there was an accident at a local factory in Brynmawr and Theophilus was the first responder on the scene. He had to run up several flights of stairs to perform the rescue and give first-aid and, although he managed to complete that task, the exertion proved too much for his heart and he died from a cardiac arrest, to the absolute devastation of Beatrice, my grandmother, and of course my sister, who worshipped the very ground that Theophilus walked upon.

So it was that I was destined never to meet not only my mother's parents, both now passed away, but also my wonderful grandfather Theophilus Hartshorn.

After all that sadness and the struggle of the war years, there was uncontrollable joy when I arrived on the scene on 1st October 1947.

CHAPTER 2

PRE-SCHOOL

My first four years of life were spent at Penbryn in Ladysmith Road, Tottenham, from which time I can actually remember a couple of things. I recall playing in the still existing air raid shelter, a big trench to me covered in corrugated roofing sheets. Apparently, as a baby, I was called "The Alderman" because I usually sat still alongside my teddy bear (which I still have by the way), and was very sedate and quiet while my demeaner was always very placid. I remember going to nursery in Tottenham and, on the way home, meeting my sister at the gates of her school - Down Lanes - which is still there today. In fact, when I took Avron to visit Ladysmith Road a couple of years ago, the flat was still there, recently renovated, and we visited Penbryn on the third floor. It certainly brought the memories of all the good times and good people flooding back to her, bearing in mind that she was 10 when we moved to Harlow.

My father was still working at the now called Enfield Rolling Mills at its base in Brimsdown, Enfield, while my mother worked for a company called Kores. In 1951 Kores opened a new factory in Harlow Newtown, Essex, an overflow town being built on the outskirts of London. People willing to move to Harlow with Kores were promised a new house in the town and, of course, that was the reason we moved. I can actually remember travelling to the new house in the removal van and meeting Avron and my parents there after they had travelled up on the motorbike and sidecar. Harlow was then a building site, without schools, shops and all other infrastructure and ours was one of the first areas to have residents move in.

Mum and dad had chosen 122 Churchfield, a house three down from the top of a block of nine terraced houses. We had a large green and a wood in front of the house, perfect for playing cowboys and taking part in games of rounders with all the other neighbours, adults and children.

Although still not complete, the only secondary school in Harlow at that time was Mark Hall, which was a secondary modern school and thus not suitable for my then high-flying sister. Therefore, to her dismay, she had to go to Herts and Essex High School for girls in Bishop Stortford which was not an experience she relished, and she went from being a top student to being a rather rebellious underachiever. In the meantime, the Spinney junior school had just been completed about 400 yards from our house in Churchfield, and so it was very easy for me to go there. In those days, parents did not escort their children everywhere and I was able, even at five years old, to go to school on my own.

Mr Angwin was the headmaster, alongside him his wife, who was his deputy. They were wonderful educators and mentors, people who really knew how to develop the children in their care and I was very lucky that they were there for me in those early years. When I moved from the infants to the junior school in 1955, my first teacher was Mrs Hammond. In those days learning times tables by rote was the key to success in education and certainly, in that first year, I knew all the tables up to 12 and displayed a reasonable gift for working with numbers.

On the home front, my sister was beginning to become very popular with the male sex, although her school work was going downhill at the same time. One Saturday evening she was playing, or rather flirting, with three of the boys who lived in the terrace opposite to ours. As far as I was concerned, she had become a prisoner in the end house opposite, held hostage by nasty teenage boys who, in order to prevent my daring rescue of her, had tied my hands and my feet together with thin twine so that, as I attempted to rescue her, I was forced to hop with my hands stretched out in front of my body. As I reached the then open door of her area of confinement, a door made half of wood and half of glass, it was suddenly slammed shut which resulted in my hands going straight through the pain of glass, creating a very loud smashing sound and a very loud reaction from me. A very wide and long cut snaked across my right inside wrist and it was fair to say that there was rather a lot of blood. The resultant screams from everyone around caused mum and dad to come running out of the house to see what was happening. Very few people had a car in those days and there were no medical facilities in Harlow and, while mum nearly passed out when she saw me, dad, well versed in first-aid, tried to stop the bleeding. Luckily someone spotted a car and flagged down the driver who kindly took me and my father to Epping hospital, where I had about 10 stitches placed in the wound.

This is a scar which I still bear today and, indeed, when I got my first passport, I delighted in writing in the section for distinguishing marks – scar right wrist, a real badge of honour! Suffice it to say but my sister, having survived her kidnap ordeal, somehow failed to learn the lesson that boys could possibly be dangerous, life changing beings.

Whether it was that incident or not, I'm not sure, but it was now that my father decided to upgrade his motorbike and buy our first car, an old 1950 Sunbeam Talbert, EJH 370, with headlights the size of dustbins and gangster running boards. We were the first ones in our area to own a car and my dad was now finally able to travel to work at Brimsdown without climbing into his flying suit motorbike gear every morning. Around this time, in my first year at junior school, it was noticed that I had, what was called, a lazy eye and I had to travel on the bus with my mother to the opticians in Epping for an eye test. Epping seemed like another continent away in those days and, after moving animated animals from one pen to another during the eye test, it turned out that I needed glasses, you know those fantastic round lens national health glasses, rather like the ones worn by Billy Bunter in the Greyfriars books by Frank Reynolds. I'd got the glasses but there was no way that I was going to wear them, and that was something that I managed to conceal from my parents for many, many years. Even when, at the last interview with Mr Angwin before I went to secondary school, they asked "how is he getting on with his glasses?", and Mr Angwin replied, "What glasses?" they realised that I wasn't wearing them, fortunately, over the summer holiday, somehow this was all forgotten and I continued to be glasses free throughout my time at secondary school.

From Mrs Hammond's care I progressed into Mr Davey's class, a teacher who was very much into arts and crafts, not really up my street, and we learned how to make pottery and oven gloves. In the autumn of 1956, I went into the fearsome Mr Bowen's class. This was the first real disciplinarian I'd ever encountered and we all learnt quickly how much better and easier it was if you simply did as you were told. I believe that my time spent under Mr Bowen at the Spinney was one of the biggest pluses at primary school because it prepared me for the no nonsense approach that would be on offer in the next stage of my education at Netteswell Grammar School. These were the days of free school milk and polio injections, not top of my list of favourite things. At that time, most of my clothes came from jumble sales, although I must say the quality of the garments was really very good, and I remember particularly a very fine mac that my mum purchased for me. In those days, plimsolls were handed out by the school for PE lessons and these were usually passed down from year to year. Somehow, I was always unhappy and uncomfortable about wearing other people's shoes and this is something that has always stuck with me and played on my mind, so much so that, later in life I even bought my own bowling shoes and ice skates in case I ever wanted to do either of these sports and had to hire the footwear. I still have both items today and indeed still use them both.

In the 1950s, winters in England were quite severe and, just after Christmas in 1957, when there had been an extremely hard frost and the roads were very icy. My dad was in the Sunbeam Talbot driving to work at Brimsdown at about 7am, having taken the route through Epping and turning right at the Wake Arms pub, going down a long winding incline towards Honey Lane. This road falls away very quickly on each side, with 20 feet sloping drops populated by bushes and trees. Because it did not hold the road very well, Dad lost control of the car and it came off the carriageway, rolling over and over until it came to a halt upside down against a tree. Mercifully Dad was okay, although in some pain around his chest area. Resourceful as ever, he walked to one of the farms neighbouring the road and got a farmer to right the car to pull him out of the wood with his tractor. The car was like a tank and was barely damaged and so he was able to get it and himself home safely, refusing to go to the doctors. Ronnie still managed to get to work that day but this accident had punctured his lung and exacerbated an underlying condition that now came to light. This was emphysema. That work during the war with trichlorethylene had made his lungs paper thin and this accident had inflamed a condition that he didn't even know he had, and to be honest, his health was never the same again.

CHAPTER 3

PRIMARY SCHOOL

My dad had always been a big participant in sports and particularly enjoyed playing cricket for Enfield Rolling Mills. In the late 50s the new sixth Earl of Verulam - this time John Grimston - also turned out to be a massive cricket fan and each year we would visit the stately home at Verulam for a match between Enfield Rolling Mills management and the workers team. There was always a magnificent spread laid on and I was very lucky that, from the age of 14, I actually took part in the match each year until I went off to university. Indeed, I still have a physical reminder from those games - a quite badly mangled middle finger on my bowling hand, sustained when a batsman from the Management team hit the ball back over my head for six and I foolishly tried to catch the ball on its way out of the ground – I got my hand to it as I desperately went for a catch. I suppose that I could count myself lucky that my finger, since then a sad and twisted affair, stayed on my hand.

I was a pretty reasonable off-spin bowler, having been taught that art from an early age by my dad. Indeed, I would practice for hours rebounding a bowl off our shed wall to perfect my off spin, as well as adding leg spin into my armoury. From the age of six, cricket had become an important part of my life and myself and my friend, Andrew Norton, who lived round the corner at 112 Churchfield, used to go to Ladyshot playing field each day on the way home from school where we would always be able to join in a cricket match with any of the many other likeminded children – no computer games in those days.

Two of these lads, brothers, were a bit older than us and lived next door to Andrew at 111 Church Field, their names were John and Michael Turner. John would precede me to Netteswell Grammar School, becoming an outstanding classical scholar before going onto Oxford University and achieving fantastic success, while his brother, Michael, went on to become a Catholic priest. However, it was John who was my inspiration and someone I really did try to emulate. Even at that early age I knew that I wanted to go to university, unusual for ordinary boys at that time, and then go on to become a cricketer.

I was to be given the present of a cricket manual containing all the facts and figures of every player dating back to the end of the Second World War. I learnt almost the whole thing off by heart and even now, without thinking I can tell you how many runs and centuries that Dennis Compton scored in 1947, along with hundreds of other bits of trivia about cricket. With all this cricket flowing through my veins, what should come along but the debut of 'Test Match Special' in 1957 a radio programme dedicated to covering Test cricket matches. I got hooked into listening to that station and have spent my lifetime searching out radios everywhere so that I never missed a ball. We were even allowed to listen to matches in The Spinney school hall and I am afraid I have been addicted ever since, a matter of great sadness for my now partner of more than 20 years, Karen, who simply cannot stand the game at all.

As I went into the final year of my junior school career, I moved into class 1 with Miss Harrison as my teacher. The Spinney was streamed and the final year pupils were split between class1 and class 2, so I was in the group able to do the 11+ exam, my first real educational challenge. I was delighted that I passed, along with quite a few others from class1, but I was the only one in the home area to achieve that distinction. This meant that I would go to Netteswell Grammar School while all the others in my area went to Mark Hall Secondary Modern School.

As 1958 progressed, I went with both of my parents for an interview at Netteswell and met my new headmaster Mr E P Bramfit. The new school was really impressive to me and had magnificent playing fields and, most of all, its own cricket square, something which I'd never seen first-hand before.

"What's the thing that makes you most want to come to school here?" said Mr Bramfit.

"I want to play cricket on a proper square," was my childishly excited reply, "plus I want to be as clever as John Turner."

I was really proud to have made it into Netteswell Grammar and I had a really wonderful time being a pupil at that school. When I returned to the Spinney for my last few months at primary level, Miss Harrison told me that I'd been appointed to be head boy of the school and I was completely overwhelmed and, even now, I regard this as one of the great honours of my life. Also, in that final summer of the Spinney, I discovered that I could run very fast, something I was aware of course, but then I'd never been in an actual race. I had always been interested in every sport as well as cricket, but although I liked football, for instance, I wasn't very good at it.

My sister had not long met a new boyfriend (now her husband of 60 years) and, true to form, my dad didn't think much of him at all. As far as my sister was concerned, he looked and dressed like Elvis Presley so that ticked all her boxes. Alan, her now husband, had a brother Mark and he used to take me to quite a few top football league matches - I remember especially going to games at Arsenal and Chelsea. The Busby babes were all the rage at that time and, sadly, I must admit that I was a bit of a Manchester United fan. In fact, Mark took me to Highbury to see Manchester United beat Arsenal 5 – 4 when my favourite player, Tommy Taylor, scored a hat-trick for United.

Tragically after that game came the Munich air disaster – where seven members of the Busby Babes, including Tommy Taylor, died among 21 people killed when their plane crashed on take-off. I recall coming in from school to that terrible news on 6th February 1958, and spending the evening next to the television set crying my eyes out. In those days, we were one of very few houses with a TV set, dad had got it in for the coronation in 1953, when everybody crowded into our living room, with the curtains closed, to watch the crowning of the Queen at Westminster Abbey - we only had one channel and it was only about a 12inch screen.

United went on to lose the FA Cup Final that year and Tottenham Hotspur, under their esteemed manager, Bill Nicholson, began to take centre stage. It was now that I did the right thing and changed my allegiance to my home-town club, as it were, and became a long term and faithful supporter of the aforesaid Tottenham Hotspur. Indeed, I'm coming up to my 50th year as a season ticket holder as I write.

At this time there were quite a few new primary schools in the Harlow area and the Education Authority decided to hold a District Sports Event on the playing fields of Mark Hall Secondary School. I would make my debut as a runner by competing in the 4th year Juniors 90 yards sprint race. I managed to achieve second place in this race and I built on that success and improved sufficiently to go on to become the district champion at secondary school level over 100 yards for the next five or six years. However, I remember qualifying for the county sports championships at one of the big National running tracks and, when I got there, I noticed that all the competitors had spikes whereas all I had was plimsolls. Also, everybody crouched down to do a sprint start while I just stood up normally. When the starter's gun sounded, all I could see was the backsides of everybody else in the race, they were a bit too quick for me!

During the summer holiday of 1958 another amusing incident took place including the whole family and the Sunbeam Talbot. We went out for a Sunday spin to a village called Hunsdon, probably only about 3 miles away but, in those days, seemingly almost the other side of the world. As dad drove down a country lane, we came across a ford, not very deep and only about 20m wide, easily navigable surmised my father. Well, it was a bit deeper than it looked. Although, in fact, probably only about 18 inches deep, the good old Sunbeam petered out right in the middle of the stream and my mother, not the calmest of people in a crisis, was, to say the least, rather panic stricken. As my dad took off his shoes and socks and rolled up his trousers to get out of the car, matters took an even more amusing turn for the worse when a herd of cows descended upon the scene. We now were faced with an abandoned vehicle, people paddling and about a dozen cows either bathing in or drinking the water.

A Samaritan came to the rescue, in the form of a man named Arthur Evans. He used his car to tow the Sunbeam clear of the ford and, not withstanding, after the rescue was completed, this man would make sure that we were always and forever in his debt. Certainly, it took a number of years to finally shake him from our lives and get some peace back. I don't think you could ever meet anyone who could ever borrow quite so many things and yet never return them.

CHAPTER 4

NETTESWELL GRAMMAR SCHOOL

Moving onto my time at Netteswell Grammar School, I was lucky that mum had managed to get me a smart, nearly new green Netteswell blazer to go with my first ever pair of long trousers. Dad had even got me a full-size second-hand Rayleigh bike, the one with the big chain guard, although initially I had great big wooden blocks on each of the pedals so that I could reach them. The day before school started, I decided to show off my new uniform and bike to the neighbourhood - big mistake! I hadn't thought through that I was the only Netteswell boy in the area, an area dominated by pupils going to Mark Hall. It was then that I received my first painful lesson in territorial loyalty and the hammering, I took that day certainly cemented my opinion of Mark Hall School, which, for the next 8 years, would be my sworn enemy on the rugby field.

The next day I met all my new Netteswell classmates who came mostly from Roydon, Nazeing and other outlying districts as well as from the newer areas of Harlow, Netteswell being situated near to the new town centre, which had not long been built and was not yet completed. I was very lucky to be a member of an extremely talented class with many of the boys and girls going on to be very successful in all walks of life. Names like John Pendleton, Gaye Crouch, John Sitch, John (Donald) Coleman, Beryl Nichol, Beryl Cairns, Francis Jarman, Jennifer Towers, John Ambrose and Linda Conlan still slip of my tongue without even thinking – they were such a great bunch of people.

Our first games lesson introduced me to rugby for the first time and, primarily because I was very quick and nimble, this turned out to be a great sport for me. Although a natural left footer, I had the advantage of being able to kick with my right foot as well and, for some reason, was able to chink past opponents very well. My position was flyhalf, no.10, and I became captain of the team and carried on being that for my entire rugby career at Netteswell.

Sport and study dominated my life and the school environment suited me down to the ground. I gained full colours in football, rugby, cricket, athletics and basketball and, along with my prefect's badge, the array of decorations on my blazer was very impressive. To say the least, as a class, we were way ahead of our time on the social side and seemed like a completely impromptu yet organised committee, able to carry out all kinds of events.

When we were 12, we organised a trip to Battersea Park to see the exhibition site and fair from 1951. We went from Epping on the tube, no parents just about a dozen of us on our own. We organised further trips to the West End and hired common rooms for parties where the boys, from the age of about 14, used to show off their manhood by displaying party seven cans of beer while boasting of their love of blues music from the likes of Steppenwolf and Muddy Waters. Strangely I was not into beer at all, I simply didn't like the taste of it. Smoking had no appeal to me either probably because, when I was about 7, my father, who smoked about 10 Players a day in spite of his health, taught me a life defining lesson.

He sent me to the Small Copper off-licence down the road to get him 10 cigarettes, quite amazing to think that in those days young children could buy almost anything without question. At lunchtime that day, a Saturday I think, we were having fish and chips for our lunch and Avron and I had walked up to the fish and chip shop in Penny Mead and bought four shilling fish and a shillings worth of chips, a meal for 4 for 25p in today's money. The chip shop was owned by the actor Larry Lamb's parents. Larry was in my class at the Spinney and was born on the same day as me, the 1st of October 1947. He always seemed to be wearing leather lederhosen, which was a subject of great mirth amongst the rest of us seven-year-olds.

After our lunch, dad was smoking one of those cigarettes that I bought him and I told him that I thought I deserved to have one too as I had had to go and get them. He agreed but said it would only be worth my while smoking one if I could get maximum enjoyment from it. With that he inhaled, took a sip of tea from his cup, swallowed it and then blew the smoke out of his nose. Now that's how you really enjoy a cigarette he said, time for you to try one. Then he passed me his cigarette and asked me to copy what he done. I inhaled and didn't get any further than that. I was immediately extremely unwell, shall we say, and that was my one and only experience of smoking, a lesson that has served me very well throughout my life.

During my first couple of years at Netteswell my sister had become very serious with her boyfriend Alan, who was a bit of a teddy boy and teddy boys liked to think that they were tough and scary. Alan was not only terrified of my father but also learned to be wary of me, only a 12-year-old but someone who could dish it out on the rugby field.

There is no doubt that my father was over strict with Avron, she had a 10pm curfew and my dad wanted to know everything she did and everywhere she went. Meanwhile I was happily getting on with my school work and at that time, I was given the choice of taking either Latin or German as my second language to French. I already was desperate to follow in the footsteps of John Turner and, when my sister told me that she had done German at Herts and Essex and that Latin was much harder, it confirmed my decision that Latin was the subject that I wanted to follow so that I could show that, not only was I cleverer than Avron, but also so that I could emulate John Turner.

My rugby was progressing well and I not only wanted to read classics at Oxford but also to become a rugby blue – I guess you must dare to dream and they were quite demanding dreams at that age. However, things at home were about to change dramatically when my sister announced that she was pregnant. Although she had probably underachieved at Herts and Essex, nevertheless she had accepted a good job with Harlow Council when she left school, and now this job and indeed her whole future was put in jeopardy. These were the days where you definitely did not have a child out of wedlock and my father, small but extremely fearsome and hard, left it in no doubt that Alan was to marry his daughter. This edict was obeyed without question and the council housed them in a maisonette in the Northbrooks district of Harlow, where they still live 60 years on. Avron gave birth to a son, Fraser, at home in her bedroom and I was there, downstairs, for the birth.

My sister told me that when I went in to see the baby I said, "Has he said anything yet?" It is quite difficult for me to grasp the fact that Fraser is now as quite as old as he is and, looking back, I believe that the complications and trauma of Avron and Alan's situation, coupled with the incredibly intransigent attitude of my father to it, had a far-reaching effect on me.

Back at school our class was so clever that the decision was made that we should all do "O" level maths a year early and progress with a an extra "A/O" level in Additional Maths in our list of subjects for the fifth-year exams. I really took to Latin, not only enjoying the subject but also because the Latin teacher, Mr Campbell, was really cool, a young sharpshooter jazz fan who was simply inspiring to our group of about 15 students.

At the end of the fourth year, after we'd all successfully overcome "O" level maths, the French department, led by Mr Hayes, organised an exchange trip to Montauban in the Tarn-et-Garonne region of France. I was a bit of a home bird and still rather shy, not particularly confident unless I was on the rugby field. My exchange student was a very tall guy named John Claude whose parents owned a fantastic bakery and this wonderful trip proved to be a turning point for me and, over the fortnight away from home, I developed lots of confidence and I even got a girlfriend, a very pretty girl named Edith Florens. This was a romance that seem to capture everyone's notice for some unaccountable reason, a romance we continued by letter for quite a few months afterwards, which was nice.

The upshot of the exchange was that I was awarded the prize for being the star pupil on the trip and, as my prize, I selected a book called "Teach Yourself Greek", an instruction which I carried out in full over the next few years until I sat the "A" level in it.

In our fifth year Mr Campbell left the school and we had a new Latin teacher called Barry Martin who was much more like your archetypal vision of a Classics teacher, rather nerdy with glasses and thinning hair, although he was again quite young and was groovy in his own way, even arranging a trip to a west end theatre to see the show "A funny thing happened to me on the way to the forum" starring Frankie Howard - we did have some really great times at school.

CHAPTER 5

RUGBY

As my rugby continued, I received the honour of being the youngest player ever to be selected for our First XV, I was still in the fifth year and a year below normal selections, although I was selected on the wing and not in my favourite flyhalf position. My debut in the First XV was in the derby match against Mark Hall, these were epic encounters and, even in those days, attracted crowds of a couple of hundred people. My father, who was now starting to suffer badly from breathing problems even though he was only in his mid-50s, used to support me everywhere I played and was my biggest fan. In a match against Brays Grove School, on the site where the new Passmores Academy was filmed for the BBC TV programme, during the game it was necessary for me to fall on the ball to defend against a breakaway Brays Grove attack. As I went down on the ball, I received a nasty kick to my forehead which all but knocked me out. This was at the beginning of the second half of the game and, after I received treatment, I staggered over to where my father was watching from on the touchline and told him that I was feeling extremely dizzy.

"Finish the bloody game" he said and then we'll have a look at you afterwards. I did just that but, at the end of the game, I passed out before I could leave the field, and was immediately taken to Epping hospital in one of the PE teacher's cars. Unfortunately for him I was sick all the way to the hospital and, indeed, was told later that the teacher had been forced to sell the car because he could not get rid of the smell pervading the vehicle. An X-Ray at the hospital revealed that I had a hairline fracture of my forehead just above my right eye, so a stay overnight and a rest from playing for a month was ordered, and then I would be okay to carry on, although I still have a bump on my head to this day, adding to my list of badges of honour. We won the game by the way,

O-level time came and went and I believe that the whole of the class got at least 10 O-levels each, with me ending up with 13, including a couple of general papers and Greek, which I had, of course, taught myself. I decided to do Latin, History, and English at A-level - sciences would've probably been the better option but I don't think I was really practical or clever enough for those subjects, the complete opposite to my father who was a much cleverer man than I ever imagined and certainly on a different plane to me when it came to being practical. Now I made a critical and who knows wrong or right decision to try and get into Oxford like my hero John Turner, firstly to read classics and secondly to see if I could achieve a blue in rugby. To do this I would need to do not only two years in the six form, lower and upper, but also continue on into a third year sixth in order to prepare for and do the entrance exams, bearing in mind that I had to get to the A-level standard in Greek. The Oxford entrance exam involved a lot of study in the subject of ancient history and this would help me later when I got to university. Clearly the grammar school system had a hierarchy of prefects who progress from being junior prefects in the fifth year to full prefects in the lower and upper six and then finally, if you were lucky enough, you became head boy or head girl with appointed deputies, and the next 18 months would determine how far up the line I could get.

Until the end of the fifth year, we had a great rugby coach in the person of geography teacher Dick Roberts, another Welshman who was to be my mentor throughout the first five years of rugby and, because of the closeness of my father to me and both being Welsh I suppose, the two became great friends. Dick Roberts was a big noise in the Harlow Labour Party and went on to become a renowned and successful mayor of Harlow - quite ironic really as I went on to become a Conservative activist and lifelong supporter of the Conservative party. In fact, Dick Roberts left teaching to go into politics full time and moved on at the end of that school year in 1964 and the new PE teacher, Ralph Hindle, took on the First XV of which I now became the Captain. All the players had a great relationship with Ralph and we played some big matches against other top-notch grammar schools in the south-east, with the derby match against Mark Hall always the major highlight of the season. Clearly each school year has its own star and there were two or three really good players in the years below me who were waiting to take their chance to get into the first 15 reckoning.

In the early months of my time in the Lower Sixth I did some work experience for a month at Little Parndon Junior School in Harlow, learning to work with junior age children and getting to know the ropes of teaching. I really enjoyed doing this and got a great deal of satisfaction from the experience and it was, in fact, to set me up for what I was going, by sheer chance, to do in the future. To complement this experience, back at Netteswell, I became an assistant to the form teacher of a new intake class at the school, helping take the register and other basic tasks the class teacher would do. The member of staff I was helping was another very cool dude of a teacher named Mr Callaghan and, looking back, I realise just how lucky we were to have quite so many cool and inspirational teachers at that school – perhaps they rubbed off on me so that I became one of them in the future. Of the same ilk as my previous hero Mr Campbell, Mr Callaghan taught English and was known to all his six form students by his Christian name, Vic. I remember in his English classes we did loads of analysis about advertising as well as the usual curriculum of Shakespeare plays.

CHAPTER 6

SIXTH YEAR

During this time the prefects set up a detention system at school and five of us took turns in supervising the detention one night a week. This detention included all ages up to the fifth year and it was when I was in charge of one of these gatherings that I met a young lady with a terrible reputation for disruptive behaviour with a penchant for causing mayhem no matter what class she was in. Her name was Jennifer Wildish, and she had the most incredible long, almost white hair which she always wore in a ponytail. Her best friend and confidante was Vic Callaghan's daughter Elizabeth, who was a little bit akin to what might be called a goth in today's parlance. Talk about opposites attract, I fell in love with Jennifer at first sight, she was absolutely stunning and her rebellious attitude was infectious, meaning that I could not help myself and fell completely under her spell, although she clearly had as little interest in boys as I had in girls. For the next few weeks, I ensured that she was in my detention every time I was on duty. Jennifer always wanted to be on the stage and was a vibrant extrovert and over this period of her constant attendances at detention we actually hit it off big time and became very friendly. Then the PE department arranged a school trip to Twickenham to see the rugby international between England and South Africa. Unbelievably I plucked up enough courage to ask Jennifer to the game and, even more unbelievably, she said she would come.

As we met at the coach on that Saturday morning the gulps of disapproval and disbelief were palpable. Here was one of the top boys, possibly being in the running to become head boy, going on a date with perhaps the worst behaved and most uncontrollable girl in the whole school, nothing short of scandalous! I remember that Jennifer was wearing a John Lennon type leather cap, bearing in mind that The Beatles were all the rage then. She was, unquestionably, the prettiest girl you could ever wish to see and there was absolutely no doubt that I was completely smitten with her. This initial date was the start of a four-year romance in which I fell totally in love with her - they say that first love is everlasting and this was the first time I had ever had feelings like this, feelings over which

I had no control and, when I persuaded her to wear her hair down, she looked even more beautiful and was just perfect in every way. Tragically a devastating event in Jennifer's life was about to happen and it started when her friend Elizabeth Callaghan was reported missing. Several days later Elizabeth was found murdered. As you can imagine, Jennifer was completely distraught as was the whole school including, of course, her father and our teacher, Vic Callaghan. It was the most shocking of events and it took a great deal of getting over for everyone in the whole school.

My relationship with Jennifer grew stronger and I bought her the record "Wild Thing" by The Troggs and the lyrics of that song summed up everything I felt about her. Unfortunately, my relationship with Jennifer was not all that well received by the hierarchy at the school and although I'd always been favourite to become head boy, what with my sporting and academic achievements along with my alleged leadership qualities, my hopes were completely scuppered. John Sitch, a great guy in my class and nothing short of a spectacular genius in maths who was very close to getting a scholarship into Oxford to read higher maths, got the extra push he needed when he was appointed head boy, with myself and John Coleman as his deputies. I do believe there was a lot of surprise at that decision but, in the end, it was the right one and I was very happy for John. Indeed, when we had a class reunion at the age of 65 at The Hare pub in Harlow, a get together organised by Gaye Crouch, John Sitch flew in especially from the United States, where he is one of the top mathematicians in the country, to join us as a wonderful surprise arrival. Amazingly he had five sons all of whom, I was told, were in top-flight sporting action in the NFL – so great! I really did have the privilege of knowing a lot of really fantastic people in my time at Netteswell and, at the reunion, where 15, or 16 of us managed to attend, we worked out that happily only a few of us had died.

Following the ghastly murder of Elizabeth, Jennifer threw herself into acting, she joined the Moot House Players and starred in lots of school plays which were well renowned events locally. She even got me to take part in the play Julius Caesar, in which I played no less than three parts - a centurion, sadly leading an army that ran out of stage before it could be seen, a nobleman with no lines and, as Flavius, speaking the very first words of the play and whose words I can still recite now, some 50+ years on – "Hence home you idle creatures, get you home. Is this a holiday?"

I achieved my three A-levels in English, History and Latin and proceeded into my third year sixth, a rarity then as now, as I was coming up to my 19th birthday. Now I was the only pupil in that year and all of my class had gone off to university. While I was determined to go after that Oxford place, I thought I would also be an asset to the rugby team with all my experience, knowing full well that I would need to step aside to make way for a new captain. Ralph Hindle had moved on from Netteswell and his deputy in the PE department, Mike Pollard, moved up from being in charge of the lower age groups' teams to take on the First XV. With him he brought a new intake from the fifth year and a couple of his former stars who played under me when they were in the Lower Sixth. Mr Pollard and I did not get on at all and, after playing me at full-back in the first two games, he informed me that he thought it was fair that he gave other players a chance and would not be considering me for future matches.

I felt greatly let down and spurned but I certainly was happy to sever all relations with Mr. Pollard and moved on quickly to join Harlow Rugby Club, playing at fly half for them until I went off to university. I worked hard on my Greek and towards the Oxford entrance exam in that year but I did also spend a lot of time with Jennifer and we had a great loving relationship. She was now doing English and drama at "A" level and had transformed herself into a model student. From my point of view sadly it turned out that I was not good enough to get into Oxford and that just proved to me just how clever and brilliant John Turner must have been. Unfortunately, I failed the entrance exam but, luckily, I had the backup of an unconditional offer at Queen Mary College, University of London, now known as Queen Mary University. I had to come to terms with the fact that I had wasted a year and had put myself a year behind where I should have been, but I did spend irreplaceable time with Jennifer and I'll take that all day long. During that last summer following school, my dad let me borrow the car and Jennifer and I went on holiday to Newquay for two weeks. My dad had taught me to drive in his dream car Rover 2000, a top car in those days, and he had given me hundreds of lessons over an eighteen-month period. In fact, I had driven back and forth to Wales four times before I took my test while my friends had all passed their tests within weeks of their 17th birthdays.

Dad used to say "It's my car you will be borrowing so I'll decide when I think you can drive," and, needless to say, I passed my test first time in the afore mentioned Rover 2000.

When Jennifer and I went to Newquay we had great dreams about sleeping in the same room together but when we got to our bed and breakfast, the helpful landlady didn't think we were old enough to share a room and put us in separate rooms. We didn't have the guts to argue with her about it, although we did sneak about at night and succeeded in breaking those rules. One romantic night out in Newquay was to provide a memorable highlight when I took Jennifer to a really nice restaurant in the town and we ordered an expensive steak dinner each. Surprisingly and disappointingly the quality of the food was not all that good and Jennifer said to me that if her father had been served that meal, he would have most certainly sent it back to the chef. I called the manager over and, having informed him of our dissatisfaction with the meal, his reaction was swift and decisive and he instructed us to leave the restaurant forthwith. I felt totally deflated having looked a complete wimp in front of Jennifer but, evidently, I didn't have the presence or confidence to get my message across. A bit too young and wet behind the ears I'm afraid, but something to gain valuable experience from. Of course, It did not matter a jot to Jennifer and we actually laughed about it as a hilarious part of our holiday.

That summer was amazing and I remember the Beatles' song "All you need is love" constantly ringing out across Newquay's Fistral beach. I was completely in love with this most beautiful and kindly girl and so it was that when, in October 1967, I left home to go to Queen Mary College, I felt far more pain than I did excitement as I was leaving behind the most important thing in my life, the girl I loved.

CHAPTER 7

OFF TO UNIVERSITY

As I came from Harlow, my home was deemed too near to the University for me to get a place in the halls of residence at South Woodford, the college being situated on the Mile End Road in London. I did think it was time to see if I could survive independently and I was allocated a room with Mr and Mrs Albury in River Way near Loughton tube station.

On my application form seeking residence advice I had, as you do automatically, listed my religion as Methodist and as Mr and Mrs Albury were staunch members of the Loughton Methodist community and were seeking a lodger, they were happy to accept me as their paying guest. Settling in at QMC, the first term concluded with an exam to confirm whether or not we were good enough to stay on to complete the three-year course. Although I was reading Latin and Greek, a large element of the first term course involved ancient history and this meant that all the work that I had done preparing for the Oxford entrance exam actually proved very worthwhile. For myself I found that I had to work very hard at the course and the translations proved very demanding. We were studying Homer and Xenophon for the Greek section and Cicero and Tacitus for the Latin one, 4 difficult authors. There was, however, not a single day that went by without me writing to Jennifer. I really missed her. She was only 30 miles away but it seemed like the other side of the world and it was almost like she wanted to treat it like a test to see if we could survive apart.

I managed to pass my first terms exams and got into the squad for the rugby team for the college, but here there were a lot of star and I mean star players - suddenly I was not the standout player anymore and had to be satisfied to play when I was picked. I can explain to you the standard of the team I was playing in when I tell you that the then current England international Alan Old had been the previous flyhalf in the QMC team.

As the year progressed into the second and third terms Jennifer was getting more and more involved in her drama although she did answer every single one of my letters, replies which, very sentimentally I have kept safe. Even when I was at the school Jennifer had always been close to another one of her acting fraternity, a boy named Edwin and his interests were diametrically opposite to mine. He had always been in her class at school and it would never have crossed my mind to consider him a threat to our relationship in spite of their apparent closeness. Looking back, I think this was the right call but, at the time my jealousy told me otherwise. I cannot for the life of me work out why our relationship collapsed but after that first summer vacation our, or my, true romance had broken down and I was completely destroyed. The love that I held for Jennifer was absolutely immense and despite my complete devastation I managed to keep going.

It helped that I got a job as "a picker" up at Standard Telephones Electrical Services Department. I had great fun winding up other members of staff by working too quickly, and also having fun delivering goods in the firm's minivan. I was good at saving and I started to put money away to see if it could be used in some further adventures while I was a university student. Actually, I returned to ESD to work for the Christmas vacation as well, getting together more money for what was coming over the horizon.

As I entered the second year at university, we had to pick one special author to concentrate on and one associated non- linguistic study area, these two choices would run alongside all the other translation work we had to do. I now visualised myself as heading towards a career in archaeology and the choices that would help on that path were, the author Lucretius, who 25 years later I would name a horse after, and Roman history. Lucretius was an Epicurean philosopher who practised the lifestyle of "live for today" a mentality that teaches you to just get on with life and deal with problems as and when they arise. I absolutely believe that Lucretius had a big influence in shaping the direction of my life and the way that I have always lived it, as did the strange contrast choice of Roman history as my other subject, which taught you a lot about learning lessons from your mistakes. Hopefully the combination of these two gave me a balance which has helped me to remain optimistic in life and made it possible for me to deal with quite a lot of ups and downs.

Sadly, for me, in the second rugby match of the new season playing for QMC against the Met Police, having made a terrific break through centre field, I was poleaxed by a serious hamstring tear. I'd never had a bodily injury before, I'd had lots of concussions and other bangs to the head but never a physical injury as such. The pain was indescribable and, literally, I could not walk. The injury was serious and I had many months on the side lines but, satisfied that I had recovered, I decided to play in a football match between the Latin and English departments. The very first time I kicked the ball the injury reoccurred and my future as a sporting icon disappeared in that moment for me. Now cricket was my only option coupled with a bit of jogging here and there. On the academic front, competition in every day studies were fierce and the Lucretius special subject demanded the assistance of one extremely special book. Unfortunately, there was only one copy of this book and quite simply everybody on the course wanted it. The copious QMC library was policed by an old dragon of a librarian assisted by a very attractive 19-year-old trainee called Susan. I have never seen a girl with such long hair in all my life, it was literally almost down to the ground and styled in a long red Indian style plait. She was extremely attractive – my taste is always impeccable, shame about me - but very aloof and very curt and all the male students tried to chat her up, all with the intention of obtaining this special book, a book with all the answers to the mysteries of Lucretius. With my appalling record with girls, I wasn't confident that I would have any chance of charming her but using my cheeky chappy approach I gave it a shot and asked her for a date. To my absolute amazement she agreed to come out with me and we dated for quite a few months but this had given me victory in the book quest and I got much street cred on campus because of that. Whatever my shortcomings, up to this time at least, I had a very good taste in women and always seem to pick the gorgeous ones. When I took Susan home to meet my parents, they too thought she was lovely but of course I had no track record for making the running and this would work against me in the very near future.

One evening, as I took her home and we travelled on the train to her house near Romford, between stations, being the only two in the carriage, she decided to become very amorous and started kissing me very hard indeed. Sadly, my automatic reaction was to recoil in shock and I simply was not confident enough to respond to her affections. The end result was that we both felt mortified and didn't feel comfortable with each other after that. I then realised that I still had the book but couldn't take it back because Susan was always in the library and I was too embarrassed to go in there apart from very late at night when she'd gone home. To my utter disgrace, I found this book in the loft the other day so, clearly, I never returned it to the library – can you imagine what the fine would be if I took it back now, impossible!

At QMC I had met a very clever boy again from the valleys of Wales named Alan. Alan was also a passionate cricket lover and we devised various ways of playing cricket with rolled up newspaper and rolled up paper balls, constantly upsetting the other students in our common room. Alan actually fell in love with his landlady while at college, even though she had four or five children and, indeed, he ended up marrying her after graduating. The two of us heard of a new organisation called BUNAC, the British Universities North America Club, who were doing a return trip to JFK airport in New York with the promise of work during that vacation, all for £69 return. This is something that not only did we gave serious thought to doing but actually decided to press ahead with. A life changing escapade! Seeing as my options for clubs and societies were somewhat limited in that I couldn't participate in any sporting activities, I joined the Conservative Association at the college, not many students are on that side of politics but I wasn't very much in favour of the left-wing agenda of the very active LSE students who were quite influential and rather over-zealous at that time. Alan and I did join the ballroom dancing Society but an incident involving split trousers and the consequential embarrassment cut that particular activity short.

CHAPTER 8

OFF TO USA

So it was, that early in June 1969 we set off for Gatwick for our American adventure. The job we had enlisted for was one which promised a very high wage - tobacco picking in Canada in the province of Ontario. That job started at the end of July, theoretically giving us time to do a bit of travelling, ending up making our way to Toronto for the last six weeks of the holiday until mid-September – hopefully to make our fortune. This was my first time on an aeroplane. When I had travelled to Denmark with my parents during my years at primary school, we had gone once by sea to Copenhagen and once across the channel and then by train all the way to the Danish capital. Before we went, my dad imparted to me the story of when he flew to Denmark on a consultancy job for Enfield Rolling Mills. The plane developed engine trouble and crash landed at Heathrow after being forced to turn back. He recounted how all the passengers got off the plane and got on another one straightaway and off they went to Denmark. Then, later that year when he went by sea with my mother to visit the friends he made in Denmark, the ship caught fire in the North Sea and had to be evacuated onto small fishing vessels. He told me that my mother kept saying "I'm not getting onto that tiny little boat." She did though and they were safe. You could say that my family has had its fair share of interesting escapades.

My first flight, a long one to start, was on Aer Lingus. The thing about Aer Lingus then, and I don't know if it is the same now, was that Aer Lingus flights could not overfly Ireland, they had to land in Dublin - no one would get off and then the plane would retake off. I was, I must admit, very nervous when it came to take off time. Alan and I were at the very back of the aircraft. No alarms, exciting and exhilarating, we were in the air! Oh dear 20 minutes in and the pilot made the announcement that we had to return to Gatwick immediately because a warning light had lit up on his instrument panel. This didn't do much to help the heart rate of all the passengers, let alone me! We landed safely at Gatwick and were all shipped off to the Grand Hotel in Brighton for the night. I have never seen such luxury! By the way, this was the hotel where the IRA tried to kill Margaret Thatcher with a bomb.

Next day, we set off again and took off from Gatwick, we landed briefly in Dublin and, about seven hours later, arrived in New York. Our ticket included a one-night stay in a hotel in New York City, I remember it was on the side street opposite Macy's. We were on the 20th floor, again and amazing new experience for me, now knowing for the first time that heights were definitely not my thing. We made a beeline for the Empire State building and this was our first real adventure in the USA.

A lift moving so fast you just reach the top of the building in the blink of an eye, an unimaginable view and the feeling that will never leave me. Absolutely fantastic.

Next day we were on our own, two very naive and inexperienced lads with the whole of the United States to choose from. For some unaccountable reason we decided to get on the Greyhound bus and travel to Atlantic City New Jersey, home of the famous boardwalk, made legendary by the pop group 'The Drifters'. As we got off the bus the first thing I saw, which I should really have noted and made a fortune from, was a pay on the spot car park. Cars were still not very numerous in England at that time and I had never seen a pay for parking car lot. It was mind-boggling!

Across from the bus depot was the food outlet called Whitetower - the menu was full of the unknown to me - we ordered, would you believe, a hamburger - a very strange and completely unknown delicacy to us. It came in a bun, with a burger on top of lettuce, a huge ring of tomato and another huge slice of raw onion - what a treat. We found a ramshackle, wreck of a hotel nearby and managed to get a room, in other words a bed in a small box. So that we could get work, we had collected our Social Security numbers which we had registered for when we got our visas at the American Embassy in Grosvenor Square. Another strange coincidence this, because in the last few years I have done numerous deliveries of electrical goods for contractors working at the new American Embassy in Nine Elms Lane Battersea. It really is a very small world.

Alan and I needed work to support ourselves in Atlantic City and we found employment at the big Howard Johnson's hotel. We got a 12-hour shift washing dishes, not as mundane as it seems because we were behind a huge multifunctional washing up machine. The bus boys would bring their boxes of dishes and waste to one end of the machine where Alan stood and remove the rubbish before sending the bus box on a conveyor down past me. I would then have to quickly put the plates and other china in one porthole and glass ware in another. The machine would go through a couple of fazes before the clean crockery etcetera was unloaded at the far end by a third guy. It was pretty constant stuff, and we did get quite a few breakages when we were busy - it was quite good fun to smash the occasional glass to relieve the stress. It was at Howard Johnson's that I did learn that all is not perhaps quite as it seems at posh hotels. I remember, on more than one occasion, the revolving door that the waiters went through to take and serve the food to the customers would cause collision accidents where food would fall to the floor in view of the customers. The waiter would apologise, pick it, come back through the door, count to 5 and then put the same food back on the plate and re-serve it. Delicious! We were quite enjoying ourselves working in Atlantic City, the money was good and we got to know several nightspots. I was experiencing discos for the first time - floors made up of flashing light squares and psychedelic decorations. This was hippy time and my hair was getting extremely long and my array of clothing started to change. There was a big drug scene at the clubs, but always having been pretty strait laced and not smoking or drinking, I honestly wasn't tempted at all. This might have been because back at QMC, in the halls at Woodford, a student had taken LSD and decided to fly from the top of one high-rise block to the top of the block next door- he died after 100-feet fall. This was not for me!

We did have one unusual encounter at a club where we did a lot of dancing with one particular girl. At the end of the night, she told us she had nowhere to go and would have to come back to our room to spend the night.

Alan, who had by now a lot more experience than with women than me, having been satisfying his landlady from the word go at college, was very keen that we did not refuse her. Suffice it to say that I did learn a little bit that night, not by choice you understand. It was however a one off and she was gone next morning. It was free love days and she was obviously working her way around the country. Our hotel was a bit of a hovel but it did have a TV lounge, and a couple of days before we were leaving for Toronto, we came home from work to witness the moon landing on the TV. That was the 20th of July 1969. It was phenomenal and to witness it in the United States made it extremely special - pride and nationalism doesn't even come close to describing it. We had done well at Howard Johnson's, we even had bank accounts at the bank of America in Atlantic City.

CHAPTER 9

WOODSTOCK

We booked a standby flight to Toronto to get there in time to start making our fortune tobacco picking at the beginning of August. When we landed, we got a bus to the farm where we had reserved employment. I don't remember quite where it was in relation to Toronto but certainly not that far away. When we arrived, we met eight other English students who had also been signed up for the work. As we were all taken to the pretty comfortable bunkhouse we would be staying in, we received a lot of abuse from some wizened old French-Canadians who felt that we had taken their jobs. They would have the last laugh! There were six concrete steps down into the bunk house and we had a bunk each. One of the new guys that we met, named Ian I remember, bragged that he had gone to Gordonstoun school in Scotland before university and that he had been in Prince Charles' class. He said it was the toughest school in Great Britain and it had taught him to be as hard as nails, both physically and mentally. We were given yellow plastic coverall suits ready for picking and informed that we had to go up and down the 200 metre lines of tobacco plants picking the leaves from the bottom first. These were the biggest leaves, most mature, and had to be picked first while the others going up to the top of the plant would develop and mature during the picking season. Each day our job would be to fill the kiln house or tobacco barn completely before we could finish work. This was going to turn out to be the nightmare of all jobs you could ever imagine. Day one, and we were out amongst the plants at 5 am. Bent double to get to the base of the plants we picked and picked, our suits turning blacker and blacker as the nicotine stained them throughout the day. It took the 10 of us until 8 pm to fill the kiln house and when we returned to the bunkhouse, we were completely black and could barely walk. Gordonstoun Ian fell down the stairs into the bunkhouse and was immediately out of action for the next day. The remaining nine of us just about managed to drag ourselves to the fields at the next crack of dawn but by the time the midday sun was beating down on us we were all but done in. Somehow, we struggled on and filled the kiln house by about 9.30pm. We had probably taken the bottom four layers of leaves from the tobacco plants - definitely the hardest part of the work because they were so low down and we were bent double also encountering all the foul nicotine extract from the upper leaves. This was a vital crop for the farmer - we were simply not up to the job. We were summarily sacked and thrown out of the bunkhouse. Those sneering French-Canadian labourers swooped in to take the jobs, still bloody hard work, but a bit easier now the bottom leaves were off.

The 10 of us split into two groups of five and our group managed to get back to Toronto. We had the two day's pay from the tobacco farm and Alan and I still had money from Atlantic City. We needed a few days rest and a bit of time to consider what to do. More than a week into August with six weeks still to go before our return to England we headed for the campus of Toronto University which was letting out rooms during the summer vacation. We managed to secure a room for two people but the other three of us entered by the window so that we had a refuge for five for the price of two.

Gordonstoun Ian and his two friends decided to head off to Vancouver, but Alan and I were not so adventurous. We decided to go back to what we knew and got another very cheap standby flight back to JFK so that we could return to Atlantic City, and perhaps get more work in Howard Johnson's. We were here to earn money as well as to travel. These were cool times - music and free love was everywhere. We had heard about a big festival coming up and when we landed at JFK we joined the throngs of people heading towards a dairy farm in Bethel, upstate New York. We were off to Woodstock! We had become a lot groovier and almost looked the part. It didn't matter we were just lost in a sea of people. I can't say that I saw or heard much of the music, but I did experience Jimi Hendrix and really fell in love with Joan Baez.

CHAPTER 10

STREET EDUCATION AND FINALS

Crosby, Stills, Nash & Young also performed there and they would give me serious credibility when I returned to the states the following year, although I did not see them in person. Alan and I got back to Atlantic City with about a month of our stay remaining and we got a room at a different hotel, right at the far end of the boardwalk, it was in a street called Ocean Avenue. There was no work available at any of the hotels so we walked up the boardwalk as far as an amusement area on a famous site called The Million Dollar Pier. Onto the pier we strode and touted for work. We were in luck Alan got a job selling tickets for the rides and I replaced a guy who had just been sacked from a small side stall called The Popguns. These guns actually fired corks which, if on target, would knock ping-pong balls off the top of Coke bottles, Coke being something else that I was encountering for the first time. I thought I looked pretty cool with my long hair and flared jeans but my biggest advantage was my English accent. I spoke reasonably well in those days, not like the lazy cockney which Karen says I sound like now. I was taught a very simple sales pitch - "4 shots a quarter, 3 off you win"- something I was shouting in my sleep within a week. I think it was the accent rather than me but my stall attracted a non-stop line of, it must be said, mostly female customers who couldn't shoot, but it was also visited by a lot of typical American guys who believed that they were a better shot than John Wayne, Americans and guns just go together. Unfortunately for these sharpshooters, corks tend to follow an unpredictable trajectory when fired from a popgun and so I didn't lose that many prizes. The prizes were actually the biggest cuddly toys I had ever seen, including a dog with glasses called Snoopy, who apparently was very famous in the USA but I'd never heard of him. I thought I was doing very well on my stall and my takings were really good, however, at the end of my third day's work, and we worked from midday to midnight on the Pier, the guy who ran the stall next to mine, the water pistol game, jumped into the space behind my counter in order to have a very strict word with me.

"This stall takes $200 a day" he said.

"I'm doing a bit better than that I think" I replied.

He repeated "This stall takes $200 a day," and this time his message, aided by a very aggressive demeanour, got through to me. What he was actually letting me know was that all the stalls had over the years had had their takings compared and rationalised so that the Pier owners knew exactly what ratios of success they had. For example, a great stall like the water pistols would normally take at least three times the amount that the popguns took because it was a more fun game and, if my stall suddenly started doing particularly well, it would put all those figures out a bonk. I was politely told that any money over the $200 mark had to remain undeclared by me and consequently I was taught how to keep a check on the amount of money coming into my stall as well as counting the number of prizes I lost, something that was already required. The guy didn't care if I cut the takings by not bothering to work hard but politely suggested that I could remove any excess money to my own advantage.

Education then gratifyingly followed on how to change the extra quarters into large denomination notes that could be removed easily at the end of the shift. Basically, the whole Pier was a money train for the guys who worked there, and I discovered that they all had dream homes in Florida and drove Cadillacs - not bad for a summer season on the well named Million Dollar Pier. In those few short weeks, I learned a lot about palming money, giving customers the wrong change and selling prizes for good money. You could say that the real world was beginning to have a serious impact on my life. I remember that the top man amongst the stallholders was a guy called Merrell, a really nice man who luckily liked me but these guys were tough and hard as nails and you did what exactly what you were told to keep them happy. My mate Alan, of course, was a bit sick because just selling tickets meant that he couldn't pull any strokes and just slogged it out for wages. In my three-week stint on the Pier I managed to collect over $1,000 to bring home, so my trip to the USA had actually produced the money I went there hoping to earn and I vowed to return the following year and have another bash. When I returned to England to conclude my final year at QMC I realised that I could do a large part of my work from home and, although I would go to college about three times a week, I decided to leave my digs at Loughton and return home to live with my parents.

We still had the Rover 2000, still a pretty exclusive vehicle, and because my dad used to start work at Brimsdown at about 6:30 am I decided that I would go with him to work and then drive on to Mile End, my habit of getting up early had begun - 5.30 am then, 2:30 am now (well until I was furloughed). Parking would obviously be a problem at college so I decided to really blag it. At that time QMC had a drive-through area in front of the main building, these days it's mostly grassed over, and there was parking available for about 12 cars in front of that main building, they would usually be nice ones, of course, belonging to top lecturers or management. My reading of the situation was that, arriving early in a nice car, there was unlikely to be anyone to see me park and then, later in the day, the area would be thronged with students so no one would notice me leave. Crazily this reading of the situation was correct and I got away with it until I left college – my course in the US about "How to be street wise" was paying off already.

Predictably I found the last year very gruelling and my avoidance of glasses was beginning to haunt me. My eyes were really feeling the strain and in the last months of my degree I had to own up and borrow my mother's glasses, still vainly refusing to go to the opticians. At the beginning of the third and last term at University, after the Easter break in 1970, we were faced with the final exams - none of this coursework or course unit easy ride stuff, this was a set of 12 three-hour exams over seven working days. The finals covered Latin and Greek translations, plus compositions in those languages, along with special subject and history papers. Pressure, pressure, pressure!

One of the ways I relaxed and which seemed to help me dissipate that pressure in this final year was a hobby that my dad had, purely by chance and with no intention of doing so, influenced me to take up when I returned from the USA to live at home for that 3rd year. At dinner one evening he was telling me about a man who worked for him on the shop floor at Enfield Rolling Mills, where, by now, my dad was the senior foreman. This fellow was, you might say, a bit of a gambler – "One day he's got furniture" my dad joked, "the next day it's all in the pawnshop, some days he's rich but most days he's skint."

He developed the story by explaining to me a system that the man had developed. It involved betting the favourites in the last three, ie higher class, races at any Greyhound meeting. At that time there were more than 20 tracks in the country and a normal card would have eight races. The system involved putting a level stake on the favourite in the sixth race, if your dog won you would stop and go home. If the dog lost you would double your bet on the favourite in the 7th race and likewise, if it lost, in the 8th. Generally, one of those favourites would win and you would end up in profit, how much depended on your level stake. This fascinated me and I set up a huge chart in our big coat cupboard at Churchfield. I listed all 20 tracks and kept a record of those final 6th, 7th and 8th races at all of them, my policy being to wait until one track had three consecutive meetings without a favourite winning in any of those races and then I will go to that track and follow the system. Walthamstow was particularly convenient as it was so nearby and I ended up going up there quite a lot for fun, even if I was not following the system, after all I had no female distractions and was quite happy enjoy my own company.

The bookies got to know me well and I became one of those punters who they didn't give a ticket to "Down to ginger" they would say, but I did have my long flowing auburn locks at that time and they did enjoy my donations. Nice memories because, if you stuck to the system rigidly, it worked, and I saved a fair bit of money over the first six months. However, greed always defeats the gambler even if appalling luck aggravates it. The system was due to go in on a Tuesday night at Romford Dog Track and running in the sixth race, the big race that night, was a star dog called Jackie's Legacy. The dog had won the Greyhound Derby that year and basically this was to be a show race for him and so I made the decision that it could not be beaten, and the system was a certainty to go in on the 6th race. So it was that I bet £300, most of my system profits and a very big bet in those days, on Jackie's Legacy to win just £75 as the price was 1/4. The dog stormed clear from the traps and as it reached the top bend before the final straight it was miles clear of the field. Out of the blue and without any warning signs the dog went lame as it came round the top bend and into the home straight. It was my hamstring all over again as Jackies Legacy stopped in its tracks - down the pan as they say, skint and crestfallen, six months of work and statistics down the river and, to make matters even worse, as I traipsed out of Romford track, the favourite won the 7th race – the system went in! Still, all this was setting me up for a lifetime of winning and losing big in so many different ways but, nevertheless, the dogs were always good for my mental health and helped me to relax and that is why, midway through my finals at QMC - in fact I think I'd done 7of the 12 exams - when I was really struggling and had almost had enough, I went to Walthamstow on the Thursday night and completely unwound by enjoying myself instead of cramming. I then completed my finals and was faced with a long wait until my results came through.

CHAPTER 11

BACK TO THE USA

Of course, I had planned to return to Atlantic City that year and I knew that if I could get another job on the Million Dollar Pier, I might be able to repeat the success of making the money I had in the previous year. Alan was all loved up with his landlady and so it was that I made the trip to the USA on my own. BUNAC again was my ride, just having to pay for the return flight this time. The flight was from Gatwick again but I can't remember who with and this time there were no dramas. I got to JFK and then on to Atlantic City by bus very easily. I went straight to the hotel on Ocean Avenue at the far end of the boardwalk and I booked in for 14 weeks. I'd arrived right at the beginning of the summer season on the Pier and, hopefully, it was a good time to go after a job. Wasting no time at all I went straight up to the Pier next morning to see If I could get hired. The Million Dollar Pier was owned by a very rich man indeed and his name was Mr Goldberg. As I arrived, Mr Goldberg was doing an inspection tour of the stalls with some of his management team and I took the bull by the horns and went straight up to him and asked him for a job, explaining that I had worked there the previous season and had come from England specially to work there again. Of course, he didn't know me from Adam and I was a bit crestfallen when he said he didn't do the hiring and for me to come back the following day and ask in the office.

Feeling a bit down in the dumps, if not apprehensive, I went across the boardwalk into a Colonel Saunders restaurant right opposite the pier entrance. I'm not totally sure, but I have a feeling that the Colonel Saunders restaurants went on to become the McDonalds chain, but anyway the cheeseburgers and hamburgers etc were still a complete novelty to me. At that time, while I was doing my comfort eating in there, I got chatting to a young lad who was really full of it and very hip. I was now 22 and he was 15. His name was Lee Cowan and his father was a doctor. The family lived in Philadelphia but had a holiday home at the opposite end of the boardwalk to where I was staying, that is the wealthy end of Atlantic City. Yes, he was very young but Lee was very much into the anti-Vietnam war scene though not an active part of it and I really ticked a lot of boxes for him when I revealed that I had been to Woodstock and seen Crosby, Stills, Nash and Young who I had soon realised he was a massive fan of. I knew a fair bit about Graham Nash from his days with the Hollies, having gone through school with loads of girls who were crazy about The Beatles, The Hollies, The Searchers and The Stones. I also struck lucky when it turned out that Lee had connections on the Pier, he came from a wealthy Jewish background and of course his father knew Mr Goldberg. Lee was a terrific guy and I spent many hours with him at his holiday home where he lent me a bike and, together, we rode all over Atlantic city and the boardwalk. I continued to corresponded with him for some years after that but sadly we lost touch and I don't know if he managed to avoid the draft but, if he didn't, I really do pray that he survived any military service and had a great life. The upshot was that Lee got me in on the Pier but, woe is me, the rifles didn't exist anymore and I was given a new stall to man, The Dime Pitch.

This was a stall just in front of the caterpillar ride, it was a square with sides about 12 feet long and consisted of about 20 three feet high stuffed animals all balancing a 12inch diameter plate with a red spot the size of a quarter in the centre on top of their heads. The aim of the game was that the player would pitch a dime onto the plate and they had to land it perfectly in the middle of that red dot in order to win a prize – I mean, really, a coin bouncing on a glass plate and looking to stop in the middle of a very small red spot was nigh on impossible, but Americans believe that they can succeed in everything they attempt and the unlikeliness of winning seemed to spur them on. The prizes, however, were enormous, the teddy bears were a big is me, there were lions, tigers and giraffes - you name it and we had almost a life-size version of it. It turned out that I would not be working alone on the stall because I had a 14-year-old kid called Harvey working with me and, interestingly, his father was a cop. I was rapidly becoming a bit disappointed that all the dodgy things I learned on the rifles might be going to waste and my dreams of making good money were evaporating before my very eyes. One of the few consolations, if you can call it that, was that we had Band of Gold by Freda Payne blaring out of the caterpillar ride every five minutes - what more could you ask for to make a summer? As luck would have it, within hours Harvey and I discovered that we were on the same page when it came to accepting that the wages for the 12 noon to 12 midnight-shift were not satisfactory enough, and so we put our heads together to come up with a way in which we could make some decent money, remembering also that it had to be shared between two people. The downside of the Dime Pitch was, of course, that it took 10 dimes to make a dollar, whereas it took only 4 quarters to do the same and, changing all those dimes into big denomination notes, was going to be a major problem. We could fall back on the old ruse of giving customers the wrong change and we could sell the occasional prize. The furry animals were really special and the customers constantly offered to buy them because they were almost impossible to win but, because the odds were so high, you couldn't sell too many in one day. In order to make decent money we had to figure out a way to deal with the dimes and considering that our stall was towards the rear of the pier, about 100 yards into the sea with water always below us, we decided that we would suspend a bag between the slats of the pier and, and as the hundreds of dimes fell onto the floor, we would push many of them through the slats and into the bag. Then every few days Harvey would swim out after work and collect the bag, changing the dimes into notes at various banks around Atlantic City. This worked very well but, being dimes, it was hardly bringing us in big-money.

Luckily for us, after about a month, the Pier management realised that The Dime Pitch was not making money. It took 1,000 pitches for the stall to make $100 and that took up a lot of time around the stall, so the powers that be decided to scrap the stall, which turned out to be a great result for me as I was moved to run a replacement stall inside the pavilion at the bottom of the pier. This was called The American Football Stall and it involved a 4 feet wide counter placed 6 feet in front of a framework supporting 10 old car tyres, going from the bottom of the frame in rows, 4 at the bottom, then 3, and 2 with 1 at the top. It cost the customer a quarter to play and for that he would get 3 American footballs which had to be thrown quarterback style through the tyres and all three needed to pass through the tyres to win one of the big prizes. On fairgrounds Americans love being tempted by something really "All American" and sports like football, hockey, basketball or shooting provided a great hook and I did a great trade. With the price of a go returning to a quarter, I could now put into action all that last year's stallholders had taught me and I could even get a refresher course because most of them were still working on the Pier, abandoning their luxury Florida homes for a summer of work on the Million Dollar Pier. Instead of a pouch around my waist, this time I had a till on my counter and there was still the bonus of being able to sell a few prizes and the opportunity to be heartless enough to short change many customers, the best ruse being to take a $10 bill in payment for the quarter charge and then give only change for one dollar, dropping the $10 bill on the floor as you rang it up on the till. Then, when the customer queried the change, open up the till to reveal that no $10 bill was inside it, so they clearly must be mistaken. After about a week on the stall I realised that there was a very large cop who would spend quite a bit of time watching me. I was not wrong and a few days later he approached me and, having told me that his name was Gus, he informed me that he knew exactly what I was doing. For a moment I wondered how could I front this one out and, as my new streetwise self, would I be capable of extracting myself from this conundrum. However, as already mentioned everyone on the Pier was there for the cash, and Gus was no exception - $50 a week was his fee for "keeping an eye on me", one hell of a result but, not surprising, when I discovered that Gus was in fact, my former Dime Pitch assistant Harvey's dad!

CHAPTER 12

MAKING MONEY

That summer I was there to try and make as much money as possible and, although I was having some great times, I really was focused on the end result. However, a small distraction did arrive one morning in early August. I was sitting on the Veranda at my hotel in Ocean Avenue when a letter arrived from my parents enclosing the result of my finals. I had passed my degree but only with a 2.2 and, although my parents were over the moon that I was now Ross Hartshorn BA(Hons), I was disappointed because I was obviously not quite as clever as I'd hoped. Looking back, not using glasses was probably a factor and not being able to see half the translations might well have lowered my marks. The silver lining was that in spite of "an ordinary" result in my degree, nevertheless I had been accepted by London University to do a PhD in Roman history - I was to do a paper on The Agrarian Land Reforms of Tiberius Gracchus. Ask me about Tiberius and his land reforms now and I would have no clue as to what you were talking about.

On the Pier we had now worked all the way up to Labor Day, the 8th September 1970, and we were having the last big push before the Pier closed down for the winter. I was going home in mid-September and I had to start withdrawing my savings from the bank I used in Atlantic City in an unobtrusive manner, planning at the same time how to get them home. I had gathered together $10,000 and, with the dollar rate at 2.5 to the pound in those days, this was about £4,000 - a lot of money in 1970 and not bad for a 22-year-old Harlow lad coming from an ordinary background. Before I came home, I also secured from the Pier, with the very best wishes of Mr Goldberg a very large black and white teddy bear, as tall as me, and a very large "sitting down" orange lion, both very special indeed. I named the bear Bill and the lion Lee. I loved everyone on that Pier and I think that I was well liked by all of them too. Fur sure, I did leave the Million Dollar Pier with the absolutely firm belief that everybody who worked on it, including Mr Goldberg himself, knew exactly how the finances worked and what everyone was doing - by keeping all the stallholders happy and letting them get on with what they did, Mr Goldberg knew full well that he would still make a huge profit and he was certainly not unaware of the fact that these guys had mansions and Cadillacs in Florida. At that time in Great Britain, Harold Wilson had just lost the election to Ted Heath but his currency legislation was still in force, which meant that you couldn't take out or bring into the country very much in the way of foreign currency. I withdrew my money from the bank in brand new $100 bills, slim enough in bundles of 50 to fit one bundle into each of my shoes. Ready to go home, I set off to the bus terminus with a hold-all over my shoulder, Bill the bear under the other arm, while I pushed the well wrapped up Lee the lion along the street with my foot. I became the intrigue of all the passengers on every mode of transport I used, the bus was fine because I had been able to ensure that Bill and Lee travelled safely and undamaged in the hold and, when we arrived at JFK, I was not short of volunteers who wanted to help with the animals. The biggest problem I had was with the baggage drop area, remember getting on a plane in those days was not fraught with all the problems we have now, but I was desperate for the big toys to travel safely. The customs officials, however, were determined to cut them open and search for drugs but, in this quest, the officers were subjected to the vented anger of all the other travellers who had fallen so much in love with my toys that they became their front-line defenders. This concerted pressure ensured that the beasts were loaded safely with the unintentional distraction of these colourful beings enabling me to get on the plane untroubled and with my shoes intact. We had a very strong tailwind on the way home and the flight back to Heathrow, this time, took barely six hours. My worries about the condition of Bill and Lee were allayed when the baggage handler put them, by hand, onto the conveyor belt and a huge cheer rang out around the baggage collection area when the lion's head appeared above the parapet. I don't think I've ever been so popular, either before or since. I had to face the same problem with the determination of the customs officials to slice open the animals in search for drugs when we landed at Heathrow, but again my fellow passengers were so vociferous in their support that we succeeded in getting past all the checks with the toys in one piece. The animals were completely "clean", had no drugs in them and it was fair and just that they got a new home in England. By the same token the distraction kept me away from any problems and questions and, as I got through the exit gate, mum and dad were waiting there to collect me and were taken aback by the size of my two friends. It was great to be home and my parents had a job recognising me with my new persona, long hair and a nice Atlantic City surfer's tan, the cool look emphasised by my blue and white striped loons, nicely finished off by red inserts in the flares. Next day my father, catching the childlike excitement from me decided to put to Bill the bear in the front seat of his car and take him to work to show him off. I don't think anyone over here had seen toys off this size before and, as he got onto Nazeing Common, only a few miles from the house, he was pulled over by the police - it was 6.30 in the morning and, believe it or not, they wanted to examine the bear. I still have both of these animals in the loft at home and, although dusty, they are probably worth millions now as antiques, large ones.

CHAPTER 13

FROM EDUCATION TO WORK

Studying was about to begin at the Senate House, London University and, after a quick brush up on Tiberius Gracchus and his gang, I was ready for action. I had changed and was a completely different person following the times that I had in the States, I knew this was going to be hard road for me to follow and, after a fortnight of studying in the library, I came to the conclusion that this life of study was no longer going to be the life that I wanted.

I was 23 and had been doing academic work for a long time and I badly needed a change of direction and another goal to aim for. I decided that the money I had brought home from the USA could be put to much better use than supporting a student's lifestyle and, having made this momentous decision to change course, it was a month on that I decided that it was time to try and change the dollars into pounds so that I could take advantage of the options the cash opened up for me. With the currency regulation still in force, this would not be a straightforward operation and so my father and I decided to go into London and try and do the conversion by visiting quite a few banks. My account with the bank was held at Mile End branch, which was next to QMC on the Mile End Road and this would be our first port of call. We went in expecting many questions and difficulties when it came to explaining where the money had come from yet, possibly because this was the start of the new student year and the bank was extremely busy, both with parents and new students, it quickly became apparent that the bank staff didn't really know who was changing the dollars, me or my father, and somehow made the assumption that the money was being used for student residency fees. Consequently, we did not face a single question and the bank changed the entire amount on the spot, I suppose the teller must have thought that he would get a bonus for getting that kind of commission, anyway we left the bank with around £3,700 in cash.

When we got home, I gave my mother enough money to buy a new three-piece suite for the front room and a twin tub washing machine, a washing machine being an appliance that she had never had the pleasure of owning. I then bought the Rover 2000 from my father, my first car, and he went straight down the road to Hills of Woodford and bought a flash new green Opel Manta, registration number FLY 258J. The rest of the money went into my bank account now transferred to Harlow.

After all these financial dealings, I had to face my dad with the fact that I had decided to give up working for the PhD because I had had enough of books and I desperately needed a change. That he was unhappy was an understatement and he couldn't get his head around why I appeared to be giving up on my dream. Lots of our relatives he knew in his early life had been academics or teachers and he saw me as following in their footsteps which meant that my decision caused him great disappointment. However, he did accept it but on the condition that I would need to find a new career path very quickly. Notwithstanding, the extremely pleasant ending to my academic career happened with the graduation event and degree presentation in late October at the Albert Hall, London. At this time, the Queen Mother was Chancellor of London University and it was her who presented me with my degree in front of my parents, a very proud moment for us all. I actually bought my Ede and Ravenscroft cap and gown, other poor students just hired theirs, and I still have both items in the back of the wardrobe, in fact I've got quite a bit of wear out of them when I have attended fancy dress balls going as a teacher!

As for my future career, I arranged an aptitude assessment at the careers information service in Chelmsford and this involved doing various tests which resulted in me receiving expert advice on what career path I should follow. This was 1970 remember and I can recall thinking to myself that I wanted to be earning a minimum of £1,500 a year by the time I was 30 - this was my father's really good salary at the time. After my appraisal I was quite surprised to find out that the recommendation for my career was that I should seek employment in a job linked with selling. That I should become a salesman of some kind is something that I definitely could not have imagined when studying classics at London University. A job interview with Avery scales in Cambridge was arranged and I was delighted that I got the job and was not concerned about commuting from Harlow.

I was still living at home and I would continue to do so until I was 29. Odd to some in those times, this did not seem strange to me at all as I suppose that, really, I was a bit of a homeboy, although I had very much learnt how to spread my wings over the last few years. I spent a couple of weeks travelling by train from Harlow to Cambridge, changing at Bishop

Stortford on the way and, after learning the basics at Avery I began to accompany the sales rep on his round to learn the ropes about being on the road. By the end of one week of this I realised that this job was not for me and I had to face the prospect of letting my father down yet again. Whatever the consequences, for the sake of my own sanity, I had to resign from Avery scales and, after working there for less than a month, I went home to face the wrath of my father.

CHAPTER 14

TEACHING

It was December and, apart from becoming a temporary postman for Christmas, there did not seem to be many jobs on offer. My sister was still working at Harlow Council and had done really well to become one of the top legal secretaries. She invited me out for lunch to have a chat about my future plans and told me that she had heard that the New Catholic Comprehensive School, built in 1965 and situated opposite my old school Netteswell, was desperate to find teachers. To be honest this was a school I didn't really know existed, I had gone to university in 1967 and the new school, called St Marks, hadn't really got off the ground by then. With nothing to lose, I told her that I would be quite interested in seeing what was available and she went back to the Town Hall to find out further details for me. It turned out that St Marks' maths department should have been four strong but, at that time, only had three members of staff and one of these, Mr Kosher, had returned to India for family reasons in December and had been delayed so that it was not known when he would return to England. Consequently, the department was now two teachers short and desperate for a childminder, if nothing else. Although maths was not one of my "A" level subjects, I had done it to "O" level and followed that with an Add Maths "A/O" level, plus I had a reasonable gift for numbers, a trait further developed by my interest in greyhounds and betting. I thought that I had nothing to lose and told my sister that I would give it a go. She arranged an interview for me with the headmaster, Mr Tony O'Shea, at his house in Willowfield, Harlow.

I went round to see him on January 3, 1971, a Sunday. Mr O'Shea was a delightful man who had won the Military Cross for bravery whilst in the army, a fact that very few people really appreciated.

As I knocked on his door mid-morning that Sunday I said, "My name is Ross Hartshorn and I have come to see you about the maths job."

"See you Monday at 9 am," came the reply and that was it.

I don't believe there has ever been an interview like that before, it certainly wouldn't happen in this day and age. Next day I turned up at school and the next 16 years of my life had begun. On my arrival at St Marks on Monday, the 4th of January 1971, I was introduced to the head of the maths department, Mr Peter Fox and also his number 2, Mr Bob Wilson. Peter Fox went on to become the headmaster of Saint Thomas More Catholic School in Wood Green, famous not only because he was given an honour by the Queen but also for the fact that Samantha Fox, the glamour model, (not his daughter) attended there.

Peter Fox gave me a great piece of advice to start my teaching career, "Go in hard and then you can ease up, you can never start easy and then get hard. If someone cries so be it."

This was so true - I always started tough and then got pretty easy but everyone knew that I had a tipping point. In reality, I probably messed about more than most of the children. Having not seen a maths textbook for about six years I soon realised that this was going to be a challenging exercise and when I was given SMP book 1 - a part of the new maths project being rolled out in schools, full of topics like binary numbers and scale factors etc - it was a book of things which I had never seen or heard of before.

Numerically, though, I did feel that I had an advantage when I discovered that these children, at 11 years of age, had not reached the level of maths that I did when I was 7, no tables, no fractions, none of the building blocks which I thought were vital for an early education to build on. Reading through chapter 1 in the staffroom before I went off to meet my class, I thought that I had mastered the initial easy binary number work, for example in binary 4 is 100, which means one 4, no 2s, and no 1s, while 13 is 1101, that is one 8, one 4, no 2s and one 1. By using a division method, you can work out any number but, here is the key, the reminders you get which indicate the binary equivalent need to be written in the reverse order to achieve the correct binary number. Unfortunately, by the time I had met my form class ('More 4' which was a fourth-year class of 14-year-olds with the house being More, named after one of the Saints we used as house names, Newman, Bede and Elgar being the others) and taken the register, enjoyed assembly and got to 1st lesson, I had completely forgotten how to do binary numbers. So, into the lion's den I went with fingers crossed and I must admit they were a great bunch of first-year pupils. There were two girls in the class worthy of note, one of them was Mr O' Shea's daughter Stella and the other, a daughter of the head of a Catholic junior school, Angela. For some reason these two in particular took a shine to me, it could have been because I had hair in those days or the Rover 2000 or the glow I still maintained from my time in the USA or, even perhaps, because I was fun. I always wore a jacket and tie when I was a teacher and many of my ties had flower designs which earned me the nickname "flower power", one of the better ones I achieved throughout my career I must say.

In that first lesson, for some reason, one of the girls did cry and thus allowed me to set out my stall as a tough guy, but when I got all the binary numbers the wrong way round, ensuring that all the homework was a disaster, I had to make a grovelling apology the next day which was something the whole class found hilarious. As I pressed on through that first Easter term, I really started to enjoy myself and feel at home in the job. I had always been "a school person" in my time at Netteswell, very sporty and a good organiser and I did, believe it or not, possess a little bit of culture from my classical studies. Basically, I just carried on being "well into school", I was still only 23 and I really think that I had found my vocation, building on that work experience at Little Parndon, so perhaps I did follow in the family tradition.

For the most part this was a very enjoyable life, but it was tempered slightly by the fact that we were in Harlow, and Harlow could be quite a rough area with some problem teenagers. St Marks had a difficult skinhead element and there was often friction with the sizeable Polish contingent at the school. At that time, I was the only non-Catholic member of staff, although it wasn't long before I knew all the prayers off by heart, and I still do by the way. Sadly, some teachers were not up to the job and my view was that if you, as a teacher, came out of a class crying then you needed to change your job straightaway. Quite a few did just that and that is why we were often very short staffed at St Marks and we also suffered because we were regarded as a very poor relation in the secondary school hierarchy that existed in Harlow. Major schools like Netteswell and Mark Hall had terrific reputations in sport and academia and St Marks, sadly, was at the bottom of the tree.

All the schools in Harlow were now comprehensives and many would not grant St Marks sports teams fixtures on the games field. The school was always seemingly struggling for a full contingent of staff and fundraising was always high on everyone's agenda. We had three catholic feeder junior schools, Holy Cross, St Luke's and St Albans and this meant that all the schools were competing for the same donations. The main fundraising event at Saint Marks was always the schools summer fete, organised by a subcommittee of the school governing body chaired by Mr

Peter Burrell, alongside Mr O'Shea, his deputies and volunteer parents. This Group seemed to be a bit "stodgy" and somewhat in a rut and, as I seemed to be showing a modicum of oomph, Mr Burrell asked me to join the team and perhaps bring some new ideas with me. The first meeting of this committee was to take place in the first week of the Easter term, building up to the fete at the end of June. However, before we got to that point, a few changes took place in staffing at the school. Firstly, during the Easter holiday Mr Kosher, the maths teacher on family leave, in India, had managed to return to England and would resume his job in the maths department, taking it up to its full contingent of 4, which was good news, but, in the meantime, because of a pregnancy and a nervous breakdown in the language department, that was now short of bodies. Because of my classics background I was now deemed as a linguist, I had I suppose got "O" level French and had won a prize for the French exchange trip at school, and so it was that I was asked to step into the breach. Miss Bourbon was head of department, a typical middle-aged teacher Miss, if you know what I mean, although that is a bit harsh, with a very stayed and conservative outlook on life. I don't think the poor woman knew that people like me existed but, somehow, we hit it off brilliantly and she seemed to get a new zing about her and it really seemed to suit her to have me around. I had some real fun convincing the kids that I could actually speak French and I remember my first lesson, just as in the maths department, was a complete disaster but nevertheless a great icebreaker.

In the language department we had something called "the Tavor system" which worked in conjunction with a projector and showed slides with the French commentary. My particular lesson today was on the subject of telling the time in French and, remembering that I have told you already, that practicality is hardly my strong point, somehow, I managed to get the film into the projector backwards so that my "il est huit heure" was actually showing "il est quatre heure" - for the uninitiated that means the film was saying it was 8 o'clock but was showing that it was 4 o'clock on screen, all very amusing.

With all this mirth pervading the classroom, I struck up a great relationship with all the pupils and two in particular, Christine and Linda, seemed quite taken with me, probably because my mistakes made me funny and I had long hair. Christine and her family went on to become really great friends of mine.

CHAPTER 15

TEAM SPIRIT

Over the years my dad used to change the car quite regularly and in fact he and mum would often go out for a drive on a Sunday and come back in a different car. He used to love visiting Hills of Woodford, a very notable top dealership where he bought both the Rover 2000 and his Opel Manta, just to look at the amazing cars that were on show there. So it was that he told me that he had seen there an Opal GT left-hand drive sports car, in azure blue, and that the salesman had told him that there were only three of them in the country at that time. We both got in the Rover that evening and drove over to Hills. We came back a couple of hours later without the Rover and in the opal GT left-hand drive. It had manual flip over head lights, only 2 seats and a couple of feet space behind the seats instead of a boot. It was quite an amazing experience dealing with a left-hand drive vehicle for the first time, using the gearstick with the opposite hand and being in a driving position with a completely different view of the road, plus of course it was hard to resist flipping overhead lights with the manual lever next to the gearstick as often as I could. How cool was I going to be turning up for school in that car!

Amusingly, when I was working in the French department, I was visited by the schools' inspector. At that time, you didn't need a teacher's certificate to go with your degree if you wanted to be a teacher, although I did do a course later on at Brentwood college in order to get one, but you did need to be approved by the Education Inspectorate. Of course, the one that came to inspect me now was the maths inspector and, because I was now teaching French, there wasn't a lot that he could do. He could not file a report on me because he was in the wrong department.

During my time teaching French, I discovered that the language department possessed 2 record players which, on some special occasions, were used to play some of the pupils' records. Coincidentally, at this time, yet another temporary teacher, named Pete Clark, arrived to help with all kinds of subjects. He was another very cool dude with long curly hair and it seemed he was there just for the crack, amazing really, because this was a guy who also went on to become a top headmaster in future years. Pete had done some music gigs in his time and he told me that he had an old valve amplifier which could be adapted so that we could run the record players through it and get a really loud sound. It was then that we decided to do a monthly Friday night get together for the pupils in one of the maths rooms and the fledgling discos had begun.

From being a school in the doldrums there was now a hell of a lot going on. I also helped in the PE department teaching games for about 10 lessons a week, and this gave me my chance to show off my rugby coaching skills. The skinhead boys were a rough tough mob and the Polish boys were gifted athletes but just not interested in doing anything at all. I decided to try to harness the two groups together and make a decent rugby team out of them. As we went through the summer term there was definitely a new bonding within the two groups and a new school spirit seemed to appear simply because the school was actually doing things, having fun and moving forward. The Fete committee got its act together and we came up with some great stalls and took a record amount of money. The big idea that I had put forward was to have a giant picnic outside, after the Fete itself, with amplified music from the record players creating an outside dance atmosphere. Sadly, this idea was nearly scuppered when the rain moved in to ruin the evening but the 100 plus people who had stayed on just carried everything into the school hall and we held our picnic and party in there. This was the original seed that led to countless, amazing, unbelievable events in that school hall, events that became legendary and are still even talked about today.

CHAPTER 16

TEACHING

That summer I managed to persuade around twenty of the about-to-become-5th-and-6th year boys to engage in a whole summer holiday of concentrated rugby training. Amongst the boys were Poles, Richard Szemiako and Chris Kisala and, from the crombie-wearing skinhead section, top man Ed Sheridan. We trained at least four times a week during that summer holiday, usually running a couple of miles down to Harlow Town Park, there doing half a dozen circuits before returning to school to do tactical rugby drills on the school field. From being a school with no team and no hope, we created a well-oiled machine with a definite will to win mentality and a tremendous team spirit. We managed to get some fixtures but Netteswell still wouldn't give us a game. After a run of pretty impressive performances, I persuaded Mr O'Shea to contact the Netteswell headmaster to try and arrange a fixture with them, something they were actually duty-bound to do because we were all in the Harlow Education Area. My old adversary Mike Pollard was still in charge of the still very good Netteswell Ist XV, who regularly came up against some of the top sides in the south-east. Mr Pollard firmly was of the opinion that St Marks was not good enough to be on the same field as his team that was definitely the case when he found out that I was in charge at St Marks. His old animosity returned with a vengeance but to no avail as the pressure from Mr O'Shea paid off and led to a fixture being granted. We were certainly massive underdogs against a team of real quality and Mike Pollard, in dismissive fashion, decided not to pick his strongest team simply because he didn't think he had to. We were in good form, with some good results behind us and we entered and continued to play this game with great confidence. It was because we were playing so well that I think that Mr Pollard realised that he may well have underplayed his hand but, all too late, because, after a magnificent display, the boys had managed to stay within one point of the Netteswell team right up to the end of the game. Then, with seconds to go, the ball found its way to Ed who, in a very rare moment in schoolboy rugby, put over a drop goal - years before Johnny Wilkinson's drop for glory in the Rugby World Cup final - and lo and behold we had won the game by two points. Mike Pollard was excruciatingly unpleasant after the game but I was dancing in circles of delight, as was our very proud team of St Marks players. We built on that success and continued in the same spirit for a long time after that and, it was not only our reputation in rugby that grew, but also that result had the snowball effect of improving us in sports of all different kinds.

St Marks suddenly had a truly great staff and a new intake of teachers brought on board Barry Sleath, PE, Brian Webster for English, American John Florens for biology and Mike Hollinsworth in the physics department, all young and vibrant guys bringing enthusiasm to their subjects and into the sports sides of the school. We founded a staff rugby team and were good enough to take on club sides like Harlow and Chingford. After the long break I'd had from competitive sport, my hamstring injury was manageable and it was great to be able to play again. In day-to-day stuff at St Marks, however, the language department was now back up to full strength, populated by actual language teachers, but Bob Wilson had left the maths department and so I was invited to re-join that department, an invitation which I delightedly accepted, and I remained in that department for the rest of my years at St Marks. Of course, there had to be a ridiculous twist to this appointment and it was that, after I had returned to teach maths, the Education Inspector for French came to check me out with the same no result as before – they didn't bother me ever again.

I was given as my form registration classroom and my main teaching base, a room which was situated as a side room to the main school hall. Called the Assembly Hall Room, this classroom had an outside passageway each side of it and had full length glass windows on running down both these sides. One utterly surreal event really illustrates how I was often in more trouble than the pupils. On this particular occasion I was taking a small remedial class for about eight pupils, this was not my strongest suit and, with classes of this type, we more often than not ended up playing some sort of educational game. This day we were playing roulette, very mathematical indeed, when one of the kids, obviously getting bored, said to me, "Sir, have you got your smoke machine with you today?"

Certainly, I had and unfortunately for us, and particularly for me, I set it up and, for a bit of fun, I proceeded to fill the classroom with smoke. It was really great and the smoke made a "pea souper" look like a mist. In a moment of incredible bad luck, a passing member of the office staff, noticing the dense smoke through the windows, rushed across the hall to the office and dialled 999. Within minutes the Fire Brigade had arrived, all suited up with breathing apparatus and everything. When they reached my classroom door, they didn't just turn the handle to open it, they smashed and chopped it down by which time, of course, all the smoke had evaporated. I must say that I did get into quite serious hot water over that incident but it has become legendary.

CHAPTER 17

PARTIES

The disco became a regular Friday night event, a sort of youth club which provided a great platform for developing a real school spirit. Girls easily develop crushes on male staff and I always had Stella and Angela on my tail, while Christine and Linda both clearly liked me a lot. I also had a great affinity with what turned out to be an incredibly gifted and talented group of boys. Tony Benner, Gerard Kenny, Jed Donaghue, Steve Colley, Chester Kamen and in Gus McKie would all go on to be amazingly successful men. At that time, we worked as a team and began to put together some amazing fundraising parents' dances.

Christine was a massive Tottenham Hotspur fan and her father, Derek, was a big mover and shaker in the Spurs supporters club. After my initial young and misguided flirtation with Manchester United until I was 11, Spurs rose to be the power under Bill Nicholson and I became ardent Spurs fan going whenever I could get a ticket, which became a great deal easier thanks to my connection with Derek, the main man in the supporters' club. Derek came to my assistance when a couple of season tickets became available in the East stand and I sort of moved to the front of the queue to secure them. These were just to the left of the halfway line in the East Stand - block E, row 3, seats 164 and 165. They were behind a central pole blocking the view a little bit each side of the halfway line but it was not long before the stand was redesigned and the pole disappeared so I had the perfect seat. I soon ended up doing all the discos for the Spurs supporters club and, indeed, some actual Spurs functions, including the party after the UEFA cup win under Keith Burkinshaw in a club along Tottenham High Road. I treasure the photograph of me holding the UEFA cup aloft and I'm proud still to be a Spurs season ticket holder and loyal supporter nearly 50 years later – and in the new stadium.

The discos now moved into the large school hall and we started putting on sensational dance events for parents. The artistic talents of Chester Kamen, whose brother Nick went on to do the famous jeans advert (the 1985 Levi's 501 laundrette one) and became a pop star working with Madonna, were right to the fore, as was the amazing stagecraft of Steve

Colley who became one of the top stage managers in the country, organising events all over the world for some of the really top pop groups. All of the lads were fantastic people and things mushroomed after our first go at parents' dance - a 1920s Gangsters Ball. At that time a lot of the fundraising for St Marks was done at Our Lady of Fatima Catholic Church by a group of parishioners called the Knights of Saint Columba. They regarded me as a bit of an intruder onto their ground and there was a certain amount of suspicion and jealousy whirling around. For this dance we created a life size, cardboard Al Capone style 20s automobile and we invited just about everybody who we could, to get our first dance off the ground. One of the big doubters at the Knights of Saint Columba was a particular parent, Mr Folan, whose son Sean and daughter Shelagh were pupils of mine. Somehow, we needed him on board and we achieved that by making "his gang" the stars of the show, something he was unaware of until he got there.

"Fingers Folan" was the nickname we gave him, having used the persuasive powers of his children to get him and the knights to come. It was terrific for us all that he had a really great time and incredibly the nickname "Fingers" stuck with him always. We had cracked it! One thing to remember about that night happened when I was giving a lift home to Gerard Kenny, who lived at Ram Gorse on the other side of Harlow. It was about 2:30am, after we had cleaned up the hall, before we got going and, as we were driving through Harlow Town Centre in the Opal GT, a sharp-eyed policeman pulled us over.

Moving to the offside of the vehicle the policeman, on checking the occupants inside, said sarcastically to Gerard, "A bit young to be driving aren't we, sir?"

In a very measured and calm manner, Gerard pointed to me behind the wheel of this unusual and left-hand drive car and politely replied to the policeman, "He's driving, officer."

The extremely embarrassed PC waved us away with an accelerating flourish, I think he'll always remember that mistake too.

As we moved through 1972 the social events coming thick and fast and our next extravaganza was an ambitious mediaeval feast. For this we unofficially took over the school kitchen which, in plain English, means that we actually utilised them without anyone's permission. Obviously, we had to be meticulously careful to make sure that the kitchen was left in its original spotless condition although, after events like this, we always believed we left things cleaner then when we found them. For that feast I cooked 46 chickens at the same time, along with a lot of other meats and about 300 sausages. We even got the butcher to supply us with a pig's head for our display and it was a very authentic and extremely boozy occasion.

This was the first of many events that our "favourite caretaker", a Mr Joe Linnen, took exception to because he disliked the disruption to his serenity. He lived in a house on site, and announced that he had locked the school gates so that no one would be able to get out. To be honest, stopping people getting in would have been a more sensible policy, no one cared about the lock in and we just kept the party going until 7 in the morning when Mr Linnen finally relented. This amazing event clearly created a fair bit of rubbish, although not in the same league as the legendary New Year's Eve Dances throughout the coming years. Some bright spark thought that it would make things easier and quicker if we burnt a lot of the waste. So, a large proportion of the rubbish was thrown into a big oil drum for incineration. Sadly, the flame wouldn't take and someone, and no one ever owned up to this, decided to add a bit of petrol to the drum. The resultant bang gave the whole neighbourhood an early Sunday alarm call but, miraculously, we all lived.

After leaving school, one of this special group of pupils, Andy, who had been going out with Linda's great friend Barbara since they were about 13, discovered that his girlfriend was in a similar situation to my sister 10 years previously. Barbara was pregnant. The couple were ecstatic about the baby and decided to get married. They tied the knot at Saint Thomas More Catholic Church in Harlow where I was delighted to be the best man and Linda was the chief bridesmaid. Of course, I did the disco. The wedding went extremely well and Linda and I each did a first-class job for the couple, getting on very well and enjoying some very pleasant dances together.

On the second day of the festivities, the happy couple had put on a sort of present hunt with places to visit and clues etc, which as chief guests, so as to speak, we were obliged to go to. I collected her in the Opal, freshly stripped of all its wedding ribbons, and we finished off the wedding celebrations by having a really nice, happy day. These would be the last hours we spent together - until 23 years later that is!

CHAPTER 18

SPONSORED WALK

On the home front, I was still living at Churchfield with my parents when Harlow Council, years in advance of Margaret Thatcher's council house purchase scheme, offered their tenants in Harlow the chance to buy their council properties, or "corporation" properties as they were then, at a discounted rate of 30% off the market price. Clearly this was a great opportunity although, with interest rates very high and wages low in comparison, getting a mortgage and paying for it was not the easiest thing to do. Of course, I still had a large chunk of my gains from my trip to the USA in the bank but, because the house was in dad's name, he had to make the purchase and, believe it or not, the price of the house was just under £4,000 after discount. I still had £2,800 which represented a large chunk of the price and, in order to complete the purchase, dad and I decided to get a short-term loan instead of a mortgage to cover the rest. Dad's Bank was NatWest, just up the road at the Stow, and we needed to borrow £1,200, choosing to repay it over only 3 years, to become a cash buyer. With me still living at home, with a good teaching job, and dad earning a good salary, the numbers added up for the bank and we were granted the loan. In that instant I became R D Hartshorn! Dad had only one Christian name, Ronald, and with me being Ross the bank needed to differentiate between our names. So, as my second name was David, I became R. D. Hartshorn and have done everything in that name ever since. We thus bought the house between us and decided to share ownership 50-50, although I paid over 80% of the money in actual fact.

Soon the next fete came over the horizon and a new member of the governing body was elected, a Mrs Chambers, a really lovely woman whose son John was in my class. Fete organisation was now a very big deal and Mrs Chambers knew someone who knew someone who knew the disc jockey Noel Edmonds, then presenting the breakfast show on Radio 1, long before his famous stints on TV. This contact arranged it so that Noel Edmonds would open the school fete this year and, in response to this news, we plastered his name in huge letters in the windows of the first-floor classroom which ran parallel to the main road which ran alongside the school and this had the desired effect of attracting a great deal of attention. We had devised some unusual stalls for the fete and were very excited to see if we could make it another record fundraiser. Unfortunately, some 10 days before the fete, for whatever reason, Mr Edmonds announced on his early morning show that he was unable to open the school fete in Harlow over the following weekend. That morning at the school saw pandemonium, disappointment and despair.

The first thing was that the sign had to come down from the classroom window! Then, miraculously, by some uncanny twist of fate, again for whatever reason, Noel Edmonds had a change of heart and announced that he would indeed be opening St Marks fete.

The signs went back up, the potential customers licked their lips for a second time and Noel Edmonds actually turned up and opened the fete. He didn't stay for very long but his appearance certainly got crowds of people to come to the event. I remember his arrival very well indeed - hundreds of screaming girls to be controlled by Saint Marks deputy head and head of religious studies Mr Murtagh, a lovely and truly gentle man, affectionately known as WAM, after his initials (Mr W.A. Murtagh). This man was an extremely good example to the Catholic faith and had 13 children, all of whom he named after saints, so his list of children could have been the roll call of a house list at St. Marks.

Completely removed and sheltered from the real world, Mr Murtagh believed that he could hold up his hand and request the surging crowd to be calm and walk sensibly, but it was just like a Tom and Jerry cartoon in which a crowd just stampeded over everything in its path, leaving him poleaxed and flattened. The poor man didn't know what hit him.

We always had a raffle in conjunction with the fete and, together with the proceeds of the day, we again topped our record take, this time making over £1,500.

As we moved into the next school year, in September 1972 our new PE teacher, Barry Sleath, lamented how we could never travel easily to other schools for sports events and indeed other events. He muted the idea of a 20 miles sponsored walk to raise funds for a school minibus. Everyone thought that this was a great idea and he became the main organiser of the project backed up of the rest of the staff. A couple of really funny events happened around this time, worth recounting because they help to reveal the real fun and great spirit that abounded at Saint Marks during this period. I don't know what people today would make of them, but here goes.

Firstly, an incident showing how careful you have to be in choosing your words, occurred when some delinquents had been given a punishment which involved redecorating two of the toilets. To announce the temporary closure of these facilities Mr O'Shea, in his headmaster's assembly, announced to the whole school that this particular set of girls' toilets would be out of bounds because some boys were "doing some touching up in them." You really can't make these sorts of things up.

Another amusing incident involved Barry Sleath, the PE teacher, who had an extremely loud voice and was a man always keen to pursue any chance of making any extra money. A few of us conned him into believing that there was a new Post Office quiz game called "Live at Five" in which you had to answer a simple question correctly to win £100 worth of premium bonds. During one break time we arranged for a member of the office staff to ring the staffroom and pretend to be presenting this very game while we made sure that Barry was the nearest person to the phone. As we exchanged small talk, ring, ring, Barry picked up the phone and immediately.

The caller interjected, "Good morning, this is the Post Office quiz game 'Live at Five', answer a simple question correctly and win £100 worth of premium bonds".

"I'm ready," replied Barry.

"What is the name of Roy Rogers' horse?"

From his mouth and reaching an incredible level of decibels came the answer "TTRRIIGGEERRRRR"! The whole staff room erupted into a long outbreak of uncontrollable laughter.

Just to show you that the pupils also were adept at playing pranks, not long after that, in that same staffroom at a special meeting attended by both all the teaching staff and all the office staff, some very clever pupils used their genius to tie the only two staffroom doors, both opening inwards with one on each side of the staffroom, to the metal railings of the staircases outside the room. Not only did this ensure that no one could exit the room because literally the whole staff was inside, but also there was no one left in the office who could be phoned for help. This prank has got to be to be right up there with the best of them and even we found it very funny as a lot of highly animated pupils blew kisses to us from the outside of the staffroom.

The final story I will impart to you before we get back to the sponsored walk, concerns the lengths that we sometimes had to go to just to keep the Friday discos up and running.

Amongst some of the staff, there was always some opposition to the discos but the money they raised and the social cohesion they produced made a huge difference to the success of the school and that is why they were supported by most parents and teachers. Now pupils from other schools were able to come along and, obviously, sometimes, there would be friction at these functions. Over the years I had several teams of great helpers drawn from the pupils and with one group of them, after one Friday night disco, I went to clean the toilets as usual. Unfortunately, three sinks had been torn off the wall and were lying on the toilet floor. This definitely could not be allowed to have happened at the disco and so, with the ingenuity of my helpers, somehow, we managed to temporarily balance them back in the correct position, a position in which they managed to survive without falling down until the following Thursday. When the inevitable investigation took place all those days later, it centred around vandalism that had probably taken place within the school and on that day and again no culprit could be found. Another lucky day or, perhaps, you could call it a brilliant escape!

Back to the sponsored walk, 20 miles out of the school gates, a 2 mile walk up to The Pinnacles area, then on past the rugby club before embarking on a 6 mile stretch to Matching Green, followed by a 10 mile roundabout journey back to the school. Nearly everyone in the school took part in the walk and we raised enough cash to purchase a 14-seater minibus. About 6 of the staff had to go to Chelmsford police academy to pass a minibus driving test and, in the blink of an eye, it was up and running and our transport problems were solved.

CHAPTER 19

WILD TIMES

More dances followed over the next few months, topped off by the magnificent New Year's Eve festivity that always went on until three or four in the morning. My classes usually spent nearly all of December tearing up paper, normally shop catalogues we acquired from town centre shops, as we needed enough confetti to put Time Square, New York to shame. We usually had at least 3,000 balloons and crowds of up to 350, probably too many for today's regulations. Tables were allotted by name and their positions became famous - they included the Meader table, the Cockman table, the Staff table, the Folan table, the Byrite table and so on. It was customary to place about 20 bottles of Pomagne on every table so that, when Big Ben struck at 12 midnight - we had a BBC soundtrack of that of course - there would be half an hour of mayhem as battles with Pomagne and confetti and balloons took place all over the hall. Skirmishes sometimes lasted into the very early hours of the morning and, in your wildest imagination, you could not visualise the total devastation and utter mess that faced me and my helpers at the end of such an incredible celebration. Whatever, the team and I would always clean up straight after the event, even if it took until noon New Year's Day, by which time we were all totally exhausted.

Over the years I came into contact with a fantastic bunch of pupils and I do believe that the things that we did, although they were more than a bit offbeat, provided a magnificent part of their education and enabled them to develop as individuals.

We held a dance set in ancient Rome where we changed the long corridor that ran past the offices into an aeroplane fuselage and sold raffle tickets doubling as boarding cards while our wonderful stewardesses seated the passengers. By the end of the corridor (flight) they had flown not only to Rome but back in time as well. We staged a classical music night when we created a full-blown orchestra, all the instruments being supplied by the music department, which comprised of pupils in evening dress miming to a soundtrack. Although the students couldn't play the instruments, they looked great holding them.

A great lad named Tom McCauley took the role as conductor and looked every inch the Andre Previn of his day.

That night my sister had brought with her the Chairman of Harlow Council Entertainments Committee and I think he must have had quite a few drinks by the time he approached me to inform me that he had never seen an orchestra with such a wide range of musical talent, playing anything from classical to pop, from reggae to heavy rock, and his view was that the conductor must be a musical genius. He thought that the orchestra was so fantastic that it would be a very good idea if he could book them for one of the Harlow Town Park outdoor concerts in the summer. Unfortunately, it was then that I had to tell him that, in fact, the orchestra was miming and that performing at the Town Park may be a little ambitious.

Tragically, it was only 18 months until the conductor young Tom passed away because of a blood disorder but, thankfully for all our super memories, he did have time to star in one more school fete, which I will describe later.

Adding to the burgeoning list of events came a "Vicars and Tarts Night", followed by a "Mods and Rockers Confrontation", at which, to the absolute fury and dismay of our favourite caretaker, we staged a mods v rockers fight on the dancefloor where 4 scooters and 4 motorbikes zoomed into the hall and screeched around for two or three laps.

I can still see the caretaker standing at the door shouting, "Those motorbikes are not coming in here!"

Wrong again, sir. It turned out be even more fun because some of the patrons thought everything that was happening was real! We also made a lot of money when local menswear shop Byrite sponsored what was surprisingly called the "Byrite Dance" where we covered the whole of the school hall - a very large area indeed - in plastic Byrite carrier bags. The manager of the shop himself came in a suit made entirely from Byrite bags, although by the end of the evening, when he was a bit worse for wear to say the least, all that remained of his garments were his pants!

Just to add, we put on a "Cowboy and Indian Dance" where I had the opportunity to dig out from the loft my toy gun and holster set which had remained unused since I was 8. I can't quite believe that, for this dance, I had the audacity to borrow some ponies and riders from the riding stable that was based just down the road from the school. Dressing up the riders as Indians, with some really cool feathered headdresses, we carried out an

Indian raid on the school hall when half a dozen horses entered the hall and charged round in a circle – it was like Custer's last stand.

This time our great caretaker was shouting, "Over my dead body are those horses coming in here!"

He did, however, survive their entry. I suppose that we were quite lucky that this poor man didn't suffer a nervous breakdown but, looking back, it was all such riotous and amazing fun and it was terrific that he actually avoided being taken hostage during the Indian raid.

The best bit of the whole night happened when, as the horses went round the hall, the cheering crowd somewhat frightened them and large quantities of horse manure were deposited all around the venue. From the safety of the stage, with regard to the slippery surface and indeed the smell, I pointed to my pupil crew and said, "Clean that up quick!", how merciless can you get?

Fair play, they did it without flinching and, recalling them now, I have to admit that these were pretty unusual but really fabulous times.

One of the first trips we decided to do in the minibus involved about 12 of the guys that I had got quite close to over these initial years at St Marks, both rugby-playing guys and dance helpers. In the summer holiday of 1972, the lads and I decided to do a tour travelling in the minibus and camping at seaside towns around the coastline of Great Britain. Richard Szemiako came, along with John, son of the governor Mrs Chambers, Eddie Howley (who married several times in future years, booking me each time for the disco), Brian O'Neill and others. We started the trip by driving along the south coast, calling at various places, including Torquay, before we drove onto the south-west, to Newquay, then turning up to go round the coast of Wales before going through the Lake District and into Scotland, where we stayed at Oban and went to the Isle of Skye. On the way back we called at Inverness and Aberdeen then travelled south through Newcastle, Scarborough and Yarmouth - six weeks of absolute joy.

We did have one bit of enormous luck on this trip because, when we were in Newquay, we decided to climb to the top of one of the cliffs at Fistral Bay. At about 30 feet up, John Chambers lost his grip and slipped and fell to the ground. Thankfully he was unhurt and, of course, we abandoned the climb. John didn't need any treatment, so we thanked our lucky stars and carried on with the holiday. I don't think he even told his mother about it when we got home.

CHAPTER 20

SCALE THREE

Still living at home, I would often get out of the house in the evening and drive to Harlow Town Park to visit a new feature in the park called "Pet's corner" which was set next to a small café beside a roller-skating area. There it was that I got to know four guys who were working in various jobs in local firms, their names being Colin Pearson, Bruce Newman, Dick Gill and Pete Conley. We were completely different types of people, at opposite ends of the work spectrum, but they were really down to earth lads and we all got on really well, meeting up a couple of times a week either at Pets Corner or at the snooker room that one of the lads had access to via his firm. Colin was a smoker (for no other reason than that he called his cigarettes "his girl getters!"). Dick had a company car because he was a rep and we often piled into it to go to Basildon Bowl, while Bruce was a landscape gardener. Pete Conley's sister was a maid at Buckingham Palace and she got us seats in The Royal Box at The Albert Hall to see The Moody Blues, apparently the Royal household allot Albert Hall tickets to staff when they are not required, a real result. On one night, when it was extremely wet and the rain was hammering down, we had set off in Dick's car to go bowling at Basildon.

Travelling down the North Weald to Ongar Road, Dick, not known for his slow and careful driving, and on this occasion his judgement was not all that good either, touched the nearside kerb at some speed and this flipped the vehicle over and we cartwheeled a couple of times before the car ended up on its roof, on the pavement next to an isolated house. I was in the back seat with Pete and Bruce and all 3 of us ended up in the tiny low space between the back seats and the front seats. Incredibly the two guys in the front seemed okay as well and, miraculously, we all walked away uninjured to the amazement of the people in the vehicles that stopped behind us. I didn't bother to mention the accident to my parents in order to avoid all the aggravation. The main upshot of the incident was that Dick, unsurprisingly lost his job. It was something we just had to put behind us and our friendship continued on, with these guys still having a role to play in a future school fete.

By the time the next fete came along, we chose to run it as a tribute to "Dads Army" but, tragically, it was organised against a background of immense sadness as school governor, Mrs Chambers, mother of John, who had had that fall as we travelled around Britain, was murdered in her house at Old Harlow.

It was a traumatic time and very difficult for everybody to move on from. So, the fete became a sort of tribute to her and we were lucky enough to secure the services of Bill Pertwee, the ARP warden in the television series, to open the fete, while we supplied the army of soldiers, led by the wonderful Tom McCauley (who played the conductor when the students mimed as an orchestra at the school dance). Tom played Captain Mainwaring and comprising of the usual gang of helpers, all dressed up in army uniform with brooms and sticks as weapons. Bill Pertwee wore his ARP uniform and we met his car at the bottom of the approach road to the school, allowing the army column to march up to the school surrounded on both sides of the street by well-wishers so that he could open the fete to a huge welcome.

This great spectacle actually made the front page of the local paper with a lovey picture of Bill and Tom at the front of the brigade. Bill Pertwee turned out to be a fantastic gentleman and a really lovely man and he spent the whole time that afternoon meeting pupils and parents. He actually spent the whole of his fee on the stalls at the fete and really was a real credit to his profession and everybody loved him.

On the teaching side, Peter Fox had moved into his new school in Wood Green and, on many occasions, he would get me to do his PTA dances at the big Irish Centre in White Hart Lane. I did quite a few functions there for Tottenham Hotspur as well, indeed, I also worked for Tottenham in a big club, The Chanticleer, which was situated under the stand at the old White Hart Lane where the players would always be in attendance. These were the days before selfies and I often had my picture taken with players and then would take it back to school where I pretended to the pupils that all the players were my mates, a great ruse.

Mr Fox was replaced by a 5 feet tall nun from Scotland called Sister Kathleen and her deputy in the department was Mrs Anne White, an extremely clever mathematician, one of whose daughters played for England at netball. Mrs White became the National Union of Teachers (NUT) rep at St Marks. A bit like Miss Bourbon a few years previously. Sister

Kathleen found me quite challenging because my interests were so varied and a little unusual, but we ended up getting on really well and the department became very successful with excellent exam results.

When Sister Kathleen first arrived at St Marks, she formed a close association with Saint Elizabeth's, a Catholic organisation set up in Much Hadham to care for epileptic children. Nowadays, it is a very large entity indeed but, in the 1970s, it was just starting to build its reputation. It was a run by an order of Catholic nuns and that is how Sister Kathleen became involved in a joint venture between St Marks and St Elizabeth's. Our school took a lot of pupils over to St Elizabeth's for a day of "getting to know each other" bonding and I was asked to provide the climax by doing a disco to end the visit on a high.

The whole day was a major success and the St Elizabeth's children loved the disco but, somehow St Marks did not really keep up the association for all that long after the initial event. However, I kept working with St Elizabeth's for some 35 years until I stopped leading my double life as a DJ in the early 2000s – a bit past it, I'm sad to say. That immensely rewarding work was a great leveller for me and a super way to keep my feet firmly on the ground - a valuable reminder of how very lucky so many of us are, even in the darkest of times.

The rugby team had continued to flourish and, via my connections with Harlow Rugby Club and my old reputation as a decent player combined with the success of the new St Marks First XV, John Davies, former head of PE at Mark Hall School, invited me to join him at his new school, Campion in Romford, mainly just to help him with the rugby coaching. The job on offer was as an English teacher, not that the subject mattered where rugby was concerned. Campion had a massive and growing reputation as a "rugby school" and John Davies saw this as a springboard for great personal success. Campion offered me a scale 3 post and I was only a scale 1 teacher at Saint Marks. When Mr Burrell, chairman of the governors and leader of the fete committee, was informed that I was on the brink of moving on, he countered the Campion offer by asking to me to become a Head of Year on a matching scale 3 salary.

I was very happy at St Marks, still living at home with my parents only 3 miles away, saving money at a great rate, it was a no-brainer to accept this counter offer although it did rather piss off John Davies. Mine was a rather controversial appointment in some quarters because I was a non-Catholic and as Head of Year it would be necessary for me to conduct year assemblies and take prayers etc. Nevertheless, everything went through and was approved.

Nigel Bovey, all 6'10"of him, joined the maths department firstly as a student teacher but then, when he qualified, as a full-time member of staff. Nigel was a Captain in the Salvation Army, adding a great deal to the religious ethos of the school and also to the success of the maths department itself. Now we were right up there with the best maths departments in Harlow and our results certainly affirmed that.

CHAPTER 21

SUPERSTARS

A new intake a of first years brought into the school a couple of lads who would test the patience of everyone for the next few years. Ryan and his mate Mitchell were as naughty and mischievous as any pupils could ever be. Their debut incident with me was when they nicked my car keys and thought it was funny when they wouldn't tell me where they were. After ages trying to get the information from them, the solution I arrived at was to split them up and play one off against the other. When separated, Ryan said Mitchell did it while Mitchell said Ryan did it, both informing me that the other one had thrown the keys onto the roof of the school. Retrieving them, at least I could get home, but this was only the beginning and the two of them would, for years, keep us on our toes. Ryan was in fact, a very gifted footballer but at that time was very small and very ginger. Quite often I would take groups of lads to Spurs and on one occasion we went to White Hart Lane when Spurs turned out to be featuring on Match of the Day. When we went, I always used my own season tickets and the lads would sit in the area wherever I managed to get their tickets for.

As we walked up to the ground, we realised that Spurs would be on Match of the Day when we saw all the BBC lorries outside the stadium. After we split up to go to our various seats and settled in to watch the game, you can imagine my shock and horror when, just as the game was about to kick off, out from the stands and on to the pitch ran Ryan. He was 12 years old and about 4 feet 6 inches tall. Up to the centre circle he ran, took the ball from the centre spot with his feet and dribbled in and out of all the players around the centre circle before replacing the ball on the centre spot and acknowledging the crowd with a wave as he attempted to leave. He was then frogmarched from the pitch by the stewards.

When I collected him from the police room later, he told me that he wanted to be on Match of the Day but, when the programme was broadcast, unfortunately for him, they edited him out! Writing this I am reminded that the same thing happened to me when I bragged to one of my classes that I had presented a trophy to David Ginola at a Spurs function, absolutely true, and that the photograph would be in the match programme at Tottenham that Saturday. On that occasion, this time it was me that they edited out, showing only David Ginola and the trophy in the photograph. Embarrassing or what?

Ryan became almost legendary for some of these antics over the years and the stories abound. For example, with his mate Mitchell he was said to have tried to rob a security van delivering money to a bank in Harlow Town Centre. Having watched the cash being placed outside the back-door time-lock area before being collected and carried into the bank, the two of them decided to help themselves to a bag of money. Typically, they chose the bag containing the 2pences and could barely lift it because of the weight. Legend has it that it was the slowest getaway in history.

Around now, St Marks assimilated quite a few staff who were good musicians, indeed so much so that some of them formed a group which performed at local functions like weddings. An outrageous idea was promulgated which involved creating a fictitious supergroup to perform at the school. The ruse was to mime to some obscure, unheard of American rock band's records with their own instruments switched on and live. This would mean that they could play riffs and audible solos in between song breaks, creating the illusion that everything was live. The teachers involved included Dave Morson and Dave Summerville and also Brian Webster and Pete Clark. The group were to be called "Grease Gun", a great name for a pretend Supergroup.

At that time in Harlow there was only one record retail shop and it was called "Startime". I bought all my records for the disco there and knew the staff in the shop really well. As we continually built-up "Grease Gun" and invented fake conversations about whether or not they were likely to tour Great Britain, the groups reputation grew – it was like "The Emperor's new clothes" story.

Pupils started getting curious and asking about how to get hold of their records and I arranged with Startime that they would "always be sold out" of Grease Gun singles and albums because, as a new band on the scene in the US, it was difficult to get their releases imported into stock. The narrative was so strong and the myth so believable that we persuaded Mr O'Shea and Mr Murtagh to give us an hour at the end of a school day to actually stage the concert. Brian Webster had some hip looking mates, we'd used them before as scooter riding Mods, who doubled as reporters for the NME and we got six trustworthy girls in on the act who would be "screamers" and pretend to pass out in the audience during the gig to create the illusion of fan mania.

We had a long rope, which was pulled from one side of the hall to the other about 5 yards in front of the stage, purporting to be for crowd control, with that expert in this field, Mr Murtagh, in charge. The concert was announced as a surprise a week before it happened and the excitement was palpable, yet not one single person questioned why it would be that a top American group would come to St Marks to start their UK Tour, especially for an hour concert at 3 o'clock in the afternoon and on a school day.

Pete Clark was a massive Chuck Berry fan and had always wanted to do the "Chuck Berry hop" on stage, this meant hopping backwards and looking cool while playing the guitar – this was his chance. We managed to arrange for a large car with blacked out windows to come into the rear entrance of the school in view of quite a few classrooms, it was empty of course but we needed to create the illusion of an arrival at the venue. By the time it had pulled up at the changing rooms, which doubled as changing rooms for the gym and the stage in the main hall, the car had moved out of sight of everybody so no one could tell what was going on. As the classes were moved into the hall for the concert, the teachers involved made their way down to the changing rooms to change their appearance and become popstars in a flash.

The crucial thing that we had to achieve was to disguise the teachers taking part making them totally unrecognisable and changing them into "pop stars". Dave Morson had really long hair with uniquely wild sideburns, and the others were all just as easy to recognise. Major cosmetic changes had to be made if we were to pull this off and, fair play to the teachers, they spared nothing and did just that, and all just before showtime!

Dave Morson had removed almost all his hair and even his mother wouldn't have recognised him as he squeezed his ample body into a figure hugging catsuit. The others too had all modified their hairdos and they all donned way out costumes. Pete Clark had become the embodiment of Chuck Berry in a flouncy blouse, while Brian Webster certainly didn't look like a hippy anymore and Dave Summerville had lost all his facial hair. Extreme colourful clothing completed the transformation.

Then they were on! Unbelievable noise, our fake NME reporters flashing their cameras everywhere, our "screaming" girls, tactically dotted round the crowd, giving it large and passing out while Mr Murtagh, not having learnt a great deal from his Noel Edmonds experience, was on the rope having very little success with crowd control.

Grease Gun bounded on stage to an absolutely riotous welcome, letting rip with an extremely loud, very strange something from some really obscure American rock band, adding the sound of their own instruments, both during and in between the mimed songs. No one recognised any of the staff as the change in their appearance was nothing short of incredible and the music was so loud that no one could tell if it was even music! It was bedlam, a totally unbelievable atmosphere. The crowd rushed the stage and one of our screaming girls actually fainted for real. It was absolute mayhem when Pete Clark did his Chuck Berry hop and hopped right off the edge of the stage only to be to be mobbed by the baying crowd. Dave Morson had his shirt ripped off and it was oh-so-real-man, a real 'happening' which made Woodstock look like a kindergarten. Within about 20 minutes everyone knew it was a con but, by now, no-one cared and the audience actually became part of the whole stunt - it was nothing short of amazing and how we got away with staging it, I really don't know! Today, something like that just wouldn't happen but then, that's what made those times special.

Fete time came around again and because we did not have anyone famous to open it this year, we decided to go for another scam. Remember my mate Colin Pearson, well he now worked in the spares department of the big Ford garage in Harlow, Gates. He had very long hair these days, wore psychedelic clothes and drove an old, navy blue transit van. We decided to change him into a superstar so that we would have yet another celebrity to open our fete. Unsurprisingly, none of the kids had ever heard of Colin Pearson, at least none of them were old enough to own a car let alone buy spares at Gates, so we kept talking about him around the school and, as luck would have it, we managed to create a connection between Colin and a guy named Johnny Pearson, who was producing top of the Pops at the time. We "suggested" that Colin was Johnny Pearson's son, who was starting to make it big in the world of pop. Fair play to Colin, he painted up his old van in rainbow colours and our other friends, Bruce and Dick and Pete, pretended to be his bodyguards/come roadies. His name had been blazoned in the same windows as Noel Edmonds, so the word was "well out", and a big crowd arrived at the school to see him open the fete. Yet again the girls were in another frenzy and, I could understand why, because I'd never seen anybody look the part better, his very own pop star look, combined with some inner belief he had created in himself that he was indeed his persona, rainbow coloured clothing, he looked as though he came from The Sweet (a pop group). With a casual wave and a confident walk, he was mobbed as a superstar and opened the fete in a blaze of glory.

After an hour he had to go back to work because the stores were open at Gates on a Saturday afternoon, but the problem we, his mates, had to endure for the next few months was that Colin actually believed that he was a superstar and it took a long time to re-convince him that he was in fact still a storeman at Gates – this was reality TV miles ahead of its time.

Things, in general, were going really well until an incident at Harlow hospital put a small spoke in the works. Mum had worked in the Central Sterile Supplies Department there for quite a few years and was a leading light at the social club, always putting on shows and funny turns. She arranged for me to do the disco at an important fundraiser at the club and she, of course, went along with my sister as dad's health prevented him from going out much Alan, my sister's husband, was not really a social creature. As the evening progressed a guy, unusually, with green hair, came up to the stage a couple of times to ask me to play something by the "Pink Fairies", a band I'd never heard of, let alone had one of their records. On the third occasion that he requested this song I leant forward over the edge of the stage so that I could hear him better but he grabbed hold of my hair and pulled me down off the stage and I fell into the middle of the dancefloor. In a split second he had planted his heavy boot into the top of my head, drawing quite a bit of blood, and, immediately after he inflicted that nasty headwound, he made a dash for the exit, which the brave doorman obligingly opened to allow his escape.

I was very quickly up on my feet and, as I made a beeline for the aggressor, I steamed past my mum and sister not realising that I was rather well covered in blood. At that point my mother apparently nearly passed out but, as I pressed on through the door and after my prey, I had forgotten that they were actually digging up the road outside the Hospital and, plop, I fell into a rather deep and muddy trench. In fact, it took me 4 or 5 goes to extricate myself from this extremely slippery and muddy morass.

When I returned to the hall, without catching the culprit, I ran towards my mother, who was just coming round after the initial shock, this time, not only was I covered in blood but also covered in mud, the sight of which resulted in a swift relapse for the poor woman. Someone took over the stage while I nipped over to Casualty to receive 6 stitches in my headwound following which, a true warrior, I returned to complete the evening's entertainment, as if there hadn't been enough festivity already. The perpetrator was actually arrested by the police later and charged with assault. In court he was found guilty of ABH and fined £500. I was awarded £100 compensation which, of course, he never paid.

CHAPTER 22

END OF AN ERA

In one of the groups that I was teaching one year there were some very bright students and one in particular, John Lewis, was exceptionally gifted, not only in maths but also, he was a very talented footballer who had been persuaded to turn his talents to rugby during his time at St Marks. John was destined to be a key member First XV and, indeed, in future years became one of the true stars of Harlow Rugby Club, gaining representative honours and masses of plaudits as a top fly half. My simple rule to follow was that, whenever I knew I was in trouble in the lesson, stuck over some explanation or solution, I would just ask John to come to the blackboard and explain how the problem could be solved. It worked really well, he understood what was happening and didn't care, and between us we ensured that everybody in that class passed their 'O' level exam, including one unconfident pupil named Shelagh, who absolutely hated maths with a passion and was so fearful of the subject that the fear itself prevented her from thinking straight. She really battled through though, and because the ambiance in the lessons was so great, she relaxed and achieved the 'O' level. Would you believe it, she actually then went on to become a tax inspector.

At the beginning of the school year 1975, Kelvin Evans, yet another Welshman joined the staff as head of PE. The rugby team continued to flourish, with a new set of players coming through in the year below, with John Lewis outstanding. Kelvin arranged for this team to do an Easter tour in South Wales, with three matches against some of Kelvin's former local schools. As a fund raiser for the tour, at Christmas, we took the team, with some girls to help, on a carol singing adventure, a bit of an off-beat thing to contemplate, but after a lot of persuasion the lads took it in good heart and we made a fair bit of money to cover our expenses.

Dad's health had deteriorated badly and the emphysema made him struggle to even lift a comb. He continued to go to work though, as that challenge gave him the motivation to keep fighting on, he was only 61 and it was upsetting to see his self-respect ebb away.

After talking with my mother about getting my dad to do something else to give him a boost, we came up with the idea that he could sit on the door at the Friday night discos at St Marks. These were big events now, at least 200 children every week, and I had become as much as a bouncer as I was a DJ. Several of the lads were able to take on the stage duties when I was required to sort out skirmishes and, indeed, there were plenty of occasions when there was a high level of disruption. There was quite a bit of disquiet among the neighbours on the main road passing the school, especially around 10 o'clock, which was emptying out time, and there would be lots of traffic caused by parents picking up their children.

My dad was able just to sit at the table by the door and keep an eye, giving a very mature presence to the festivities. It was great for him because the kids really took to him and talked to him a lot and, in fact, gave him the major boost we were hoping for.

Then, one Friday night, a very unpleasant group, not from our school, decided that they wanted to gate-crash the disco. George, another great right-hand of mine at the time took over the stage and I went down to the door, which was always visible from the stage, to sort out the aggravation that appeared underway. There was no major difficulty until one of the gate-crashers decided to draw a knife and threaten everybody. I have mentioned before that my father was probably the strongest man I have ever met and feared nothing, and notwithstanding his small stature and the state of his health, he rose from his chair, grabbed the attacker by the arm and jammed the hand with the knife in it down onto the table with such force that he was powerless to use it. The intruder was unable to move a muscle for the 10 minutes it took for the police to arrive and arrest him and allow the disco to continue. The incident was over but it gave me a lot of problems again trying to justify the disco's existence but, luckily, the fundraising necessity and its success in that matter always managed to hold sway.

When the case went to Harlow Magistrates Court dad and I received threats from the attacker and his mates and, when we all passed each other at the courthouse, we were advised that the guy would be pleading not guilty. However, the fact that my dad and I had turned up and weren't frightened off by the rabble and their threats ensured that the defendant changed his plea to guilty and neither of us had to give evidence.

The rugby team made its trip to Wales, winning two of the three games, and it was a great success both on and off the field, where our boys made a very good impression when they were put up in opposition players homes. Kelvin and I shared the minibus driving on the trip and the parents, and boys, were quite happy because it was a well-known fact that I was a non-drinker.

After one of the games, we had a meal at a local pub and, for a bit of fun, we decided to see what would happen if the lads knew we were both over the limit to drive. Kelvin had a few pints and so everyone knew that I would have to be the driver. Just before we left, and in full view of everyone, Kelvin bought me a snowball, probably about 1% alcohol content and, after I'd had a sip, we made out that I was so drunk that I could barely stand. It was hilarious as two of the lads carried me to the bus and put me in the driver's seat while the rest of the team got in the back without question. I made sure I drove in a zig zag to start with and even though no-one complained, they weren't quite sure they were totally safe. We did get one over on them after that meal and it was great for team spirit and bonding.

As the school year went on, Dad's health was not all that good and was definitely deteriorating, so much so that he began to mention that he might need to retire but a serious incident at his work changed that mindset. One of the workmen on the shop floor at the Rolling Mills, a very big man, well over 6ft and more than 16 stone, had been sacked for stealing. It must be stressed again that my father was barely 8 stone, wore glasses and was very unwell with emphysema. Yet when the guy learned that he had been sacked, he lashed out viciously at my dad's head smashing his glasses, blacking and cutting his eye simultaneously. Ill or not, this was not a wise thing for that miscreant to have done. My father knocked him out with one punch and, when he came home that night, battered and bruised as he was, his self-esteem had grown immeasurably and, all of a sudden, he was the man I had known all my life and he was motivated to continue working, which he did for another 18 months.

I was fortunate enough to be talking about my worries over my father's health to one of the lads from the rugby team, Vince Ferrie, another brilliant guy from a wonderful family who also went on to become a stalwart at Harlow Rugby Club. His father was a police officer, a sergeant in fact, and it turned out that Sergeant Ferrie was also a faith healer. So it was that he started visiting my dad every week to see if he could help him. He worked absolute miracles over the next year or so and my father's quality of life was immeasurably improved. On one occasion, after Sergeant Ferrie had left the house and my sister had called in to see how dad was, she told me that dad had said to her that lots of Japanese people, with large colourful cushions, were in our hallway calling him to go with them, but he decided but he didn't want to. This vivid description is something that is haunted me ever since and has forced me to give very serious thought as to what may happen after death.

In September 1976 I was doing all my usual things, working with the rugby team and sorting out what we could do in the way of fundraising and dances. Around the time of my birthday, early in October, I was driving out to Bishops Stortford when I noticed that there was a new housing development being built at Thorley Park. Just the Harlow side of Bishops Stortford. "Rialto" were the builders and they were moving on to phase 2 of the development with some show homes available to view in phase 1. My curiosity stimulated, I popped into the site to look around and the thought of finally moving out of my parents' home had jumped into my mind. Because mum and dad had allowed me to continue living at the home, although I did in practice own half of it, I was in a strong financial position, especially as I had virtually every Saturday booked up with discos, mostly functions for people connected to St Marks or the stuff that I did for Spurs. Thorley Park was a small niche development and phase 1 was just starting to be occupied with phase 2 just getting underway.

Phase 1 had a showhouse of the type that I liked and could afford and I went in and looked around. I really liked the floor plan, and the house was ideal for a small family. Phase 2 was being built just up the road, designed around a courtyard system with 10 or 11 houses situated around a square with a small grass area in the centre. There was generally a small terrace block with three or four houses combined with a mixture of several detached and semi-detached ones. I came across the first courtyard in from the main thoroughfare, where none of the houses had been built but the foundations were in the ground, allowing you to see the actual layout of the square. After turning left into the courtyard, there was a terrace of 3 houses on the centre right of the square. The middle house of the group of three was the cheapest in the courtyard, priced at £15,100, while the two semis either side were £15,600. The next courtyard along was effectively behind my square and the back garden of the mid terraced house actually backed on to the open side of that square meaning that the house that I would choose would not be overlooked at all. Although it was the cheapest house it was, in fact, the best house in the square, position wise at least, and when my father came over with me with me later, and checked it all out, he agreed.

I decided that I liked it and would go ahead and buy it. I would have had enough money to buy it in cash but obviously I needed furniture, never having owned any property or furniture before and, in that case, I had to arrange a small mortgage before the house became mine in February 1977. I would now have lived in three houses only in my 29 years, all new builds, the flat in Tottenham which I was born into, the house in Churchfield and now my own house in Thorley Park, Bishops Stortford. Indeed, I have still only lived in three houses in my entire lifetime because, against all the odds and somewhat unbelievably, I still live in Bishops Stortford some 43 years later.

It wasn't long before the disco, at which we sold refreshments including drinks, chocolate and crisps, branched out, so as to speak, into a tuckshop/common room in my classroom which meant that, at break times and lunchtimes, loads of pupils made a beeline for the assembly hall room which became a sort of school-based university refectory area. Unfortunately, the dinner ladies in the kitchen were not at all happy and they complained that their trade had fallen because the kids were spending their dinner money on sweets and things. But the profits helped the school finances and that always took precedence. Now was also the time that I had to finally surrender and be forced into making a small change in my appearance. When my latest nickname, Mr Magoo, gave me the hint that I might need some assistance with my vision as, apparently, I spent my life squinting at the blackboard and had to write on it from a distance of about an inch away, and I realised that Elton John had perhaps made it cool to wear glasses, I bit the bullet and progressed into a 10 year phase of wearing very colourful spectacles. White frames, red, purple etc - obviously I was hoping for a nickname connected with Elton John but the one I got was Joe 90.

The Hartshorn family always had a cat at home and we had some really nice ones. Our first one at Harlow was named "Taffy" (welsh connection) and she had three kittens actually on the day that mum was making our

Christmas cake, December 4th, I recall. She delivered a black one, a shorthaired tabby and a normal tabby with a fluffy tail. We named them Sugar, Spice and Sultana. The black one, Sultana, went to a neighbour at the far end of the road while Sugar went to Trevor Price, one of the men that dad had brought from Brynmawr to get a job at the Rolling Mills and who, via my mum, managed to get the house next door but one to us in Churchfield. He and his family renamed Sugar as Lucky. We kept Spice, a great cat, who lived till he was 16 and was notable for the time when his tail got set on fire by the gas feed to our fridge, after which he walked about for about a minute, with his tail in flames, before we could put it out.

Along came Friday, the 9th of December 1977, the school had a day off for Christmas shopping and I was going to go to Romford for the day. Romford being the last word in shopping in those days with a C&A and a BHS. I was woken at 6:30 am by phone call from my mother, remarkable in itself because my parents had only had the phone installed a couple of months before, when I left home, and I only had my phone connected the week before.

She gave me the tragic news that my father had passed away in his sleep that morning, having finally retired from the Rolling Mills only three weeks earlier. He was only 63 years old. I firmly believe that it was the challenge of having to get up in the morning and go to work that actually kept him going and then, when he retired, that desire and necessary effort had been taken away from him and he wasn't able to carry on.

It was before I arrived at the house that the ambulance had got there to remove my father's body and this really was so beneficial to me because I would not have been able to go into the room where he was lying and, in fact, I was unable to bring myself to visit him in the chapel of rest.

My sister and my mother both had the courage to say their goodbyes but I know that I would not have been able to handle the grief and it would have been far too traumatic for me to bear because I was actually very close to him. As it was, it was quite surreal that, within a couple of hours of his death, there I was in Daniel Robinson, the undertakers, organising a funeral and a burial plot while in a complete haze of despair.

Remarkably I had never been to a funeral in my life nor had I experienced the death of any family member. The following week was like a tornado doing things that I cannot even remember doing. The staff rugby match against the school was the following Wednesday and Kelvin Evans was very surprised when I went back to school on the Monday and said that I wanted to play. My father had been my biggest fan when I played rugby, he supported me at virtually every match I played in and I felt that I had to play in this game as a special honour to him, and I did just that. It was fantastic to participate and, although I cannot remember what the result was, I do know that I played well and my father would have been proud of that.

My mother was now in an emotional turmoil, she had been married to dad for 39 years and he was her rock. Dad did have a small pension, a portion of which transferred to her, and she did have her job at Harlow Hospital but, even though she had no rent to pay for the house, it was going to be tough times for her.

Within days I organised a re-mortgage on my house in Bishop Stortford - The first of many re-mortgages to come over the future years - and borrowed £10,000 against the house over a period of 10 years. When it materialised a month or so later, I gave all of that £10,000 to my mother so that she could have a more comfortable life although, with more experience now, I realise that it would have been far better if I had given her a weekly amount instead and saved all that interest as well as protecting against the terrible family weakness of spending money. At least I was happy that, as I went to my Father's funeral, I had done the right thing. The actual service and burial took place at Harlow cemetery and his mother, Beatrice, came from Brynmawr accompanied by dad's brother Vernon while his sister Betty came from Kent. It was a sad but moving event with us exiting the chapel to the strains of "The Lord is My Shepherd".

After the coffin had been lowered into the grave, my sister told me that, as all the mourners moved away from the graveside, Arthur Flight, her godfather and the foundling who was the other man that my dad had brought from Brynmawr to the Rolling Mills in the early 1930s, stood alone by the graveside and cried his eyes out. An image which brings me to tears as I write at this moment, all those years on. On that day, for me, when the coffin was lowered into the grave, I can only say that it felt like a massive, and I mean massive, weight had been lifted from my shoulders. It was an uncanny and strangely physical experience but, mentally, I was completely satisfied that I had not let my father down in any way. What a great man he was.

CHAPTER 23

FIRE

St Marks had a couple of feeder primary schools which were 2 or 3 miles away and, because of this, a private hire bus service to shuttle the pupils to and from the school was organised, the theory being that the parents would pay weekly for the service which would be non-profit making. The owner of the coach firm was himself the parent of children at the school and was putting on this service as a big favour to the school and the other parents. Mr O'Shea, a really great headmaster but not the best of businessmen, was badly let down when very few of the parents paid their fees and, of course, they couldn't be chased because nobody knew who was actually on the bus let alone when they travelled on it. Mr O'Shea turned to me to try and sort out the puzzle.

I found a couple of hundred small, wooden oblong shapes about the size of a domino that the woodwork department had used for something or other and these would serve as my tickets. The bus provided was a double-decker with room for about 120 passengers and, when it arrived in the morning, I would take a return fare of 50p, giving each passenger a wooden ticket to present for the return journey. When the passengers got back on the bus in the evening, I simply collected their ticket at the door as they got on. With this easy and efficient system, we collected around £250 each week which not only paid the coach firm but also made a profit for the school fund. It of course meant that I had to be at the bus in the morning and in the evening, which wasn't a problem unless there was bad weather, which often was the case, and for this eventuality I got a fisherman's yellow waterproof suit, resulting in the rather appropriate and affectionate nickname of "Banana Man". This system carried on for the whole of my time at St Marks and, who knows, it might still be in operation today.

Time inextricably moved on and one Sunday afternoon, when I was watching TV in the lounge, I heard a loud crackling sound coming from the kitchen. I jumped up and rushed into the kitchen to see what it was, only to be confronted by the chip pan going up in flames, the fire caused by me having left the pan on the heat. I tried to smother the flames with a damp cloth but without success and so I decided to get the pan out of the house. I needed to get it out of the kitchen, through the lounge and into the back garden, a distance of about 30 feet. I picked it up by the handle with my right hand and it was unbearably hot as I headed towards the back door. The backdraught I was creating by walking sent the flames up my arm and burnt the sleeve completely off my jumper. I got to within a couple of feet of the open back door before the heat and the pain defeated me and I had to put the pan down on the carpet which instantly melted, creating a large round hole in the lounge. The oil had largely burnt away by now and the flames were not high enough to be a problem in the house as the fire brigade, called by a vigilant neighbour, arrived and read me the riot act for not just calling them and leaving the pan to burn.

I was taken to hospital and my right hand was completely black, with severe burns to the area between my thumb and forefinger, where the handle of the pan had laid as I carried it. The doctors had doubts about the long-term future of that hand and, as I was bandaged up, I was warned that I should not use the hand at all, and that included driving. I did lose a couple of freckles on my face because of the oil splashing, but they were cosmetic injuries. I actually went to school as usual the following day and drove as normal. I had no time off, however, I could not participate in any sporting activities for three or four months after that and had to endure a lot of shooting pains going up my arm for a long time afterwards. Thankfully my hand recovered fully, apart from a now unnoticeable scar on the webbing in between my thumb and forefinger. Yet again, I was very lucky boy.

During that initial decade or so at St Marks, it is quite remarkable how amazingly talented were, not only a great number of pupils, but also the staff. These factors all contributed to a really fantastic spirit at the school which you would have to say was nurtured by the, shall we say, light touch management of a truly gifted headmaster.

At the end of 1982 Mr O'Shea retired and a new headmaster took the helm. He was radically different to Mr O'Shea and the atmosphere and feel of the school changed. It was soon evident that he and I would not get on and then it was that I was approached by one the priests on our governing body to relocate the discos to his church hall to help bolster his finances. This was a big endorsement for me and I did not refuse. The church hall was half the size of St Marks school hall but you could still get around 200 people in there although it was in need of some renovation. I arranged for some contractors to build a stage and check the wiring, plus we also made removable blackouts for all the windows to ensure the maximum effect for our ultra violet lighting. We were up and running and soon attracted the attendances to make it very viable for the church coffers.

By December we had run a "Teddy Boy" dance for adults, replacing the old parents' dances at St Marks but basically with the same cliental.

One incident of note during these discos was brought on by the fact that church hall was across the road from a local evening youth club, a club with a reputation for having a very tough crowd. One group in particular took great exception to there being a thriving disco across the road.

One night, after the evening function was over, and I was walking alone down to my car - which I parked a fair distance away for security reasons - I was confronted by pretty large lad and four of his mates. In gang culture, the leader always instructs his lackeys to do his will while he actually never gets involved. On this occasion, the four henchmen surrounded me and were obviously going to give me a good hiding. However, muscling them aside, I stood and jabbed my finger at their leader as I calmly asserted, "I'm probably going to get a good going over, but only one person is going to go down here tonight and that person is you!"

The incident ended there and then, the foes melted away into the darkness and I went home safely in my car.

CHAPTER 24

DOG RACING AND DENTISTS

1984 came along, things were all going along well and I was watching a lot of football.

Spurs had reached the two-legged final of the UEFA Cup and, although I had not been to any of the away legs in Europe, I was present at every home match. The second leg of the final was at White Hart Lane, starting with the score tied at 1-1 after the first leg in Belgium. Anderlecht was the opposition and this was the Tony Parks final because, after the match finished 2-2 on aggregate, after extra time, Tony Parks, the stand-in goalkeeper that night, saved two penalties in the shoot out for Spurs to lift the trophy 4-3 on penalties. Not only did Tony Parks go ballistic but everyone in the stands did as well. I didn't get home until about 2am.

That final had been a fantastic and memorable night for every Spurs supporter and the joy was carried forward to the weekend when the supporters club threw a big party for the team in a nightclub at the top of Tottenham High Road. I was lucky enough to provide the music and joined in the festivities when we were all given turns to carry the UEFA cup around the dancefloor in a lap of honour. I had pictures taken with manager Keith Burkinshaw and various players, including Steve Perryman, giving me even more street cred when I got back to school. The picture gallery in my classroom was growing and I continued to allow the students to believe that all these people were actually my mates.

Now it was that I decided to change the garden at home. I planted about 20 conifers at the back of the house, seven of them were in front of the small patio - which was in turn, in front of patio doors - while the rest were shared between the sides and the back of the garden. Over the years, as they grew taller and taller. My neighbour, Doris, became rather unhappy about this because she said that they blocked all the light from her garden and, it must be said that, by the time I met Karen in 1999, they were all about 25 feet tall and she thought I was living in the black hole of Calcutta.

It was during this period that I stepped up my Interest in greyhound racing again and when a Mr Alf Mowat joined the school staff, as head of the art department, we discovered that we had a shared hobby. We actually progressed this interest by buying a couple of greyhounds who we placed with the greyhound trainer Pam Heaseman who was based down the road in Nazeing.

Naturally, we thought that these dogs would be our ticket to riches and the two that we bought were called Gary Magpie and Proud Boots, the second one being a bitch. Gary Magpie looked to be a really good buy and won a couple of races very quickly but, unluckily he injured his leg soon after and was unable to race again. Proud Boots was a really solid long-distance bitch and she became a big favourite with the Walthamstow crowd. One night, we were told by the trainer that Proud Boots was coming into season and although, by the rules, she was not eligible to run because a bitch in season apparently runs a lot faster with all the dogs staying behind as they chase her, she would be taking her chance. As she had not run well in her last few races, we expected a big starting price and went to the track armed with £500 pounds to win big! Unfortunately, it seemed that everyone and his brother knew the situation and the dog started at 1/2 favourite. She did win but we only won £250 and not the thousands that we were expecting. That evening rather tempered our expectations on how rich we would actually become from owning dogs but, the fascinating offshoot from this interest came when Pam Heaseman's head lad offered us the chance to buy a young but experienced bitch, plying her trade at Hackney Wick Stadium. She was called was called Lady Lano.

Pam Heaseman's man - and they are all great salesman, whether it's dogs or horses - told us that, although the dog was £1,000 to buy, we would get our money back first time out because she would definitely win. How did he know this? Lady Lano was "a very quick away dog", very fast out of the traps, and also a railer, a dog that hugged the inside rail. He would ensure that Lady Lano was drawn wide in stall 6, so that when she "hit the box" her early pace would take her directly across all the other dogs as she headed for the rails, severely impeding them so that she could go clear and then hopefully lead all the way and hang on. It all sounded very, very plausible indeed.

With my work at the church hall and connections still strong with the fundraisers at St Marks, quite a few of whom were interested in greyhound racing, including my wonderful friend Anne White, our NUT rep and now a great friend of my mum and sister, we broached the idea of buying the animal with various parents who partook in gambling. The idea got rave reviews and we collected the money to purchase Lady Llano and she became "The School Fund Dog"!

When word got around about what we had done, loads of parents got on board with the idea and Lady Lano became an icon of betting for the whole school family. For that first "nailed on race", 6 members of staff came with me to Hackney on the Saturday morning to make sure we got our bet on professionally. We took with us £2,000 in cash from the school fund which we managed to spread around the bookmakers at virtually the same time, achieving odds averaging about 9/2. It was a hell of a job, but we all knew what we were doing and Hackney was the major Saturday morning draw for live TV greyhound racing in all the bookmakers across the country. There used to be around 20 bookies on the rails, which made it easier to get the bets on quickly without losing the odds. All very mathematical! The excitement peaked as the bell rang to indicate that the hare was running and, with a crash, the stalls opened and the dogs were on their way. Right to plan Lady Lano flew out of the traps, across the other dogs and headed for the rails. 2 of the inside dogs were knocked over and the other 3 severely impeded, there was no stopping Lady Lano, she stuck to the rails like glue, went clear and stayed on to win comfortably. You could only hear the St Marks staff celebrating at Hackney, there was a hush around the Bookmakers area.

The school fund was £9,000 better off, parents had made a killing and all was good. Of course, it wasn't that easy all of the time, mostly because the Greyhound Racing Association introduced seeding for wide, middle and rail runners, meaning that a railing dog could not usually be allowed to run wider than trap 3, whereas wide runners could only go into 4, 5 or 6. The school fund and the parents were all sensible enough to make that the biggest bet we ever had and other bets were very much smaller, bird in the hand, so as to speak. Over the next few years, Lady Lano won quite a few races and gave everyone at St Marks a great deal of pleasure. When she retired, Anne White took her home as a pet and I remember her telling my mother that Lady Lano had completely devoured her sofa. However, she did forgive her and the greyhound lived a long and happy life.

One great favour that Anne White did for me, at this time, involved the dentist of all people. I never had problems with my teeth and had not visited the dentist for decades until, all of a sudden, I had toothache in one of my back molars. I was able to get an appointment with the dentist at the Nuffield House practice at the Stow, about a mile away from the school and, when I sat in the dentist's chair, he looked at the problem and decided that the tooth needed to be extracted. It was only then that I realised that the reason I had not visited the dentists for years was that I was utterly terrified of them. After I had accepted that I had to have the procedure, the dentist told me he would give me a couple of painkilling injections in the gums to nullify the pain and then get on with pulling the tooth out. In went the injections, out came the "pliers" and, excruciating pain as he bore down on my jaw.

He simply did not believe that he was hurting me and could not understand why I was screaming that the pain was intolerable. Eventually he stopped work and decided that it would be better if I was given a gas extraction, but now I was now very discombobulated and, as he tried to get the gas mask over my face, I left the chair with considerable force, tossing the nurse mercilessly to one side and pinning the dentist against the wall.

I am afraid that was the end of the consultation, and the amusing part was that I found out that the dental nurse was, in fact, a parent of children at St Marks, another embarrassment to add to my long list of stories.

As it was the dentist arranged for me to have an extraction under a general anaesthetic at Epping hospital, safer for everybody involved and it was Anne White who had to drive me there and take me home afterwards because of the anaesthetic. She was a brilliant lady and a magnificent friend to me. Sadly, she passed away after the turn of the century, a great loss to my whole family.

CHAPTER 25

DRIVING FORWARD

This was the time that personalised number plates were first hitting the streets and I thought it would be cool to get one to go on my Renault Fuego. So it was that I spent a few grand on my first personalised number plate, 923 RH. It did look pretty good in the car park, although there were still some members of staff at St Marks, management in particular, who did not think much of me and this number plate really got under their skin – tough!

Onto 1985 and everything was running smoothly at school, it even had been requested for me to move the discos back to St Marks, both for financial and social bonding reasons and New Year's Eve dances would also return in 1985 and 1986. I lived in my home at Bishops Stortford on my own and, when he had a domestic problem, this caused a new English teacher at St Marks to ask me a cheeky and quite provocative question. His name was Keith and he was a young, good looking bloke with flowing blond locks, a teacher who had, at least, taken the pressure off the rest of us as regards crushes. He had not long been married but he began to have a serious affair with a very attractive domestic science teacher at the school and this caused a marriage breakdown.

He, therefore, decided to approach me with his desire to move into my house with me, his view being that, as I was living in a three-bedroom house alone, it would be the perfect place for him to crash, rent free, of course! I could not believe the consternation he showed when I refused to let him move in and he did not speak to me again.

Thoughts turned to those New Year's Eve events and the new Friday discos. A new team of helpers was required and my main man was a guy named Tony Daniel. Tony was an absolute gem and there was nothing he wouldn't do for me. He was so big hearted that at Christmas time, off his own back, he would put on a Santa suit and deliver a little gift to each of the small the children who lived on his estate at Millwards. He was not an academic person but he was extremely street-wise and I knew that he would make a success of his life. Indeed, it was very gratifying to me that so many of the people who I was fortunate enough to come into contact with at St Marks went on to achieve great things. 20 years later, Tony made the headlines in the Sun newspaper when, as a lorry driver driving a 40 tonner down the A 414 near Harlow, he prevented a suicide attempt by a man jumping from a bridge by moving his lorry underneath the structure and sealing it off. This is a tactic which the police have gone on to use many times since then. I think that Tony worked for Comet at the time, and that company gave him a special award in recognition of his actions, very well deserved.

It was around this time that I met a new girlfriend at a wedding where I was providing the music. Her name was Jessica and we were about to embark on a ten year association which is probably best described as a really loving friendship rather than a romance. It would be Jessica who would, unwittingly, lead me to follow a journey that would completely change the direction of my life. The most significant event in our relationship happened almost at the very beginning of it when we returned to her house after a night out and met her sister Mary along with her boyfriend Patrick Simmons.

Patrick gave off the air of success as he was a local electrical contractor who ran a very successful company. The company had large contracts with Essex County Council and was involved in much of the Essex school work, including new projects. One odd coincidence, helpful to me on one occasion, was that we both had the same colour and make of car. I had changed my blue Fuego for a black one with the red racing stripe down the side while Patrick had a plain black one. I could still be a target for some of the nasty elements of society and I used to park my car away from the area on disco nights. On this particular night, thinking it belonged to me, someone decided to vandalise Patrick's car - you could say it was one of the few occasions that he would ever "take one for me".

Jessica was a really special, classy woman who came from a loving family who had led a really sheltered life away from the real world. Her older sister Mary was a gifted musician and worked for the BBC, a place to which Jessica followed her. She was a gifted artist and craftsperson, very much into music and was a massive fan of The Doors, being crazy about Jim Morrison, and Led Zeppelin, where Robert Plant was her main man. Phil Collins was another huge icon for her at that time and no doubt she'll still be going to Glastonbury, a custom that she took up after departing from me. I was very good at taking her to gigs though and I managed to get us seats for Live Aid in 1985, a pretty iconic concert to have been at in person. Then we saw Robert Plant at the Apollo and even managed to get in at the Albert Hall to see Phil Collins in 1990, when we spent £160 on 2 tickets from a tout outside the venue. The tickets turned out to be front row seats in the stalls, the best possible position she would ever sit in for any concert she ever goes to in her life.

Amidst all this, we even managed to spend a week at Disneyland Florida before fitting in the most daunting challenge of all, which was teaching Jessica to drive. This is something she definitely did not want to do and I had to be very forceful with her in order to persuade take it on. Never even having ridden a bike, she had absolutely no idea, nothing, zilch about how roads work, had never heard of the highway code and how she ever managed to cross the road, I'll never know. She was totally lacking in confidence and I had to be really firm, if not nasty, with her to even get her behind the wheel at first. It was a massive learning curve, but she did start to get some satisfaction from the progress she was making and, suddenly, realised how many benefits being able to drive would bring. Despite all of the of disagreements we had over the months and after a lot of heartache, she passed her test first time. It had all been worth it, she was over the moon and her parents couldn't believe it.

I became intrigued with Patrick Simmons and his electrical business success. It all seemed so straightforward, in spite of the fact that he would often ask me for a loan to help with cash flow.

This insidious curiosity began to make me think that the time might be arriving for me to make a change in the direction of my life. I had continued to do well making money on the side and rarely touched my teachers' wages, apart from buying the occasional new car. Some of the teachers at the school were a bit jealous of me because they thought I was loaded but, then again, none of them were prepared to get off their backsides to put in the hours to earn that extra money.

The runes were aligned, bigtime, for me to make changes in my life and fate certainly intervened one lunchtime in the middle of the summer term in 1987. I had gone out in my car to get a sandwich and have a break from school when, as I drove back towards the school, I could see a mass gathering of people in the front car park, in and around the cars and near the front entrance of the building. As I entered the gate, I could see that, in the hub of the crowd, a fierce fight was going on with about five or six people involved with many onlookers baying for blood. It later transpired that this fight was, in fact, caused by an invasion of Passmores pupils from half a mile up the road, undoubtedly over some minor incident that had happened elsewhere.

I drove my car gingerly through the crowd to the centre of the disturbance, got out, forcibly separated the protagonists and, within seconds, the fight was over and everyone had dispersed. After this had happened, I realised that standing at the edge of the affray, watching with his obnoxious deputy head, was the headmaster himself. Nothing was said and those two heroes returned to the safety of the building while I parked my car and went to the staffroom.

Within half an hour I was summoned to the head's office. I made sure that I was accompanied by the NUT rep, my great compatriot Anne White, as I was quite aware that my relationship with the new head had reached the point of no return. The upshot of my interview with the two gentlemen was that, in their opinion, I had been too aggressive with the milling crowd and should not have made any physical contact with them. My retort was, "You both just stood there and watched it, someone could have been seriously hurt while you did nothing – pathetic!"

I realised immediately that there was really no coming back from that statement and that I would have to consider my position forthwith - at least I had Anne White as a witness to that whole farce. What little respect I had for that management team had vanished, I was now 40 years old had been at St Marks for 16 years, it was time to move on and seek another challenge. That very night I ran into Patrick Simmons at Jessica's house and asked him if he would like a partner and fancied teaching me about the electrical business. When he replied that he could do with someone to do the books, we concluded that as I was, allegedly, not only a mathematician but was also a good fundraiser, we were, it seemed, a perfect fit.

The next day I went in to see the management at the school and gave my three months' notice, my flirtation with teaching would be over in July 1987. To be honest, I didn't hold my breath for a nice send off when I left St Marks and, indeed, after a very perfunctory thankyou and goodbye, the silver lining came when the pupils presented me with the largest model of Flymo, a piece of equipment that helped me keep my garden in very good order for many years.

CHAPTER 26

NEW BUSINESS

It was out of the frying pan and into the fire for me. Sad to say that during my three months' notice period Patrick's company, had gone into liquidation and that we would be starting up a new company. I must admit that that was a bit of a shock start but, apparently, this is how business works a lot of the time and, already, I was starting to appreciate that I had an awful lot to learn.

So it was that we had to set up a new company which we called RP Supplies and Electrical services Ltd -, R for Ross and P for Patrick, supplies because we sold fixings and the main bit, electrical services, which was self-explanatory.

In those initial years I was full of enthusiasm and wore a shirt and tie as I lived my life as a director, sitting behind a desk with my own computer, which was nothing like today's ones but more like a big TV with green writing on the screen, like the ones you see in Murder She Wrote.

I still lived at Bishops Stortford and though my relationship with Jessica was now quite serious, she rarely spent the night at my house. I had money behind me because, basically, I saved all my teachers wages and these savings I had invested via a financial advisor, Richard Van Marle, in an Abbey Life investment plan.

Patrick's old company had been based in a small industrial unit at the Stow, Harlow, and for its first few months RP took over that unit. We grew quickly and changed our premises to a newly refurbished second-floor office at a block called Shenval House, in the centre of Harlow's main industrial area at Edinburgh Way. This move involved an investment of some of my money to get the legal work done and to buy office furniture but, par for the course, dismal fate would strike again and two calamitous events were about to take place, with devastating consequences for my life.

Firstly, on Thursday night, October 15th, 1987, came the great storm. A violent extratropical cyclone with hurricane-force winds which swept the UK, France and the Channel Islands to devasting effect. As it moved into

Black Friday, the damage to the country's infrastructure was horrific and there was misery and distress everywhere.

On the lighter side, when I turned on the Southeast News on BBC 1 that evening, there being interviewed was my former pupil and now busy roofer, Ryan (the one who ran onto the pitch during Match of the Day). He was telling everyone that he was snowed under with work and was ready to be assistance to anyone who needed it. For Ryan, sadly, it transpired that he was wanted for questioning on a matter of VAT fraud and his celebrity TV appearance had alerted the police to where he was and, as a consequence, he was detained as the interview came to an end. Typical Ryan!

Worse events were to follow – Black Monday - only four days later, on the 19th October 1987. That day all my savings disappeared! I told you that I had developed some super inner strength and, considering what had happened, I believe that I coped with that despair very well indeed. Nothing could be done, the stock market crashed - end of story - start again.

What a strange dichotomy I seem to be, I like to have money for security but I honestly believe that I am not materialistic per se. Things for things sake don't really matter to me at all. Some things are more important than possessions but, then again, that may be the gambler in me. I realised that I needed to pick myself up and carry on, the only difference now was that I just had nothing to fall back on anymore.

Having made the move to Shenval House, Patrick used his old connections to get us some good contracts and we added quite a few subbies to our workforce. Teaching had been a world in many ways sheltered from reality, the business environment was a completely different animal. Especially when you were creating your own work in order to earn your income and then have to collect that money in before you got paid, and then only after you had paid your men. It took me a long time to understand how contracting worked, or rather didn't work. Each contract has stage payments which usually works alright but, when you come to the last payment, that's when all the arguments happen and it is very hard to extract that last payment from the client.

Unfortunately, that last payment is where any profit lies, that's the profit that pays your overheads, including your own wages, and that is the reason why contractors need to move onto the next contract as soon as one ends, because they always seem to miss out on the very last payment and so need a new first payment to keep the cash flow going. That was, I found out years later, what caused the demise of Patrick's former company but, of course, he never pointed out these quite major flaws in contracting to me, although my lack of due diligence lays these shortcomings at my own door.

Sometimes things do happen to give you a boost and restore your faith in humanity and, amazingly, I had loads of requests from parents that I knew from St Marks to try and organise one final New Year's Eve dance at the school, despite my appalling relationship with the management.

I think that, after the events of Black Friday and Black Monday everybody in the country needed something to lift their spirits. Apparently, several influential people had mentioned it to the headmaster and so, when I telephoned to ask him about running the party, he was quite amenable to the idea - although it was probably all about money yet again. However, this wasn't to be a school event, I could hire the hall and run the dance as a private function. The cost for the hire of the hall was £2,000, with an extra £500 for caretaking and electricity.

A quick calculation told me that the figures added up, 300 people at £20 a head gave a £6,000 budget, a viable proposition for someone like me to make a quick couple of grand profit at a time when the money would be very useful. I would need help but I still had plenty of pupils at the school who would be very keen on coming along, especially now as I would pay them for their time. It was all systems go, selling the tickets didn't prove to be any problem at all, I still managed to organise the confetti and decorations in the normal way and ordered the food and Pomagne.

Everything went just like clockwork as always. The dance went really smoothly, without a single hitch, and was a great success but, as always, there was a huge amount of mess for us to deal with. For years we had become used to cleaning up far worse and the policy was always to get on with it immediately the dance was over. That's the procedure that we followed this time and we'd completed the job by about 10am New Year's Day.

Never in the past had we overlooked anything and the venue was always cleaner when we finished then when we started. We always worked to a gold standard and nothing was different this time, everything and everywhere was spotless. When I got home that lunchtime, I reckoned that

I made about £1,500 profit for my efforts, a return that I was delighted about.

Into the happy new year of 1988, back behind my desk at Shenval House beavering away. 10 days into the new year I received a letter from St Marks which stated that, owing to the terrible state the school hall was left in after the New Year's Eve Party, they were demanding £2,000 in additional fees, for returning the school to its normal standard of cleanliness. To say that I was unhappy would be a gross understatement, absolutely fuming more like. I sent a very terse reply saying that what they were alleging was completely untrue and that, under no circumstances, would I pay the money and, if they wanted to take it further, they would have to see me in court, where I would have been quite content to confront them. Belligerent aggression was always a good way to unsettle this headmaster and, within days, I had a reply from him in which he agreed to drop the demand but informed me that I was, from that day, officially banned from St Marks and, under no circumstances, was I ever to set foot on their property again.

I absolutely knew that this had been coming for years and I was completely fine with that outcome. However, I sort of had the last laugh in the future because I was to return to St Marks on two occasions, in 1998 and 2011, and both by invitation!

Jessica had followed her sister to the BBC and worked at Broadcasting House on Kingsway in the West End. I would often drive there to pick her up, just off the embankment, and we would go onto Tottenham for a mid-week match or park up and go to the theatre or the cinema in the West End on a Friday night. Jessica became quite a dedicated Spurs fan, a very good job as I had two season tickets, and I did have the satisfaction of converting her from being a Liverpool supporter – well almost.

As we worked to get RP off the ground, not only did we get a large contract via Tower Hamlets Council, just off The Mile End Road in the East End of London, but we also made a promising contact with Boots the Chemist, at their head office in Nottingham, about carrying out some day work jobs in their pharmacy departments. The job in the East End involved the renovation of a tower block with a large garden refurbishment including a lot of outside electrics as well. As a new company, we were having a great deal of difficulty opening accounts with the electrical wholesalers who supplied our goods. Contractors do the work and then, theoretically, get paid 30 days after invoicing though 90 days is far more realistic. To support the operation, you need credit accounts with the suppliers and you need a good track record and good references to achieve those accounts. RP had neither. In reality, it is all about image and what you can make people believe. We derived a strategy in which I would appear to be the new "money man" backing Patrick Simmons who, because of his electrical expertise and knowledge, was well-known to be a top-class electrical engineer and very skilled tradesman, and of that there was no doubt. Unfortunately, it was the lack of financial acumen - and, shall we say, his inability to explain how money was lost or just vanished - that always let him down.

To convince people of my resources and standing, we decided to lease a red Porsche 944, a nice addition to put alongside my Renault Fuego at home. To save money, however, the Porsche being an expensive acquisition, I gave my black Fuego to my long-standing helper Tony Daniel. He had always had an eye on it, loved cars and he became one of the youngest drivers of a flash car in Harlow, following which sort of apprenticeship, he went on to drive huge lorries thousands of miles all over Europe.

The Porsche had an amazing impact on our ability to get credit, confirming that it is, indeed, all about perception. I would turn up to a supplier in the Porsche, nice suit and tie and I would be able to open an account almost without question and this happened time after time. The one statement that Patrick made at that time and that has always stayed with me and was probably the truest thing he ever said was, "Remember a car is just a payment, it says nothing about you."

That is an absolute 100% true fact, if you don't make the payment you don't keep the car. It reminded me of a boy at school whose dad used to pick him up after lessons perhaps in a Ferrari one day, a Maserati the next, then a Lamborghini and so on and, when I asked him what his dad did for a living, he told me "Oh, he repossesses cars!"

CHAPTER 27

FOOTBALL

One of the first trips for pleasure in the Porsche was to take Jessica up to Anfield to watch her beloved Liverpool play Tottenham. It was my first chance to see what the car could do as the journey to Liverpool is all motorway - M11 to M25 to M1 to M6 to M62, you could say it could be a very fast drive if you wanted it to be, around 220 miles, doable in under three hours with favourable traffic and in the right car. This was in the middle of September 1988, a lovely day, early in the morning and light traffic. M11, M25, M1 all came and went in a flash and we were zooming along at between 90 and 100 miles an hour overtaking virtually every car on the road. The Porsche travelled like a dream and it certainly was a dream turning into a nightmare for me as we sped onto the M6 and I overtook a dark saloon. As I did so, I noticed that the two men in the front seats of that saloon had gold epaulettes on the shoulders of their shirts - unmarked police car flashed into my brain. I was probably doing more than 100 miles an hour, which meant an automatic ban so, basically, I slammed the anchors on to slow the car down as quickly as I could, without making it look too ridiculous. The saloon overtook me and signalled me to pull into the hard shoulder. The people in all the cars that I had overtaken on the way took great pleasure in giving me a happy wave as they continued on their merry way whilst the nice policemen issued me with a ticket. I remember, in my letter in reply to the notification of the intention to prosecute, in mitigation I said that I was "keeping up with the traffic", now I think "what a cretin". Of course, I got three points on my licence, my first ever points, but the actual offence was speeding at 99.16 mph for 0.9 mile and I think the gods were smiling on me, as always, to allow me to miss the automatic ban by less than 1 mph. Spurs lost the match 1-0, by the way, at least Jessica was happy, although she pretended not to be.

A small hiatus in our relationship happened at the end of 1990. For years Jessica had supported events put on by Patrick and Mary's music society, in fact many members of that society plus quite a few celebrities from the BBC had attended their recent wedding and then the reception at the Churchgate Hotel at which I, of course, provided the music. Jessica had always rather liked one of the guys who played guitar at the music society but he was quite a shy individual and was probably unaware that Jessica had a boyfriend. When he overcame his shyness and asked her out, having himself obviously liked her as well. It was a request that she felt that she could not say no to and so I had to accept that our relationship was over.

It was just another kick in the teeth for me to take and I was crestfallen and upset but I was big enough to decide that we should not fall out over it, we were extremely good friends.

Luckily, I had the Spurs to fall back on and in January 1991, not a bad year in which to throw myself into supporting the team, we embarked on our FA Cup run, with the first match being a 3rd round away tie at Blackpool. There was a howling gale behind me as I drove up the M6 again, this time alone and within the speed limit, with scarves billowing from both sides of the car. In those days I wore the Spurs' shirt, two scarves tied to my wrists and even had my white glasses to go with my blue and white cap with a yellow pom-pom on top. I recently showed a photograph of myself in all this gear to the guys I work with now and they reckon that I look better now, as an OAP, than I did then. I'm hoping that it was just the gear that made me look ridiculous. I had booked into the Imperial Hotel at Blackpool for the Friday and Saturday nights, this being the hotel where the Spurs team were staying. I got a good parking spot near to the hotel reception so I wouldn't get blown away by the wind and the gods were smiling on me once again because, as I was signing the hotel register, a small chimney stack was blown off the roof and landed as a pile of bricks about 6 feet away from the Porsche. It was about 7pm when I arrived and I learned that the Spurs team were already there but had a private room for their dinner so that they could prepare for the next day in peace. I had my dinner in the hotel restaurant and went to try and get to bed early so that I could get up at the crack of dawn and perhaps catch the team at breakfast and do a bit of hobnobbing.

Obviously, some fans had seen me getting out of a Porsche wearing a Spurs shirt and that might have been a clue that I was member of the team. As I approached the impressive staircase festooned in my replica Spurs shirt, clearly word was about that the players may have been at large in the hotel. Mistaken as one of them, I was mobbed by half a dozen young ladies whose desire was simply to get near to and touch a star footballer, illustrating how so few of these so-called fans really know what their idols look like and whether or not they are players. It rather reminded me of the Grease Gun con that we had pulled all those years previously. Suffice it to say I did not bother to inform my new entourage of admirers who I was or rather, who I wasn't, and I must admit it was quite a rewarding and pleasant experience being the subject of such misplaced adulation.

Next morning, now more exhausted than refreshed, I went in for breakfast and sat down at the table next to Eric Thorstvedt, Eric The Viking, our Norwegian goalkeeper. He was the earliest arrival at breakfast but others soon followed Paul Gascoigne, Paul Stewart and Gary Lineker amongst them. The morning raced by and soon it was time to walk to the ground in conditions that were probably reaching gale force 8, conditions that reduced the game to a farce.

For me the most memorable thing that happened in that match, which we won 1-0, was that when the first goal kick was taken, about a minute into the game, the howling wind simply grabbed the ball and blew it straight over the stand and into the sea. The win meant that we were on our way and I made sure to keep a very low-profile that evening at the hotel following the match. We had a very straightforward run to the semi-final after that, a home win over Oxford, an away win at Portsmouth and a home win over Notts County. So it was that we were drawn against Arsenal, on the 14th April 1991, in the semi-final at Wembley.

Wembley was chosen because there was no neutral venue anywhere in the country that could cater for both sets of the London club supporters, not even Old Trafford, and this became the first ever FA Cup semi-final to be played at Wembley, something that happens all the time nowadays.

Happily, by the time that game came around, Jessica's dates with her other friend had ceased and, although I think she probably missed the football more than she missed me, nevertheless we got back together again. Of course, she came to the semi-final with me.

This semi-final will always be remembered for that Gascoigne goal and we had brilliant seats, second-tier above the corner flag, a perfect view of everything, especially that Gascoigne cracker. We had a diagonal view from behind the freekick right into the corner of the goal it arrowed into. It went like this, five minutes, free kick to Spurs 35 or 40 yards out from goal, it looked almost to be on the halfway line, David Seaman, the Arsenal and England goalkeeper, England's number 1, was popping up and down on his goal line as Gascoigne tore up to the ball and blasted an unstoppable rocket of a shot into the top corner of the net. If Seaman had got a hand to the ball, I'm sure that it would have taken that hand into the net with it. Bedlam ensued, absolute euphoria, we're never the favourites against the Gunners and never have any luck. This was our day, 2 goals from Gary Lineker and we had won 3-1 and would be going to Wembley again, for the final on the 18th May, but going there again would not be without incident.

Because of my contacts in the ticket office, we got two superb seats, top price, first tier along the side of the pitch right at the front, near the touchline. That year a lot of tickets went missing in the post and ours were amongst them. So it was that we had to turn up for the match without a ticket, but instead with a letter, sent to us from the Spurs ticket office, explaining what had happened to the expectant staff at Wembley. On entering the stadium, the Wembley stewards took us to the seats known to be allocated to us initially to see if they had been occupied. To be sure they were occupied by two guys who had paid a lot of cash to a tout outside the ground to purchase the tickets. Regrettably for them, they had to go - they didn't have a valid ticket, they were ejected from the stadium and we took our seats for the match.

In the final Spurs were playing Nottingham Forest and typical of Spurs they started very slowly. Paul Gascoigne, the main man in the semi-final, went for a ridiculous tackle right in front of us and, if he hadn't injured himself so badly, there is no doubt that he would have been sent off. Although this injury forced a substitution, the bonus was that we still had 11 players still on the field. From the free kick Stuart Pearce drilled home a shot and Forest were in front. We put on some pressure after this but Lineker had a goal disallowed and then, of all things, missed a penalty. In the second-half Nayim, you know "Nayim from the halfway line", fed Paul Stewart to score the equaliser and take the match to extra time and, during this period, we won the match courtesy of an own goal by Des Walker and that produced another day great day for the lads and the whole club was in cloud cuckoo land.

CHAPTER 28

ACCOUNTS

Back on the RP front, 1991 was really the year that defined RPs whole life history – a year of problems, with money and the banks, problems with the Inland Revenue and the VAT office, problems with bailiffs, in fact problems everywhere and mostly of our own making because, at the heart of things, we had a very good business with very good customers. By now we had won the Boots contract for virtually the whole area of England south of Nottingham and employed a dozen subcontractors to carry out the work, some earning over £1,000 a week, even in those days. However, for whatever reason our administration and paperwork were not up to scratch and we were constantly having really major cash flow problems. The problem started big-time in 1991 when that major contract for Tower Hamlets in the East End started to unravel alarmingly. Invoicing and organising the work itself was Patrick's domain, whereas I processed the paperwork and tried to collect in the payments. This Tower Hamlets job was using a huge quantity of resources, we were paying wages and buying supplies but no money was forthcoming from our claims for stage payments to Tower Hamlets. This created an enormous cash flow pressure and the bank would not increase our overdraft facility.

We were just entering the very bad recession of 1991 which was about to cause major problems for every industry in the country. At that time the VAT rate was 15% and every invoice raised created a 15% VAT liability. We had invoices out to Tower Hamlets for their contract totalling some £191,000, of which more than £25,000 was VAT. We were struggling big time without any payments, wages were a nightmare and, clearly, we did not have the cash flow to pay the VAT return when it was due. At this time, the serious problem created by not paying VAT was the fact that a 10% surcharge on anything outstanding would be due on your next return, moving to 20% and 30% on the subsequent returns. We desperately needed to stop the escalation of that bill which was bad enough in itself. My suggestion was that we should approach the bank, Midland as it was then, be upfront about the VAT problem and see if we could get a loan to cover it - we were talking about Tower Hamlets here and the European grant that, allegedly, they were using to fund the project, so surely the money invoiced would be 100% secure.

Patrick Simmons was adamant, "Tell the bank nothing," he said.

I suppose, he did have far more experience than me on how companies had to operate on some occasions. Anyway, my opinion prevailed and off I went to the bank to see our new bank manager. Gary Timpson had taken over from a chap named Des Smith, the manager who had set up the business account 4 years earlier, one of those nice, friendly, helpful bank managers that no longer exist. On hearing my submission, Mr Timpson's immediate response was simply to freeze our account, we could pay money in but nothing, absolutely nothing, could be taken out. In other words, this decision effectively would shut us down. So, Patrick had been absolutely right, although that wouldn't have solved any problems either but, in hindsight, it probably would have been the best course of action for us to be shut down and prevent all the future misery that was to follow. As it was, this decision by Gary Timpson initiated a record-breaking chain of events over the next 15 years. Following my debacle at the bank, the next morning I had to drop off some gear to the guys doing a job in the Boots store on Chancery Lane, we still had plenty of work with Boots but, of course, any money they paid us would just vanish as we paid it into the bank. For some inexplicable reason a sign for The Temple caught my eye and immediately the thought "Law firms" came into my brain. I waited around Chancery Lane till about 9 o'clock, having my customary crispy bacon sandwich in one of the very nice small cafés in the area, and then went in search of some legal advice. I managed to get in at the very first building I came across in that legal quarter and, amazingly, secured an appointment with an elderly solicitor, probably in his 70s, whose name, disgracefully, escapes me, which is very bad because he was absolutely first class during our briefing. It transpired that this man also had been a graduate in Classics some 50 years earlier and his special interest was, incredibly, Roman history – yet another of the most peculiar coincidences that had and were to happen throughout my entire life. Clearly the amazing parallels in our lives made it very likely that we would hit it off big-time and that is exactly what happened.

The solicitor was calm, collected and calculating and nothing was too problematic for him to get his head around. He was on to the VAT office by telephone almost immediately and, in what seemed like minutes, he had arranged a moratorium on our account, with an agreement to pay the outstanding backlog without surcharge over a two-year period. Out of nowhere he had achieved an incredible result. He made the decision to send a fax to the Midland bank detailing the new arrangement with the VAT office because then, in his view, the bank would then have no option but to reopen our account, there being no impediment to prevent it from doing so. The fax was on its way and I drove back to Harlow with all speed to go to the bank to progress matters. As I entered the banking hall at Midland bank, a large area fronted by a big glass expanse, it so happened that, amongst the queues of customers, was Gary Timpson, our manager. I waited for him to finish his conversation and then politely approached him to ask if he had received the fax from my legal team. He gave me a rather vacant look before he dismissively stated, "We won't accept that communique, it's probably not genuine anyway."

Red rag to a bull doesn't come close and fortunately, I forcibly I held Mr Timpson by the neck against the large window area amidst, it must be said, scattered applause from a somewhat stunned group of customers. Mr Timpson was left in no doubt as to my opinion of him but things calmed down and we went into an office with a couple of his assistants, probably accompanying him as bodyguards. I suppose I was lucky not to be arrested.

The upshot of all this mayhem was that our account was reopened, allowing us to trade again but, just to punish us further and throw another major spanner into the works, our overdraft was to be repaid within seven days, effectively shutting us down all over again. Notwithstanding, as I said earlier, my previous experiences had given me the strength of character to handle and solve most pressure situations and this was one of them. Even in those days, the banks were getting severe criticism from the media about the way they treated Business and 1991 was a really problematic recessionary time and TV programmes were constantly airing the plight of all types of businesses.

I approached the Panorama programme about running our story but I didn't get anywhere. However, I did tell Gary Timpson that I had been to the BBC and that they had taken on board my proposals to do an expose on the Midland Bank's treatment of our company, RP. I neither confirmed nor denied that they had decided to produce that programme but planted the idea. Whatever, it had the effect of concentrating Mr Timpson's mind and our overdraft was indeed converted to a loan. We could now trade but, now, we had even bigger problems with the cash flow with a debt of about £50,000 to find over the next two years for the VAT and bank loan. I really believe that a diligent and experienced businessman - and sadly most businessmen basically are failures - would have definitely known to call it a day, but when you are in the driving seat you somehow believe that you can solve all the problems and emerge with success. Utter rubbish, believe me!

Patrick just relied on me to solve all the money problems while he sorted the work and all the invoicing (huge mistake). We should have made a fortune, what with the wages we were paying for the Boots work but, somehow, those wages never seemed to be reflected in our turnover. I re-mortgaged the house up to the hilt, something I would have to do another four times over the years, and this gave us nothing more than breathing space, as it always did. It was at this time that I got very active with the Federation of Small Businesses and I used my Conservative Party connections to liaise closely with Harlow MP Jerry Hayes about pressuring the government to enforce, in law, 30 day payment terms for business.

Indeed, Jerry Hayes arranged for me to have a couple of meetings with the then Chancellor of the Exchequer, Norman Lamont, at the House of Commons itself to talk about this issue. Unbelievably, that was 30 years ago and still the same argument goes on today, promises of action on this problem have been, and still are, well and truly empty.

At this point, it is probably worth pointing out that when we set up RP in 1987, the accountants we used were Price Bailey. We changed our accountants two or three times over the years, one change was to Barnes Roffe, clever accountants for business, but the common strand linking all these different accountants was Brian Dobby. He started at Price Bailey as an assistant on our account and, as he moved from accountant to accountant, RP was always one of the clients he used to sweeten any deal and that is why Brian Dobby was on the scene with us for such a long time.

CHAPTER 29

ADDING UP

On the lighter side, in 1991 I had a few requests from fans suffering withdrawal symptoms from the lack of dance activity at St Marks and I organised a cowboy dance at Burnt Mill School. that was a large comprehensive school on First Avenue Harlow where Glenn Hoddle, the famous Spurs legend, went to school. It was because of this dance that I became aware of a disused storage space in the basement area underneath the school hall, access to this space being via a gate that allowed entrance to a back playground. I knew the caretaker at Burnt Mill from the days when I used to take St Marks sports teams to compete there and also because he lived 50 yards up the road from my mother. The negotiations were easy and the headmaster was up for making money from this disused space so RP took it on for £200 a month.

This was a very convenient site for us as all our subbies could access the stores at any time, we could also keep our plant and the larger equipment in there safely and access it more easily than before. Within about a year, we came to a fresh agreement with Burnt Mill School whereby we paid them £10,000 up front for 10 years rent and this was to help the school develop new ideas for their curriculum and showed our confidence in our own business because we were prepared to save over 60% of our rent over those next 10years. By 1992 we had come to terms with the fact that the Tower Hamlets money was a bad debt, we did take legal action but, because of the rules surrounding European grants to councils, although we won a victory in court, we got absolutely nothing and, even worse than this Pyrrhic victory was that it cost us even more money.

We had to look seriously at our expenditure, we needed tighter control over our resources and a more effective way of using them. Rent and rates were clearly a big drain on our finances and we were lucky enough to hear that CD Rose, previously a pretty big concern occupying a large warehouse behind the Shenval House building, was downsizing and looking for a tenant to share their space. Mr Rose, the proprietor, who had continued to run his business well past retirement age, was prepared to let us have an office and a small store area for less than half of our current outgoings. The office was big enough for three desks, my own, Patrick's and one for the secretary.

The smallish storage area was big enough to be used for all our screws and fixings etc, the value of that stock being about £15,000. As well as doing my office work, I was now added to our workforce on the tools which meant a lot of night and weekend work had to be added to my hours. Unfortunately, I was not be paid for this extra work, unlike our many subbies who were all on enormously better money than me.

It was about this time that I realised that I could get unsecured money using credit cards. It was the beginning of the big credit boom and I certainly got in on the ground floor. I had quite a few mortgages and loans by now and so, although I didn't really understand all the ins and outs of credit ratings, I had built up a good, possibly even terrific, credit history and, apparently, the more credit you had the easier it was to get more – something that I would be able to exploit with almost unimaginable success. I started with a couple of cards, each with about £1,000 credit limit, but the supernova was about to explode!

Unfortunately, the credit card revolution did not arrive quickly enough to help our cash flow while we were the guests of Mr Rose. Finding enough money for RP at that time was next to impossible, and it was a matter of great dismay to me that we even found it impossible to keep up with our reduced outgoings to Mr Rose, a really kind and lovely man who we treated disgracefully. We had been extremely remiss with Mr Rose and, quite justifiably, finally he lost patience with us and sent the bailiffs to visit us in his own building.

Unbelievably, this visit came on the morning when I bought my portable television into the office to watch the test match later on that day. That morning both Patrick and I were at meetings and away from the office, leaving the secretary there on her own. Thus, when the bailiffs turned up, they came up against no opposition whatsoever and it was a simple "fait accompli". They confiscated all the fixings and all the furniture, including of course, my portable television. I honestly think that this was our, and definitely my, least-finest hour in business, and to make it even worse, I believe that, after fees etc, Mr Rose only got about £1,000 for all that gear.

Jessica was doing well at the BBC and had made a friend of one of the radio sports reporters, a lady called Isabel Cunningham, primarily a journalist with the Scotsman newspaper but someone who did horse racing segments for the BBC overseas service. Jessica had spoken to her about my forays into the betting world and Isabel used to give her tips for me to bet on. This lady was very friendly with a Scottish racehorse trainer named Sue Bradburne and I began to follow her horses which were mostly ridden by her son Mark. There is little doubt that Isabel knew her stuff and her tips were always there or thereabouts.

Early in December 1992 Isabel told Jessica that The Fellow would win the King George VI Chase for the second time in a row on Boxing Day and, via the credit cards of course, all of a sudden, I could get money again and, showing my total restraint as always, I put £500 on the horse taking odds of 6/1. The Fellow won the race and that meant £3,000 in my pocket – nice! Although The Fellow was not one of Sue Bradburne's horses, I continued to have a soft spot for them over the years.

By now Patrick and Mary lived in a bungalow in the country and Patrick managed to get RP office premises nearby in a warehouse conversion development. Based in this really rural and peaceful area, we were now covering a very large swathe of the country for our Boots contract and we worked a lot of the time in tandem with a large shopfitting company based in Clacton. This meant doing lots of refits during the nights and lots of weekend work. I was a labourer on these jobs and the hours were very demanding although the hard times were mitigated, somewhat, by the number of McDonalds and kebabs we were able to put away.

As we went through 1993 and 1994, and I still just cannot believe that we did not make a fortune, I was trusted enough to go to any Boots store on my own and blag my way through electrical checks, as long as nothing actually electrical needed to be done, it was easy enough to "talk electrician" and convince the shop manager that I knew exactly what I was talking about.

My speciality was doing emergency light checks and, in a nutshell, this is how straightforward it was for our guys to stack up the wages that they pulled in. We used to pay the guys one hour travel each way to a job, plus any parking charges and fuel, plus their time in the shop logged onto the job sheet.

My task on one occasion involved me doing emergency light tests in several West End Boots stores. I was heading for two shops in Holborn, one in Chancery Lane and then two the Tottenham Court Road area. For this work I knew where to park for free in one of the Holborn shops and, having done that, I signed in at the first three shops one after the other, the distance I had to walk being barely half a mile, so I was actually in all three of them at the same time. The light check involved switching the emergency lights on and leaving them on for 45 minutes before counting how many had failed after that time and needed replacing. That would mean getting a work sheet with "an hour and a half in-store time" booked on it. Because of their proximity and the fact that I was in all three at once, it took no longer than three hours to complete all three jobs. It was the same principle at the two shops in Tottenham Court Road where I'd get an hour and a half on each time sheet and do both jobs at the same time. Access to Boots London stores starts at 6am so, because I started early, I was on my way home before 12 o'clock noon. Had I been an electrician this is what I would have booked on my invoice for the work – five jobs at an hour and a half each for work in-store, 10 hours travel (5 x an hour each way), and £15 parking with probably £10 for fuel. That is seventeen and a half hours pay (at very good rates) plus £25 for a bit of fuel – not too bad for half a day's work. I would have been delighted to pay the wages that we did, if only we had we passed those charges on to Boots but I couldn't work out why that didn't happen and we just failed to make the money we should have.

CHAPTER 30

£8 BET AND JURGEN

By mid 1994 my credit card count had gone up to around 20 and it became a ritual for me, every few days, to go into the bank and relieve the cards of any spare money that might be available on them. In the bank, tellers used to shut their windows when they saw me coming because they couldn't take the pressure. The route to success with credit card manipulation was always to have one spare and completely empty card and religiously to stick to the steadfast rule of paying the minimum payment bang on time. I always knew exactly what the limit was on each card and how much cash was still available, I also knew when the payment was due and never, ever missed a payment. The use of my credit cards was very successful in helping RP trundle along and, of course, all the money I took out on them and paid into the business went into my director's loan account so, on the books and in the accounts, it was beginning to look like I was a very rich man. A difficulty was that I did feel very well off as, theoretically, I could get almost whatever I wanted at any time. Perhaps the biggest problem of all, in that scenario, was that I actually lost the concept of the value of money completely. I was dealing in such big amounts of money that reality went completely out of the window. In actual fact, so much money was going through my personal account at the bank that I became almost their top premier account customer.

On the work side of RP, there were some incredibly funny but also astounding things that happened on occasions when we were doing Boots refits. One such event happened on a Sunday morning when we were doing a re-fit at Boots Romford. The shop next door was a big electrical goods retailer selling TVs and other appliances and a couple of their staff were in reorganising their stock display. Halfway through the morning, when the shopfitters and RP boys were out front having their usual McDonalds, a large but empty lorry pulled up outside the TV shop and four guys, dressed in cleaning company uniforms got out and went into the shop. The shop manager didn't seem to know why these people had arrived but, we were told later, that boss of "the cleaners" had informed him that they had come to clean the carpet while the stock was being repositioned, as this was the most opportune time to carry out this job. Of course, while they were cleaning the carpet, the stock needed to be moved and the best and safest place to store it would be on the lorry, where it would be completely out of the way.

We watched on from outside, fascinated to see what was going on. Everything seemed above board so that's exactly what they did, all the stock was loaded onto the lorry for safe keeping and it really was safe keeping because then the four guys got into it and drove away, while the shop staff just stood there with their mouths open. This just shows you that, sometimes, all you need is a rock-solid nerve and a lot of a cheek to be a successful criminal – and a lorry, of course.

There were other times when things were not quite so amusing as, for example, during IRA bomb attacks in London. The worst one for us was when a bomb exploded at Liverpool Street station in 1993. The Boots store was totally wrecked and it seemed uncanny to me that I was one of those crawling through the debris, helping our guys disconnect the power supply. That was a very frightening start to, what you might call, a very big refit.

It was all very surreal, too, in July 1994 when Spurs signed the famous German football star Jurgen Klinsmann from Monaco, what you would call a real marquee signing. At the same sort of time, I was alerted by the caretaker at Burnt Mill School, where we had our stores, to the fact that there was a small kitten wondering around the school site, seemingly homeless. I kept an eye out for it when I was picking up stock and, indeed, this gorgeous little creature turned up quite a few times, always looking a bit forlorn and unkempt but a lovely little bundle of ginger and white fur. I made the decision to bring him home and the school caretaker was very happy that the kitten had found a good home.

My cat, Candy, was getting on now, incredible that she had been with me through all those ups and downs over16 years and, unhappily, she would soon pass away, but at least the new tiny kitten brightened up her life for her last few months. The question now was what to call this white fronted ginger beast? Jurgen, of course, after the mighty Klinsmann and he too was destined for superstardom like his namesake.

The surprising events just kept coming thick and fast and, worthy of note around this time, was an incident that occurred when I had to visit Royston Boots, one Wednesday morning, in order to carry out one of my fabled emergency light checks. As I mentioned not long ago, these annual checks at all Boots stores involved turning on all the emergency lights in the shop and leaving them running for about 45 minutes before counting up the number that had failed to remain illuminated and, thus, needed replacing. In practice, I turned the lights on and then went for a walk or a coffee to kill the time and then came back to the shop to do the count up. On this particular day, as per usual in Royston, I suspect, there was not a great deal happening although, on that Wednesday, I did have something to look forward to because Spurs were playing Liverpool that night and I was picking up Jessica from the BBC on the way to the game. During my time killing period, I happened to go into the Ladbrokes bookmakers to have a cursory look at the days' horses. I picked out selections in six races but in two of the races I couldn't make up my mind between two selections. These extra two horses resulted in me having eight separate accumulators to make sure all my selections were used and this bit of fun bet cost me £8, £1 pound for each of eight accumulators. Having completed my investment, I returned to Boots to finish the light check before returning to my van to do a few more jobs on my way to London to pick up Jessica and go on to the Spurs. The match was another cracking 0-0 draw and, by the time I dropped Jessica off at her house and came home, it was getting on for midnight. I really hadn't given a thought to the bet I had done at Ladbrokes that morning and it wasn't until I sat down with my pre bed cup of coffee that I suddenly remembered my bet and had a look at Ceefax - now there's a word from the past - to find out the results.

Crikey I thought, I recognise the names of some of those winners, so I got out my betting slip to have a careful check, only to find that I had had six winners. Because of the combinations I had done, it meant that one accumulator had all six winners in it and (because one of the horses was a 25/1 shot) my winnings would be come to just under £12,000.

You could describe me as being very excited when I returned to Royston the next day to collect the winnings, but the manager at Ladbrokes told me that a little shop like theirs did not keep that kind of money on site and asked me if I wouldn't mind going to the main branch in Harlow Town Centre to collect my winnings. Not even the tiniest of problems – off I went and duly collected my £12k, happiness personified.

This was when we were pursuing Boots as a customer big time and we used corporate entertainment as a lure. One weekend in late spring we hired 20 rooms at a plush hotel near Bar Hill, just north of Cambridge, and invited 20 lots of couples from Boots management team to stay over the weekend, arriving on the Friday night from Nottingham and leaving on the Sunday morning after breakfast. On the Saturday we had hired a coach and took them all on a jolly to Doncaster races, a really brilliant place to go as a bloke because the women who go to northern racecourses hardly wear any clothes at all, even in the middle of winter and, even if you lose your money, you can have a really great day taking in the sights. A really good time was had by all that day and when we returned to the hotel after racing, I put on a disco for everyone until the early hours. This event cost a tidy sum but there was no doubt that we recouped it all and more in new work.

Over the years I had, always under instruction, bought Jessica the same Christmas present, it was a classic Estee Lauder gift box, which was an amazing value myriad of perfumery products, always presented in a glorious carrycase, unbelievably affordable but only while stocks lasted and always in great demand. I always bought this present at the major department store Liberty, which is in Regent Street, in Soho. In those days there was no such thing as online shopping so, as you can imagine, I was well pleased when, purely by chance, someone told me that the very same product could be obtained at our own local Department store, Pearsons, in the High Street, Bishops Stortford Bishop Stortford. This afforded me the opportunity of meeting the lady in charge of the perfumery department at that shop who turned out to be the Christian Dior rep for the whole of the South East of England. Her name was Val and, over the next few years, she became a bit of an "agony aunt figure" for me, trying her best to advise me against all the mistakes I would soon be making with some very, shall we say, ill-judged relationships which seemed to afflict me over the next 4 years.

The actual bombshell which was to cause these howling errors was about to drop from a clear blue sky just like the Enola Gay payload in 1945. Jessica announced that she was going to leave the BBC and enrol at Middlesex University as a mature student so that she could experience the student life that she felt that she had missed out on when she left school. I was really surprised by this decision as she had always been determined to follow in the footsteps of her sister's successful career at the BBC and was doing extremely well there. She was an extremely gifted artist, not only was she a superb painter but textile art was her real speciality and now she needed to develop that talent. Jessica desired a move away from everyone, live away from home and "find herself". I suppose, looking back, that this was a very reasonable outlook to have considering that we had been boy and girlfriend for more than a decade, yet we had never really thought seriously about living together. She probably loved Jurgen more than me – but then everybody did.

CHAPTER 31

NEW BUSINESS, BAD RELATIONSHIPS AND TAX

By now, I was the proud possessor of about 50 credit cards, a total which reached 89 at its peak. When the numbers reached those levels in the early 2000s, I had a combined credit limit of over £1million and I worked out that, over the 12 or 13 years adventure with these cards, taken in conjunction with my mortgage interest and loan interest, the total interest I paid to banks during that period was in the region of £1.3million. Perhaps we were making a lot of money at RP but we were giving it all away to the banks in interest.

No wonder I was a top premier account at the bank. My directors loan account on the RP books was also monstrously large, especially when you compared it to Patrick's zero amount, and the figures seemed to indicate that I was a millionaire – shows how wrongly numbers can be interpreted. A constantly recurring problem for RP was that we were always on stop with wholesalers because of late payments or because we were at the top of our credit limit. It became patiently obvious that we actually needed to be our own wholesaler. One of the main suppliers that we used at the time was a wholesaler called North Electrical which was run by a guy called Paul Jessop. We had dealt with this company for many years and we were friends with Paul, at least for most of the time when we weren't on stop or because we hadn't paid. I particularly used to have lots of friendly banter with him about who was driving the better car, seeing as I still had the Porsche, although It was getting old now. (Indeed, I kept it for 16 years, after buying it out from the lease in 1990.)

When he announced to me that he had put in an order for the new model BMW Z3, which had a two-year waiting list on the orderbook, I instinctively told him that I had actually done the same thing and that we would have to see which one of us got the car first. Straight from that meeting I went to Sewell's BMW garage at Bishop Stortford and ordered a Z3, not just an ordinary one either, but a Z3 with everything, absolutely everything on it, including the super wide rear wheels – I suppose I was being over the top but it's crazy what pressurised business men do for kicks and I was being one of them.

The manager of North Electrical was a very able chap named Ken Roberts. He had been in electrical wholesaling since leaving school and now, in his early 30s, there was nothing that he did not know about the trade and everything connected with it. However, Ken was in the middle of a very unpleasant divorce, most unsettling because two young children were involved and buckled severely under the stress of all this and took to drinking a lot. He had gone downhill rapidly and reluctantly Paul Jessop had to make the decision to let him go. I knew Ken well, and tried to put a tiny bit of order back into his life by regularly taking him with me to Spurs. I still had my two tickets and, with no Jessica anymore, I tried to use them sensibly with customers and friends. At one of these trips to Tottenham I ran the idea past Ken, of RP starting up an electrical wholesaler. He also thought that it was the right way forward. Then I suggested to him that he should consider coming on board and become the front man in the business. For a contractor like RP to be a wholesaler was a complete nonstarter because, if we wanted other customers so that we could make a useful profit, other contractors would definitely not trade with us as RP were their competitors and they wouldn't want us to get wind of their work and probably steal it.

Lots of contractors knew Ken well from North Electrical and it seemed logical to call the new company KR Electrical Wholesale, using Ken's initials as the title, indeed, everybody thought that Ken was the owner of the company, and that I was his assistant, and this remained true for the next 10 years. He was paid an excellent salary from the word go and it was Brian Dobby who set up the new company and became the accountant for both RP and KR, while I split my time between the two of them, prioritising deliveries at KR in my nice new van, registration number R10 SSO, keeping up my penchant for personalised numbers. We found a small unit, classroom size in fact, for the new company in the business estate converted from the old Latton Bush Comprehensive School on Southern Way in Harlow and, when Ken and I collected the keys to the unit, we had with us one box of 5 double sockets as our stock.

As we entered the unit and placed the sockets on the floor, the door opened again and we received a visit from Paul Jessop, Ken's recent former boss who had got wind of the venture and called in to pour scorn on our entrepreneurial spirit.

"I'm afraid you just won't last," he said, "you've made the wrong decision." Then he turned and left.

Luckily for us and unluckily for him he was wrong, but the real irony here was that Ken would repeat these words to me himself 15 years hence, when he stabbed me in the back, figuratively of course. We were up and running and, in due course, most of North's customers turned to us because Paul had placed too much reliance on Ken as his manager, a mistake that, in many ways, I was to repeat. Customers were pleased to see someone that good at his job back on the straight and narrow and especially owning his own wholesaler. It wasn't all that straightforward underneath though, as Ken had serious lapses in behaviour. At times when he had his children staying in his flat, I had to go and sort them out for him when he was too incapacitated to do so.

He had also made some poor choices in friends and this was illustrated when, after four months of working at KR, his new Renault company car was torched and destroyed outside his flat. This was pretty annoying, to say the least, especially when we found that, although we had insurance, we had no "gap insurance" and that cost our fledgling company a cool £3,000. By and large we were flourishing and RP was getting its gear and not getting any grief from non-payment or credit limits. The fact that KR had a credit card machine also meant a lot less stress for the bank tellers, as I didn't have to use them quite as much because I paid RPs bill direct to KR, instead of having to move money everywhere.

However, nothing goes along smoothly for too long and the Inland Revenue decided to perform on me one of their friendly investigations into my financial affairs. Based at a large office complex just up the road from my house in Bishops Stortford, I must say that they turned out to be not the most pleasant of people, guilty until proven innocent was undoubtedly their motto and they wanted to go through everything I had ever done with a fine-tooth comb.

After about six months-worth of shenanigans costing the tax payer God knows how much, the good old revenue came up with a £12,000 discrepancy in my financial dealings. That was £12,000 worth of income that was not traceable and would be eligible for tax at a rate of 40%, leaving me with a bill of £4,800 plus interest to pay. In some ways I was philosophical about this and believed it not to be too bad when so much money has actually gone through my accounts during the past six years that they were examining.

In an unprecedented flash of inspiration, I realised that the £12,000 was, in fact, the winnings from that fluke accumulator bet that I did when I was doing the emergency light check at Royston those few years ago. In the twinkling of an eye, 5 weeks actually, I managed to get an appointment with the so efficient people at the Inland Revenue and confidently went into the meeting with them to explain where these ill-gotten gains had come from.

"I won it gambling," I explained.

"Oh yes, everybody says that," came a very terse reply, "Goodbye sir, just pay the tax."

I absolutely knew that I was in the right, but the win had happened two years previously and, when I collected the winnings, I had to hand in my ticket to the bookmaker to get them, so I could not possibly present any paperwork to prove my story. However, it did occur to me that companies have to retain their invoices and records for as much as six years and I wondered if Ladbrokes fell into that category. I visited the main Harlow betting shop where I'd had to go to collect my winnings two years previously and explained the situation. The manager asked me to give him a couple of weeks to look into the problem for me and, I must admit, I did wonder if he meant what he said or if it was just talking platitudes.

The couple of weeks passed and I popped back into the shop and he had only gone and found the ticket! Eureka! Surging with the energy of total justification and righteousness, I ran back to the car and sped over to those impressive Inland Revenue offices. I think you could say that I burst in, much to the chagrin of the receptionist who told me, as I brushed her aside, that no-one could see anyone without an appointment. Too late Mrs, I was already into the main man's office in the blink of a very noisy eye.

Purposefully I strode to the boundary of the investigator's desk and very, very deliberately placed the evidential betting ticket on the said desk.

"I take it that will satisfy you," I said, possibly with a few expletives added for effect. As the important official sat statue like in stunned silence, I left with all haste before I was ejected. A few weeks later I got an inland revenue bill for £4, due in respect of unpaid tax – it probably cost them £20k to get that result. What a brilliant organisation!

CHAPTER 32

FOUR YEARS OF MAYHEM AND CATASTROPHE

Before embarking on, shall we call it, the adventures with females over the next few years, there is another amusing incident that happened, this one involving Jurgen the superstar cat. My next-door neighbour Doris was a widow whose husband had died a few years before. She was in her late 60s at the time. How ridiculous that that seemed old to me when I am older than that now myself.

She seemed to have, shall we call it, a soft spot for me, although I really don't know why. She often took care of Jurgen for me because my hours of work could be erratic and she had a key to my house for that reason. Doris' house was one of many houses that Jurgen would visit and spend time in as he was the most popular and gregarious of cats and, as I have said before, national fame awaited him in 2001.

On this particular morning, I had a long ladder tied to the roof of my van and obviously set off for work in the normal way, out of my cul-de-sac turn left onto the main road, left at the roundabout and down the steep hill to the trunk road at the end. As I pulled up at the fortunately red traffic light, a frantic pedestrian ran towards me flagging me down to stop. Wondering what on earth was going on, I got out of the van to be greeted by the sight of Jurgen gripping the ladder for dear life with his claws, looking like one of those cartoon cats when it's been startled and all four legs stick and its fur is like a punk rocker's haircut.

Safely, if meeowingly, inside, I brought him back to the house only to find Doris having palpitations outside her front door as she waited for the expected terrible news.

"I saw him on top of the van," she screamed, "and phoned your mother to tell you to stop."

I think that by the time my mother had phoned me after Doris phoned her, the worst may have happened but the thought was there. Never mind, all is well that ends well.

Not long after Jessica's decision to move on, I called into the Harlow Town Centre branch of the bank to do some of my normal credit card withdrawals and was served by a person I had not seen for over 20 years.

it was Linda from the wedding that we officiated at together at St Thomas Moore church all those years ago. It turned out that she had worked at the bank for most of those years and was extremely well thought of. She had normally been based in another branch, a branch that I had never visited. Fate decreed that on that day, and at that time, she would be working at the Harlow branch because of staff shortages. What could not be explained was that there was some kind of chemistry or zing when she served me and, I must say, it travelled both ways.

We had a brief chat at her window and agreed that it might be nice to meet up for a cup of coffee and a catch up. I can honestly swear that I did not give a single thought as to what her situation might be, I just thought that it would be quite a nice thing to do and when she suggested meeting in the snack bar opposite tomorrow lunchtime, I didn't see a problem with that.

Next day at the appointed time she came out of the bank and we went to the snack bar, our first rendezvous since that wedding all those years ago. It was now that I learned that Linda was in fact a married woman with three children and, as I brought her up to date about my life, I felt quite pleased that we could catch up in such a pleasant and uncomplicated way. She remained at the Harlow branch of the bank for quite a few weeks and we met up a few more times for lunch and, probably stupidly, I did give her a couple of presents. It was always common knowledge, even in those early years at St Marks, that I was a big Spurs fan and it transpired that she asked me if I would take her to a match, assuming that I was still a supporter, because she had never been to one.

When she asked me to do that, I absolutely remember saying to her, "As long as your husband is fine with it, I will take you."

She waited a day and then told me that her husband had said it would be ok for me to take her to Tottenham, so we decided to go to the next mid-week game. When I told her the time that I needed to pick her up at her house she said that it would be better if she met me at the bank car park because she would be working that day and it would be easy for her to leave her car there.

Whether I was just plain thick, even with those arrangements, I did not smell any kind of rat whatsoever. We met at the car park and drove to the game for her first experience of a top football match. It was a very pleasant evening and I returned her to her car at the car park with no overt display of affection. It was a few days later at the bank that she suggested that it would be nice for her to come over one evening to see where I lived and what my house was like and, perhaps, this Saturday would be a good time because her husband would be working that night and she could easily get a babysitter.

It was now that finally the penny dropped and, all too late, I realised the glaringly obvious direction of travel. Conversely after 20 years, I was very attracted to her and I could not resist the idea of her coming over and this was major because, believe it or not, I had rarely brought any other woman home to my house, let alone one that was married with 3 children. I am reminded that she was smitten by the song "Runaway" by The Corrs, have a listen to the lyrics of that song and see if you, like me, connect them to subconscious psychology.

When Saturday night arrived and having made all the arrangements at home, probably going for a meal with the girls from the bank, she presented herself just after 7pm. We had a really lovely, romantic and nostalgic evening together and it was now impossible for us to keep our hands off each other, which in itself was an extremely unusual state of affairs for me. Very quickly I had to face the fact that this relationship had escalated into something significant and I was definitely not in control. I was forced to consider all the options available to me, complicated by my fast-slipping morality that told me that I was not a marriage wrecker. This was not my style at all.

Events were taken completely out of my hands when, the following Monday night, Linda turned up at my house with not only her bags but also with her children.

The die was cast, my brain was addled and I'm sure I was just a robot. First things first, I had two double bedrooms and a small third bedroom. We took one of the bedrooms, and fitted the children into the other rooms. My lifestyle was "home alone" and this was a totally different ball game for me, especially when I was still working the most peculiar hours and spent a lot of time away from the house. Now I had to deal with all the extra people.

Within a day Linda had got us an interview at the Bishops Stortford branch of her bank to arrange a mortgage. She had already found, and God knows when she did that, a four bedroomed house in Harlow, not far from where she lived with her husband, and that is where she wanted us all to live. My mind was gone, I was in a complete whirl, unbelievably I even took my mother and sister to see the house and although they thought I had gone totally insane, they did like it.

Surprisingly, the five of us did exist acceptably in the house for that first week, avoiding the topic of Linda's husband and the children's father. When I got home on the Friday, now with time to take stock of what had happened during this week's hurricane, I had to really bite my lip and maintain control of myself as I discovered that Linda had been through all my cupboards, drawers and possessions, searching out, destroying and removing any traces of any previous girlfriends from the house. I tried to be understanding and reasonable in the face of all this, and although I didn't think about it at the time, looking back, this was all a very similar chain of events to the film Fatal Attraction.

A sad case, I was completely discombobulated, swept along in a typhoon of misjudgements, leaving me almost unaware and oblivious as to what was going on. Mercifully after the weekend, on the following Monday when I returned home from work, something totally supernatural happened to me. As I entered what was my house, Linda greeted me with the words "One of my children is allergic to the cat, Jurgen will have to go!"

In a lightning strike, the electrical impulses in my brain reconnected and without a millisecond of hesitation I retorted, "NO - you lot will have to leave!"

Within minutes I had them all outside, them and all their belongings. The neighbours were well entertained – all those years of peace followed by this riot. Where they went, I have no clue, but for me, the nightmare in Bishops Stortford was over, sanity returned. Jurgen was safe and sound and, without any doubt whatsoever, this wonderful cat had been my saviour.

Leading the solitary life was not to last, however, and I then crossed paths with an old colleague from St Marks, although colleague was not the correct description because she worked as an assistant in the music department all those years ago and I can't say we bumped into each other that often. Her name was Amy and when we met in the Town Centre, she reminded me of the fact that we were in the same class as each other at the Spinney Junior School in the early 1950s, which in her mind meant that we had been friends for over 40 years.

The oddest thing though, was that she was a big fan of greyhound racing, which had been cemented even more when the school was involved with that Lady Lano project. It really is quite amazing how many things in the story intertwine and coincide. The long and the short of it was that we ended up going to the dogs, mostly Romford and Walthamstow, quite regularly over the next four or so years and we were both very competitive over our abilities at selecting winners and would battle it out to see who was the best gambler, and it wasn't usually me.

Following the Linda fiasco and with Amy holding a torch on the periphery, I now took a fancy to a bank teller called Jane at HSBC, formally the Midland, where RP's account was held. I guess I had some sort of innate weakness for bank tellers or perhaps, all my screws had come loose at the same time. I really can't understand what I was striving for during this manic period, as I certainly would never have classed myself as a woman chaser, not so suddenly at my time of life anyway.

Jane was devastatingly pretty. I knew nothing whatsoever about her and I thought she was about 25. Hopeless romantic that I was, I began to take her little gifts of chocolates and flowers, but she really wasn't that interested, I suppose I wasn't that attractive although, appreciating her character from hindsight, she definitely would have me marked down as a well-off business owner who drove a Porsche.

Clearly, over the years, I had got to know many of the staff who worked at HSBC and one of them told me that Jane was, in fact, divorced and the mother of two young children, 4 and 6, and closer to 30 than I thought. Apparently, her husband was a very nice chap but Jane had got involved with a bit of "a bad boy type", possibly involved with drugs, and this had resulted in the end of her marriage. She was, however, a clever girl and was getting her life back on track. I had accepted that I had drawn a big blank with Jane and was all set to abandon my quest.

In all honesty I was feeling a bit low and rejected when, one Friday night, as I was just about to leave home at about 6.30pm to go for a cricket net at the Essex County Cricket club in Chelmsford, there was a ring on the bell just as I was in the act of opening the door. It was Jane. She explained that she just had a row with her boyfriend and had decided that I may be able to offer her some solace.

"I'm really very sorry," I said, "but I've got an important cricket practice that I just can't miss." I shut my front door, got in the car and drove to Chelmsford – perhaps I had learned some lessons at last, I wish!

After this masterful performance, I remember going into Pearsons and having a chat with Val, the perfume lady, who advised me, in no uncertain manner, that this was a relationship doomed to failure and her portentous assessment was that Jane was a very dangerous user who should be avoided at all costs. She analysed that, by being hard with her on that Friday night, it would in fact attract her to me more than ever and that I needed to be extremely vigilant - what a very wise woman Val proved to be!

Ignoramus that I was, I did feel badly at the way I had treated Jane that Friday night and, the following week, I trumped those mistaken feelings, by getting up the nerve to ask her out on a date.

Whether or not it was my new forceful approach that, as Val had suggested, seemed to have changed her mind about me or, more likely a very calculating mind, she agreed to come out with me and we ended up seeing a lot of each other. We went for the day to Brighton without the children and went to Walthamstow greyhounds with the children. These outings were very pleasant occasions but I did feel that I had to try and work really hard at trying to build a loving relationship. Then, all of a sudden, HSBC underwent a staff reorganisation and Jane was one of the staff to be let go.

Erroneously feeling responsible for her, I gave her a job as an office assistant at KR where she proved herself to be very meticulous and conscientious, and it seemed like it might turn out to be a good appointment. Plainly I had on intensely rose-tinted spectacles as far as she was concerned and my liking for her grew out of all proportion and rationale, so much so that, when her car gave up the ghost, I treated her to a new Suzuki jeep.

Ken at KR correctly thought that I was off my rocker but I'm afraid I was smitten and quite irrational. I was under the impression that she liked me a lot, but how wrong could I be and how right had Val been. Very soon afterwards, my adulation was completely and utterly blown out of the water. My sister phoned me on a Saturday night with the revelation that she had just been to the Oasis Hotel, a Chinese restaurant in Old Harlow, for a meal with a friend and, as she and her friend had pulled up in the car park, the aforementioned Jeep had turned up and parked next to them. The Jeep was being driven by a man with Jane in the passenger seat and, of course, they had no knowledge of who my sister was and, therefore, had no clue as to who was parked next to them. My sister said that she felt obliged to phone me because, after the couple went into the restaurant and were eating their meal, they were extremely "lovey-dovey" and she thought that I needed to know. It turned out that this was the drug dealer boyfriend that she had apparently 'escaped' earlier.

I'm glad to say that I wasn't having any of that and, after calmly considering what to do, I decided that I needed to take direct action. At 6am that Sunday morning, I drove round to her house in Harlow, banged on the door and got her and her man out of bed and proceeded to repossess the Jeep. My demand for the keys was, shall we say, uncompromising. The drug dealer boyfriend knew absolutely not to give me any bother because he could clearly see, from my unhinged and aggressive demeanour, that I would most certainly take him out if he tried to refuse me. Meekly the keys were handed over and, in that instant, I also sacked Jane from KR. To put it succinctly, that was the end of that – except that now I had two cars to get home. With my back against the wall with regard to these women, it appears that I could be just as much of a bastard to them as they were to me and, with my rekindled strength of mind, I sold the Suzuki back to Hilton Garage at Spellbrook, took the loss on the chin and moved on.

For my decisive action I received some serious brownie points from Val at Pearsons and she even took me out for lunch to celebrate. At this lunch, Val confided to me that she been let down badly by a financial advisor and actually lost money from her investments. Highly trained over many years to always be on the lookout for cash flow help and realising that one day the credit card situation may prove problematical, I asked her if she would consider investing some money in KR. She thought that it was a great idea and we agreed an investment of £15,000 at 1% per month, that is a £150 repayment per month with a capital sum remaining the same. £150 would be payable on the first of each month until the full amount of capital was repaid in one go. I hoped that this blinding investment for Val would be quite short term but in actual fact it went on for some 15 years and turned out to be an absolutely incredible deal for her, especially as I stuck to the terms of the agreement throughout those 15 years. She retired from

Pearsons a little bit later but I always kept in touch with her, apart from through my standing order, and we would meet for lunch every so often.

This 4-year period had been interesting at best and a recurring nightmare at worst and, with my disastrous record in romance over this period of madness, my neighbours in the square at home started to feel really sorry for me.

CHAPTER 33

NUMBER PLATES

During this manic period, as 1998 drew to a close, I received a phone call from Reg Transfers, the number plate company, from whom I had purchased 923 RH to start my collection, followed by R10 SSO for my KR van at work. When I purchased that number, Reg Transfers got to know that I fancied getting a number plate which spelt the name Ross. R10 SSO was good, but people used to ask me if I was an Italian gangster. It was around that time that the registration number ROS 5 came up for auction and Reg Transfers phoned me to see if I was interested to join the bidding for it. They thought that it might sell for £6,000 to £8,000 and so I agreed to let them bid for it on my behalf while I listened in to the auction on the telephone at work. When the first bid came in at £20,000 clearly, I wasn't in the game and this number plate actually sold for £35,000.

A couple of years later, I got a call to tell me that ROS 55 was going under the hammer, not quite as good as ROS 5 but, with a screw in the right place to make an apostrophe, the plate would spell "ROS5'5" and that seemed pretty cool. I agreed that I would let them bid for it but stressed that my limit for the purchase was £10,000. My cash availability on the credit cards was under pressure and even 10 Grand would be a big ask. As I listened on the phone, the bidding went up in £500 units as the bids clocked up, £13,500, £14,000, £14,500, £15,000.

Disappointed but thankful, I knew that I was out of the running as the auctioneer said those classic words, "Going once, going twice," and then, during the interminable last pause before the third statement, the Reg Transfers man shouted down the phone to me, "It's with us at £15k".

"Gone!"

What? I had bought ROS 55 for £15,000. How, how had that happened? Should I be happy or should I be mad? Still, no pressure, I had seven days to find the money in order to complete the deal. Definitely not enough clearance on the cards to collect that kind of cash so there was nothing else for it but for me to try and get yet another loan. I made an appointment at the bank and, as a bargaining tool, I was prepared and ready to point out the huge sums of money passing through my account, transactions totalling more than a quarter of a million pounds that year, should have made it quite straightforward for them to grant me the loan.

"I've done something rash," I admitted to the manager.

"What's that?"

"I've bought the personalised plate ROS 55."

"What did you have to pay for that?"

"15 Grand!"

The poor soul needed resuscitation, especially knowing full well how I seemed to hoover up money all the time and that I had a loan with the bank already then.

"How much do you need to borrow then?" he enquired

"The whole 15 Grand," I replied.

If you are too young to remember it, let me tell you that this was credit jamboree time, "To borrow that amount" he said "you would need to be earning £85,000 a year."

"That's funny" came my retort "that's exactly what I do earn."

Of course, the incredible sums flashing through my account, almost daily, totally confused the computer so that, when the manager pressed the magic button, "Agreed" popped up on the screen. He was dumbfounded but I had achieved the loan and 'ROS 55' was added to my collection of plates. Almost immediately, I got a call from Sewells, the BMW garage, to let me know that the new Z3 was being delivered to Bishops Stortford forthwith. That bill was a paltry £43,000, I'd paid the deposit and had it on a three-year HP deal, easy-peasy, and how much cooler would it look now with the new number plate on it. But that wasn't the end of the story.

On the following Sunday, I bought the News of the World, then still in existence, for my weekend educational study and, as I opened the front page to look directly at page 3, this headline bludgeoned its way into my eyes, "Offer of £1.2 million rejected for number plate ROS 5". The story went on to explain how there had been a battle between some wealthy bidders to get this number plate, probably because, at that time, Ross was still a relatively unusual name, a situation sadly to change with the onset of the Poldark series and then Friends. The article went on to say that Jonathan Ross had tried to purchase ROS 5, but had his offer turned down. I knew that Jonathan Ross had a show on Radio 2 on a Saturday morning and so I got through to the programme and succinctly put it to Mr Ross that, as I knew that he was disappointed for failing to purchase the number plate ROS 5, and because I had the sister plate ROS 55, he might want to buy it from me for the knockdown price of £500,000. I must say that we did have a laugh but, it wasn't my day and he said that he had changed his mind about personalised number plates, they were just too expensive.

Time yet for another laugh though and, pretending that I was deadly serious, I took the News of the World cutting about ROS 5 to HSBC and asked our RP account manager to grant us a much bigger overdraft using my number plate as collateral against the new facility. He certainly did have a very good laugh and gave me the answer in two words, one beginning with F, and the second ending in F.

Being the least practical person ever, when I became a valued labourer and sweeper-upper on our Boots refits, the lads used to love to take the rise out of me by telling me to connect wires that were still live. I, of course, being too dim to check them out first with a volt stick first, would create a great laugh when I rebounded with an electric shock but I never seemed to learn and this made the shocks even funnier. It was doing this refit work that prompted me to change from glasses to contact lenses because constantly changing from simple close-up work like wiring plugs to sweeping up meant that I was also changing from my reading glasses to my distance ones over and over again. By the end of a night's work, I often forgot which glasses I was wearing and, many times, I drove home wearing my reading glasses, all very demanding for my eyes.

My sister, who is six years older than me, had recently changed to contact lenses and I thought that if she could do it, then so could I. I made an appointment with the optician, tried the lenses and never looked back! I obviously and instantly became even more attractive to the opposite sex and that is probably one of the reasons why I had so much emotional upheaval in those late 90s.

CHAPTER 34

HORSE OWNERSHIP

Then came the most life changing moment I had lived through, a rather big statement considering various past events. It arose from one of those nightshifts at Boots, when we were carrying out a refit in the branch at Saffron Walden. We were working with the shopfitters as usual on that Saturday night and a complete counter change was to be done on the shop floor. Between the two contractors, the shop fitters and RP the electricians, we were creating a great deal of rubbish which was being removed into large skip outside the back of the store. This was quite unusual because normally, during a refit, the shopfitters would take the old counters back to their yard for refurbishment but, on this occasion, the counters were in such a bad state that they went into the skip with all the other debris, hence its size.

My main job during this refit was to ferry the rubbish to the skip and I was working with one of the shopfitters top labourers, Richard, who I knew as an acquaintance from previous jobs although I had never spent a whole shift working with him. As we came to the end of the job, at about 5am on the Sunday morning, Richard casually asked me what I would be doing when I went home. When I said that I would be going to bed and asked him the same question he told me that he was going to visit his horse. Fascinated, I asked him what he meant by that and he told me he was a twelfth shareholder in a horse racing syndicate run by the trainer Peter Harris in Tring Hertfordshire. Peter Harris, by the way, was the pioneer of horse syndicates in the late 1990s, designed to give ordinary people the chance to experience racehorse ownership. He suggested that I went along with him to meet the horses and happily, as I still lived alone and still had no commitments, I agreed to go with him straight from the job and watch the horses have a training spin. We went in my little van to save him going back to Clacton in the lorry to collect his car, and I would take him home from Tring. There was a beautiful dawn and, as the sun came up and we drove through the picturesque village of Newport only a couple of miles outside Saffron Walden, we were pulled over by the ever-vigilant police for a routine check on my van, before we were allowed to proceed to Tring. Having never been to a stable, let alone a racing stable, before, I was amazed by the luxury of the owners' area at the Harris yard and the overall facilities on offer for the horses.

After coffee and toast - it was 7am on a Sunday morning after all - we went to see the horse in her box before she went out on the gallops for a spin. Her name was Nora's Cottage and she was gorgeous. When she went out on the gallops and worked with a couple of other horses over a mile, Richard and I were the only people on the premises apart from the stable lads, the work riders and the syndicate manager for Nora's Cottage.

Would you believe there was a vacancy in the syndicate which, it was suggested, I might fill at the cost of £220 per month which covered training, keep, race entries and transport. As part of the syndicate, you would "probably" be able to attend most race meetings when Nora's Cottage ran, although there was a limit on tickets and all 12 owners sometimes might not be able to go all at once. Readily I agreed to become a syndicate member, a decision which had far-reaching consequences for me in the long run. Not only would I now be spending an awful lot of money and time on racehorses but also this would enable me to meet the best animals and the best people in the world, enjoying some of the most amazing, wonderful and unexpected experiences.

My start with Nora's Cottage was inauspicious as she turned out to be an injury prone filly. However, the syndicate contract meant that you kept the horse for two years and, after that two years, the horse would be sold with any money going back into the syndicate. Unfortunately, in the two years that we had Nora's Cottage she did not run a single race and then had to be re-homed and given away, so the first two-year investment resulted in a loss rather than a financial advantage. We did not even get a visit to a racecourse but we had a lot of coffee and toast. I had caught the bug and Peter Harris met with me in early 1999 to suggest that being a twelfth share owner had been a good introduction into racing but, to have more say and input into the horse's career, a quarter share owner would be the way to go. He offered me a quarter share in a new filly in the yard, the owners would name their horse and also decide the colours that it was to run in. I was in and became a quarter share owner along with my three other partners. Each partner then put forward a name for the horse and each partner choose a colour and design for the racing colours, all suggestions submitted anonymously in an envelope. A couple of us, including me, put "magic" in our name choice and she ended up with the name Misty Magic.

I also chose green as my colour and three of us went for a plain jacket with three diagonal spots and so it was that racing colours of our four-way partnership ended up being a plain green Jacket with three red spots. Misty was a lovely soul but, although she had a few places and actually got us to the racecourse, she was not the most talented of racehorses although she always tried 100%. In October 2000 Peter Harris suggested that the horse should be sold, thus dissolving the partnership because she was not good enough to generate enough prize money. This meant that there was a problem as to who would keep the racing colours or if they would disappear. Racing colours must be lodged with the British horse racing board and must be either transferred or cancelled in the event of the dissolution of a partnership.

It was decided that we would draw lots as to see who would keep the colours in their name and, true to all known form, as usual it was lucky Ross who won the draw and so the racing colours of a plain green jacket with three red spots became the colours of Ross Hartshorn, another step on my road to racehorse owner immortality.

Unbeknownst to me, two of the other owners had decided to bid for Misty at the sales with a view to keeping her and moving her to the yard of Trevor Black. It turned out that they had known Trevor for some time and really admired him as a successful trainer. When I found out that this was in the offing, I contacted the other two and asked to join them in the attempt to buy Misty, effectively from ourselves. She certainly wasn't at all in demand at the sales, we succeeded in buying her for a pittance and so off she went to the yard and into the care of Trevor Black.

CHAPTER 35

KUMAKAWA

At the end of 1999, after those four rollercoaster years of madness, a truly angelic being was about to enter my life although, in the first instance, it appeared as though it would only be a fleeting meeting.

It was only after three or four appearances at our trade counter at KR that I realised that one particular female customer was coming in every couple of days. My desk was in the small office adjacent to the trade counter and if I was concentrating on my work as, of course, I always was, I sometimes wouldn't be aware of who it was that was being served. Apparently, this lady was ordering bits and pieces for her home but I thought that she was actually there so that she could chat up Ken. I couldn't resist winding the two of them up and, the next time that she was in, I made a point of joining them in their conversation and doing a good bit of stirring.

It turned out that her name was Karen, divorced with two sons, one at university and one about to go to university. She was a bit taken aback when, cheekily, I enquired about what progress she was making with Ken and, it was then, that she made it abundantly clear that her purpose at KR was simply to purchase electrical goods and nothing else. The next time she came in I made a point of having a decent conversation with her and found her to be a very intelligent, as well as attractive lady, although way out of my league as usual. She mentioned to me that she had attended a few meetings held by a high-class singles organisation and that she was not impressed with the standard of male that was on offer. With both feet in first, my mouth again working without engaging my brain, I said, "If you've tried those meetings without success, why don't you come out with me?"

Blown away and in complete shock, that's me not her, I still almost didn't believe her when she actually accepted my invitation.

Apart from the bog-standard dinner date, I seem to be a man with few options and very limited ideas and I therefore plumped to ask her to come to see the Spurs with me. What a top guy I am - well at least if the date is a flop, I haven't completely wasted the evening.

Karen had never been to a football match in her life and, unusually, didn't know any of the rules at all let alone the offside rule. It turned out that her sporting prowess was in the water, she was a canoeist, a kayakist, a lifesaver and, of course, could swim like a dolphin so, when we went swimming, as she was turning to do her 10th length, I would still be struggling on my first. Our first date was a Monday night trip to see Spurs play West Ham, certainly not the friendliest of fixtures dotted with lots of nice people exchanging pleasantries. This, in fact, was a full-scale battle zone. Fortunately, we did survive and, although the game ended in another pulsating 0-0 draw, at least she experienced the excitement of all the fighting going on down Tottenham High Road. I'd probably say that a score of 2 out of 10 for the date might be a bit on the high side. When we got back to Harlow, we went to Karen's house for a coffee and she introduced me to her dog Pepa, a beautiful grey schnauzer who was extremely pleased to see her.

I was very taken with this woman, I thought that she was a lovely, very elegant lady and had hopes that we might see each other again. Organised as always though, I didn't bother to get her number but, I did now know where she lived and also that she worked somewhere in the Latton Bush Business Centre, where KR was based. Unlucky Ross this time, she simply disappeared and was nowhere to be contacted or seen and, fearing rejection, there was no way I was risking visiting her home. The millennium came and went - I did attempt to organise a dance to celebrate the year 2000, but it didn't get off the ground and my days as a DJ were limited to request appearances for friends and St Elizabeths, which still was always very rewarding.

Now was time to concentrate on racing, I put the huge disappointment of missing out on Karen behind me and got myself back into the mindset of considering that bothering with women was a pretty bad idea for me and a sensible non-starter.

Having made this rock-solid immutable decision, some months later it came to pass that, as I was visiting the rubbish bin area at Latton Bush, which turned out to be mid-way between KR and where Karen worked, who should appear with her own rubbish but the invisible Karen. We got talking and both of us were surprised that the other had not been in touch. It turned out that Karen's dog, Pepa, had been quite unwell and, although he was fine now, he had needed a lot of tender care and could not be left alone at any time. This fateful meeting led us to the decision to give our relationship another chance to get going and at least horseracing offered a bit more than football. My first job was to introduce Karen to Misty Magic and after quite a few days out at the stables Karen really fell in love will the horses. This whole experience somehow brought us close together and a close relationship quickly developed between us.

In the context of horseracing, soon Karen and I were a designated couple and she became a great fan of racing and the people concerned with it. As regards Misty Magic, we visited Trevor Black's racing yard to confirm our new partners' views on placing her with him and, having met the man himself, we agreed that it would be a great place to have a horse in training. Regrettably, Misty seemed to go backwards after joining the yard and, after half a dozen unsuccessful runs the other owners lost faith wanted to move her on. But Karen and I are softies, we loved Misty to bits and decided that we would buy out their shares and keep her going at Trevor's yard. This was in the summer of 2001 and the decision we made was with the heart and not the head. I guess we were just not hard-nosed enough but, a good business decision it was not, because poor Misty kept coming in last and there was no option but that she needed to retire.

By this time, Trevor Black had also retired and the yard was taken over by his son Damien, with whom we were to have a great relationship and valued friendship for a considerable time.

When Misty retired, Damien found her a great new home and, in fact, she became a polo pony for the American Olympic team, finding a fabulous outlet for her courage and tenacity and having a great life. Karen and I were really loving being in the racehorse environment and clearly Damien saw an opportunity to keep us as customers in the yard and we became a very good, and willing, target for horses that, basically, needed rescuing. Like a car, however, it is not the buying of the horse that makes you skint, but the running costs. All horses in the yard have to have their training paid for, as well as their keep, whether they are good or bad and we took on a couple of real rescue jobs, bought and named by us.

One we called "Lucretius", after my special subject author at university, and the other "Life is Rosie" because we transformed her from being a very poorly horse to a very healthy one. Unfortunately, neither of them made the grade.

Misty Magic's last but one race was on 14th March 2002 where she came 11th of 12 at Southwell in a six Furlong maiden at 50/1. This was her 28th race without success but, on the same card that day, was a 6-furlong claiming race which was won by a horse called Kumakawa, trained by Mark Polglase.

When a horse runs in the claiming race, any horse in that race can be claimed, ie bought out of that race, it does not have to be the winner and, if the owner wishes to retain the horse if it is claimed, he or she must put in a counterclaim and then the claims are drawn by lot to determine who wins the horse. The price of each horse is predetermined in the race card and a percentage of the claim price goes to the racecourse itself, so it would still cost an existing owner money to claim his own horse. With Misty Magic running at Southwell, Damien Black was at the course, along with Karen and I, and he suggested to us that Kumakawa, would be a good acquisition as replacement for Misty.

Kuma was in the race card at £6,000 and consequently we put in a claim, as did trainer Mark Polglase, who clearly wanted to keep the horse for his owner. Kuma actually won that race and then the balls went into the hat for the draw. Lucky Ross was back, and my ball came out and I was now the proud owner of Kumakawa, who had been brilliantly named by his original owners. He was from the line of Nijinsky the famous stallion named after the Russian ballet dancer, his sire was Dancing Spree and so the owners named him Kumakawa, after the most famous of all modern-day Japanese ballet dancers and, indeed, he too was to have headlines to go with his famous name in the years ahead.

Kuma had run five times in my colours with no success until, at the beginning of June 2002, he was entered in a race at Wolverhampton. Karen and I decided to travel up the night before the race and stay in the lovely hotel which was on site at the racecourse. As we ate our breakfast on the morning of the race, we received a phone call from Damien to tell us that Kumakawa had cut his face open from top to bottom in a collision with his stable door as he was on his way to be loaded onto the horsebox. No race for him that day and an enforced break of nearly 6 months. We were at Wolverhampton without a horse and with no race to run in, still that's racing, as they say, and similar things would happen many times in the future, what with horses refusing to come out of stalls and the like, and we would experience them all.

CHAPTER 36

CLAIMING

Nonetheless, a strange episode was about to unfold, both uncanny and supernatural being good words to describe it. Just after the mishap at Wolverhampton, Karen dreamed that she herself owned a horse and, in this dream a horse with no tail somehow had a prominent role.

On the Saturday after the Kumakawa debacle, we went to Damien's yard, as usual, to visit the invalid and there, in one of the paddocks, was a new little foal running and jumping around the field and, as is common with foals, it had virtually no tail at all. All very eerie! In that instant Damien met us and said that one of his owners was having financial difficulty and was worried about being able to afford the fees for her horse, concluding that it would be best for her to sell him. Grasping a good opportunity, Damien suggested that it might be an idea for us to take on half of this lady's horse with him as our partner and he told us, as was his wont, that the horse had great ability and that he did not want to lose him from the yard. This horse's name was "Hard to Catch" and Damien agreed that, if we purchased the half share, he could run in our colours and our name. This whole morning was turning out to be quite surreal as Karen's dream unfolded before our very eyes and we decided to follow through with the dream and make hers the name on the paperwork. Now she had become the "owner" of Hard to Catch, she was faced with the problem of designing her very own racing colours. She liked the pattern of my colours and came up with a similar design, to have a lilac jacket with three dark purple spots - the famous racing colours of Mrs Karen Graham were born.

Damien then informed us that Hard to Catch was entered in a 15 runner handicap at Yarmouth on June 13th and so the new colours had to be made pretty dam quick, within a week in fact. That job was entrusted to Mr John Waterfall, proprietor of the Horse Requisites business in Newmarket. Also, by coincidence, on the night of the 13th after the race at Yarmouth, I was providing the DJ services for Trevor Black's birthday celebration which was being held at St Albans golf club. It was certainly going to be a pretty busy day and the number 13 was always auspicious for Karen because she was born on Friday the 13th, everything good happens for her when the number 13 is about.

First, on our way to the racecourse, we had to collect the new Karen Graham racing colours from John Waterfall at Newmarket so that they could make their debut in the Yarmouth race as, indeed, would Mrs Karen Graham as an owner. Funnily, I also remember this day for the rather silly reason that this was the first time that I heard the famous track and TV commentator, Derek Thompson, use his stock joke in commentary "Mystic Meg sends her apologies that her horse will be a non-runner today due to unforeseen circumstances", it's difficult to count how many times I have heard that since.

I had been involved with horses for five years since that fateful day at Saffron Walden Boots and, apart from one second and a few thirds, I just had to enjoy the flavour and excitement of being a racehorse owner. We arrived at the track and unwound in the Owners and Trainers Bar, chatting to people we had met before at other racecourses and unwrapping the brand-new colours, which we delivered to the Weighing Room for the jockey to wear. Soon it was time for Hard to Catch to go into the stalls and set off to see if he could bring glory to his new owner. Incredibly it was all one-way traffic, he pinged out of the stalls and flashed home to win by a neck as we went apoplectic with delight. The feeling of having your own horse win is indescribable and we were speechless with joy as Karen received the first of her many trophies. First run, first time colours, horse first - quite a result, stupendous!

We returned to St Albans golf club that evening to a standing ovation and I did one of the best discos of my career. What an unforgettable day, a day to illustrate that happiness and joy is the most efficacious medication.

Onto November that year and Kuma's return to racing. On his fifth race back, he managed a good second on the 14th January 2003 at Southwell, his favourite track and the track where he would end up winning 8 races. At that time Damien had entered him into two races at Southwell, two days apart on the 14th and 16th of January 2003, this double entry was to cover the possibility that he might not get into the first race on the 14th. However, naively, I did not realise that the second race of the two was a claiming race and, having ran so well to come 2nd in the race on the 14th and obviously being in good form, Damien decided to take our chances in the race on the

16th. I was really concerned about this race being a claimer and I feared that someone might put a claim in for Kumakawa.

Damien's view was that the horse had not been that successful since I claimed him before and following that 6 month layoff, he felt that no one would be interested in claiming him. The difference between my thinking and that of Damien was based on sentiment. We loved Kuma while Damien saw him in a business light, quite rightly I suppose. Karen was working that day and so I went to Southwell on my own, while Damien was represented by David Gray, his chief assistant and an ex-bank manager. On arriving, I noticed the presence of Mark Polglase, the trainer and, always suspicious of everything, I decided to follow him, discovering that he went to the weighing in room where he put in a claim for Kumakawa. This happened even before racing started and so I had some time to consider my plan of action. As it was a claiming race, it did not matter if Kuma won or came last, every horse in the field was up for grabs at the advertised price and Kumakawa was in the program for £4,000. From a strictly business point of view, it would have been a good financial return to win the race and collect an additional £4,000 for the horse which, in all fairness, had not been a financial asset by winning lots of money. The problem, though "problem" is completely the wrong word, was that Karen and I loved him dearly and he was a very special animal to us both.

The time to the off just raced past and now, from nowhere, I was being consumed by incredible time pressure. I made the decision that the best way to proceed in order to prevent the possibility of losing the horse, was to maximise my odds of winning the lottery against Mark Polglase. As a "mathematician" that meant the more balls I had in the hat, the better my chances of winning the draw. So it was that I put claims in in the names of Ross Hartshorn, Karen Graham, David Gray and one in David Gray's wife's name. Of course, only two of us were there. It was written in the stars that Kumakawa would win the race and he ran a blinder that day and did exactly that. The key result was, however, that we all, that is me and Mr Polglase, trooped into the Weighing Room to draw lots for the horse. Out of the hat came the ball with the name of David Gray on it and I punched the air with delight. Theoretically, I had kept the horse but of course, as you know with me, nothing is that straightforward. The rules of a claiming race state that a claimed horse must change yards for 6 months and so I had to swiftly get Damien on the phone and get him to pull a few strings, so that Kuma could be taken to Eric Wheeler's yard near Reading, to run in the name of David Gray. Eric was a friend of Damien's and, conveniently, was at Southwell that day and so was able to pretend that David Gray was a prospective owner of his and perform the necessary duty of removing the horse from the track.

I would continue to be the ghost owner and pay the bills while, Kumakawa would run in David Gray's colours, he already being a racehorse owner with horses at Damien Black's yard and, as such, had his own colours. We successfully overcame these few surmountable complications, all very straightforward you would think but after a few days Mark Polglase, who was clearly a very unhappy man and was determined to get Kumakawa back in his yard, realised that David Gray was, in fact, connected to Damien Black's yard and put in a complaint to the British Horse Racing Board alleging that skulduggery had been afoot at Southwell.

An enquiry was launched and investigators were dispatched so that we could all be put through the ringer and all the misgivings could be examined. Obviously, I was well aware that I had infringed, perhaps 'broke' might be a better description, the rules, even though it was with the best intentions towards our beloved Kuma and the question, now, was how to mitigate the result of the enquiry. The enquiry could not invalidate the draw for the horse and so he was legally owned by David Gray, legally placed at the yard of Eric Wheeler and so was able to run in races in the normal way. At that time Karen and I each lived in our own houses and we were both owners in our own right but, with regards to the claim, we were not allowed to be connected and, only if that was the case, could we have put two claims, one each, that is why us living in separate houses was a plus. The whole thing was like being in Perry Mason episode and my assertion about Karen's presence or not at Southwell that day was problematic. The reason for this was based on my insistence to the investigator on his initial questioning at my home that all the information I was giving to him was based on my photographic memory, and I hope that you appreciate from what I have written so far, that I do have an excellent memory for detail.

The amusing bit now is that, having invented the fact that Karen was at the course that day, I had to somehow override that statement by saying that I couldn't quite remember if she was there or not. I must admit that, since then, I have taken a lot of stick over the years from Karen over "my photographic memory".

When the investigator actually visited my house, just like Paul Drake (Perry Mason's private eye), he made an excuse to go upstairs to use the toilet but was obviously checking the wardrobes to see if any of Karen's belongings were stored here. He did exactly the same when he visited Karen's house and checked for my belongings. Amazingly, the combination of these investigations did not reach fruition until early 2004 when we were summoned to the Jockey Club whose offices were then situated at Portman Square in London.

I had to attend along with Karen and the unfortunate David Gray, who had become the unknowing owner of Kumakawa while being completely in the dark about "his claim" but, nevertheless, had been so important and supportive in our success in keeping the horse. We were all petrified at the thought of what might happen at the hearing, especially when it was conveyed to us by the court ushers that the Jockey Club took a very dim view of such shenanigans in claiming races. Conversely, soon into the case itself, it became obvious that there had been tens, if not hundreds of cases where there were, shall we say, unorthodox methods used to preserve the ownership of horses running in claiming races. This was a fully legal case where we represented ourselves against the Jockey Club's solicitors and the cross examinations did get a bit tetchy. However, it didn't go on for all that long and the upshot of the trial was that all three of us were found guilty. By the way, this was not a criminal case, just a sporting tribunal of sorts.

I was fined £200 for being the ring leader of the misdemeanour while David Gray and Karen were each fined £100 for their, suffice it to say completely unwitting part in it. Kuma was still safe in our hands, about to go on a long losing run, but we really didn't care because he was so greatly loved by everyone and the stories about him were turning into legendary status.

My faith in life and horseracing was rubberstamped that day when, as we were going down to the street in the lift at the Portman Square building, one of the Jockey Club bigwigs, who had been present at the hearing and was now in the lift with us said to me,

"Do it a bit better next time - good luck to you all."

The irony in all this was that, in the middle of March 2003, way back before the trial, when the horse had only run three times from Eric Wheeler's yard, Kuma actually escaped from the stable area in the yard and ran down the main road towards Reading. During this escapade he slipped and fell onto the tarmac and this caused an enormous swelling on his back end, above his hind leg keeping him out of racing for 260 days before he came back in November 2003. What a character that horse was and, thankfully, still is today at the age of 22.

On the 29th January 2004, after the conclusion of the Portman Square case, as if the devil somehow needed to punish me further, Eric wheeler, to our complete disbelief and dismay entered Kumakawa in another claimer at Southwell racecourse. I suppose Eric was quite correct in thinking like a trainer seeking a winnable race for the horse and his rationale was that, because Kuma had run so badly after his exceptionally long break, coming 14th of 16th at Southwell and 13th of 15 at Lingfield, and because the swelling on his back end had failed to clear up and was, as well as forcing him to have another seven weeks off, clearly an unsightly and visible blemish, for certain no one would be interested in claiming him this time, while he would have a winning chance in a relatively low class race. Of course, nothing ever works out as planned, especially in my case, plus Eric Wheeler had not factored in the Mark Polglase component.

Kuma was put in the race card for an advertised price of £3,000 and the race was over his favourite distance, a mile at Southwell, his favourite track. Karen and I both went to the course with a feeling of trepidation because we were terrified of losing our idiosyncratic and wonderful horse, and this was a grave possibility. Those fears were unfortunately proved justified when the first person we saw entering the Weighing Room that day was Mark Polglase. Although it was nearly two years since I originally claimed Kumakawa from him and a year since my dodgy claim to retain him, there is no doubt that Mr Polglase was there at Southwell for one reason and one reason only and that was to settle the serious grudge he held against me in this matter. This was in spite of the fact that Kumakawa had run 16 times in the period since he left Mr Polglase for me, only winning that one notorious claimer and in spite of the fact that he had come closer to last than first in all of those races.

In the Weighing Room, we witnessed Mr Polglase put in his claim, he really was absolutely determined to get the horse back. The only option open to us to counter this manoeuvre was to submit what is known as a friendly claim but this time, there would only be two balls in the hat, mine and his. In the event the horse came 5th of 10 at 50/1, no one should have been interested in claiming him but, no matter, we both went into the Weighing Room, yet again, for the draw. A lot of people crowded in the small space because the needle involved had generated a sort of feverish excitement at the track. Karen was almost shaking with nerves and my heart was racing - would you believe it my ball came out of the hat!! Really and truly how lucky am I, we had kept him again.

I was not in control of my emotions at this stage and, even at the risk of upsetting the now overjoyed Karen, I approached Mr Polglase with some alacrity and uttered the immortal words "That's twice I've done you!" hardly gentlemanly, but full of some of the strongest emotions of joy I have ever experienced.

We had won nothing, paid commission to the course for buying our own horse back – but it couldn't have been a better day. Kumakawa carried on losing for Eric Wheeler but served his time at that yard and returned to Damien Black in my name again, now not under the pseudonym David Gray.

It was in early May 2004 that Kuma continued his career with Damien Black after another 151 days off because he still had a problem with the swelling at his backend, something the vets had never been able to get to grips with.

Karen's horse, Hard to Catch - or 'H' - had begun our list of winners at Yarmouth on that special day, the 13th, and had continued to run very well indeed, with two wins at Brighton already and another at Brighton on the 28th May 2004 followed by a win at Folkestone 10 days later. Hard to Catch took us to many tracks over the years, Bath being one of the more unusual ones.

Set away from all the normal amenities, Bath is, I believe, the only race-course in the country without an irrigation system, it cannot be watered and because of that it is a perfect course for firm ground horses and indeed, sometimes trainers describe the going there as "like a road". In late August 2005 it was H's turn to give it a try - fast ground, testing uphill finish, 5 furlongs. H put in his usual solid performance, actually coming second in the race, but this day was more memorable for me for what happened off course and in the restaurant.

I may have mentioned that I have always been a massive cricket fan and over the years I have had many idols, Ken Barrington being my all-time favourite player. But I had many other favourites, one being Ted Dexter, who I thought was really terrific cricketer. As Karen and I entered the quaint racecourse restaurant at Bath before racing that afternoon, a gentleman was sitting alone at one of the tables enjoying an aperitif.

"That chap looks like Ted Dexter," I said to Karen who had no clue as to who Ted Dexter was. "I must go over and see if it is him."

Over to the table I went and, yes, it certainly was Ted Dexter, the former captain of England and someone who I never thought I would meet. What a fabulous gentleman he turned out to be and he invited us both to join him for lunch. He was completely humble as I impressed him with my knowledge of his achievements, and I think that he felt genuine pleasure that someone actually remembered and appreciated him. He was 70 at the time we met him and is still going strong as I write this story, which is really great news.

CHAPTER 37

GUNS BLAZING

In 2003 Hard to Catch, on a few occasions, came up against a relatively low rated horse named Guns Blazing, a horse that was improving with every race and had got the better of us a couple of times. Damien approached the owner of the horse and persuaded him to let me purchase him, with David Gray as my partner, for £12,000. He joined the Black yard in April 2004 and his debut for us was less than inspiring when he came in last of 15 in an inauspicious performance at Brighton. After another poor run at Warwick, Damien entered him in for 5-furlong sprint at Nottingham on the 15th May 2004. In the meantime, Karen had acquired another horse to add to her list, another sort of sentimental purchase from a claimer, this horse was called Supreme Salutation. To make it a good day for us at Nottingham on that 15th May, Damien entered Supreme Salutation in the last race of the day which was over a mile, in spite of the fact that he was carrying a double penalty for winning his previous race, a claimer out of which, as I said, Karen bought him. Also, on the 15th May, Damien had another horse, Silver Prelude running in the first race and our friend, Mike Murphy, had his horse, Bucks, in the third while another owner and friend from the yard, Helen O'Mersa, had her horse Azreme running in the fourth race. So, Damien had a nap hand and the order was Silver Prelude, Guns Blazing, Bucks, Azreme and then a gap to Supreme Salutation in the sixth and last race. A new young apprentice jockey, Mark Howard, was riding our two horses and also Bucks.

As my previous history shows I had, and still sometimes do have, though very rarely these days, a penchant for doing complicated multiple bets and, on Friday the 14th May, the day before the Nottingham meeting, I decided to do a Super Yankee on the five horses from the yard.

A Super Yankee comprises 26 bets altogether, 10 doubles, 10 trebles, 5 four timers and an accumulator. Karen and I were going to travel up early on the Saturday morning, arrive before midday and check in to the Premier Inn before going to the racecourse in a taxi and then returning to stay overnight at the hotel after racing. Rather than having the pressure of getting the bet on hanging over me, I decided to place the bet by using my William Hill telephone account on the Friday afternoon.

We had quite a few customers in on our trade counter that day and, being excited about having five horses from the yard at the same meeting, which was quite unusual, I was busy bragging to them all about how much money I was going to make - always a source of great amusement amongst our customers who did not share my expectations of gambling success. I decided to do my Super Yankee with a unit of £10 so that my 26 bet Yankee came to a total of £260 and, because I placed the bet on the Friday afternoon, I was not able to fix the starting prices of the horses but just had to rely on their odds when the race went off. As I used the phone to put the bet on with William Hill, I made sure that everyone could hear me, showing a bit of bravado and trying to make them jealous at the same time by me investing such a large sum. Several of the guys seemed impressed by my confidence and took a copy of the bet that I was doing, none of them knowing what a Super Yankee was, and then they went off to Jennings the Bookmakers to do the same bet as me, only with a £1 pound unit, that's a cost of £26 in total. One of the customers, a one-man band electrician called Dave Wilson, lived in a small village nearby which had a tiny, local, village bookmakers and did the £26 bet there. He actually told me later that the bookie himself did the same bet with Ladbrokes, just in case. The scene was set and we went on our way to Nottingham races arriving, as planned, at lunchtime on Saturday 15th May 2004. We left our luggage at the Premier Inn, changed into our decent racing clobber and got a cab to the racecourse in order to avoid the busy car park. It was a really beautiful early summers day and, at the track, we met up with Damien and all the other owners. We were like a coach party, Damien, David Gray and his wife, Mike Murphy and his wife Denise, John and Helen, owners of Azreme and, of course, Karen and me. To add to the occasion the whole race meeting that day was being covered by Channel 4 Racing.

We enjoyed a bit of socialising before racing but it was really surprising how quick the first race came upon us. Damien had high hopes for his 2year old, Silver Prelude, in that first race, he was quite a dark horse who would become silver grey, almost white, as he got older. Silver Prelude was a 25/1 shot who usually broke quickly, but today was not his day and he missed the break and trailed in 7th of 7. A bit of a disappointing start for everyone and a big let-down as the first loser in the complicated bet. Guns Blazing was next up in the second race, coming off the back of two poor runs he also was 25/1. As was my wont in those heady days, and much to Karen's usual chagrin, I placed £100 in cash on him to win, notwithstanding my other investment on the Super Yankee. Guns was drawn nine, my lucky number, in an 18 runner 5 furlong handicap, on a straight track where high numbers often held an advantage on fast ground, which it was today. Mark Howard, the apprentice jockey, had little experience and was just starting to try and make a career on the track. Today he got Guns out of the stalls like a rocket and he made a beeline for the far rail and just kept on and kept on and kept on. About to come to the end of his tether, he held on to the line and won by half the length at the aforesaid 25/1 and I was £2,500 richer. That was a lot of cash to stuff into Karen's hand bag.

Our £12,000 purchase had started to give us a return and this was the start of a glorious day. It certainly was a rush to get the trophy in the parade ring and then we moved swiftly up to the top bar at Nottingham racecourse to watch Mike Murphy's Bucks in the third race, another 18-runner handicap, this time over a longer trip of 1 mile 6 furlongs. Bucks was also ridden by Mark Howard and this time the jockey allowed Bucks to travel just off the pace all the way round. Then at the 2-furlong marker, Mark brought him out to challenge but, as he did so, the horse was severely hampered as he made his move. Mike and Denise were visibly disappointed as it appeared that Bucks' chance had gone but, somehow, the horse rallied and came again in the last 50 yards to get up and win in the last stride. To this day, I still believe that Bucks was second, but the announcement came over the tannoy that he had got up to win by a short head at odds of 8/1.

Unbridled joy amongst the group, hugging and kissing and sheer exuberance and, while Mike and Denise were cheered on by us all as they received their trophy, it suddenly dawned on me that one of my doubles in the bet had come in. That £10 double on Guns Blazing and Bucks meant that the initial £260 won on Guns was going onto Bucks at 8/1 producing a winning double of £2,340, adding that to the £2,500 in cash we weren't doing too badly already, but would more follow? Azreme was next up and the anticipation was intense as he had been running really well and Helen expected him to go very close. This time, however, although he was in with a shout throughout his race Azreme faded in the last furlong and came in down the field.

That left Supreme Salutation as the last of our five runners and in the last race of the day. This was the very first time that Supreme Salutation was running in the now legendary colours of Mrs Karen Graham and, wearing number 1 as the top weight he made his way down to the start of the 14 runner 1 mile 2 furlongs handicap. Worryingly, he drifted alarmingly in the betting market, which was surprising considering that he was carrying a £2,340 bet into a treble on my super Yankee. On the upside, the bigger the price the more money we stood to win and so we were confused as to whether we should get more excited or more concerned. Of course, not only was I hoping for a treble but also Mark Howard, an apprentice jockey previously without a win, was now looking for a treble of his own, and all this being witnessed by Channel 4. Nottingham's 1mile 2 furlongs race is a long sweeping course with a smooth final curve leading into a 3furlong finishing straight. Supreme Salutation sat at the back of the field as Karen and I stood on the raised viewing platform opposite the finishing line looking straight down the track.

As the horses came round the bend towards the finishing straight Mark Howard sent Supreme forward to take up the running just before the 2-furlong marker. Surely, he had made his move too soon, with Supreme having to carry all that weight. The only noise that could be heard on the course was the screaming of me and Karen as our horse went further and further and further in front, winning comfortably and sending us into cloud cuckoo land.

Seriously, when we watched the video of the race all you could hear on the soundtrack was us - absolutely incredible! A treble for Mark Howard and a treble and 3 doubles for me. Mark made the headlines in the racing post the next day and I was interviewed on Channel 4 and, after Karen collected Supreme's trophy, I found out that I had won £43,385 for my Super Yankee and it turned out to be a very, very good day, especially when you add in the two and a half grand cash-bonus from Guns Blazing. Not only had I won £43,385 but the lucky customers at KR who had had the nerve to invest £26 had each won £4,385.

The next bonus came when Karen announced that, for the first time ever, she had copied my bet and done it for £1 like the customers, adding another £4,385 to our coffers. My winnings came from William Hill but, apparently, quite a few of my customers and their friends had all placed this bet with Joe Jennings bookmakers in Harlow and he was rumoured to have lost in excess of £30,000 on that day. I was quite well known in the Jennings shops and I received an immediate ban because it was suggested that I had inside information, when all I had was one hell of a lucky streak on that day. Besides, if one of the other two of Damien's runners had won that day, the return would have been over £1million.

The other nice thing that happened was that Dave Wilson's village bookie told him that, if he hadn't laid the bet off at Ladbrokes, the result would have put him out of business. To finish off that wonderful day at Nottingham, after an interview with Channel 4, at last I had time to visit to the toilet, that wasn't the wonderful finale by the way, and standing at the urinals were two guys who were slightly the worse for wear.

As I entered the facility, I heard one say to the other, "I'd like to meet that bastard who won the 43 grand."

"You have," I said, "I'm here!"

Very sheepishly they slipped away – there will never be another day like it! The strange things that followed after that 15th March were that Supreme Salutation didn't win another race after Nottingham and retired two years later. Guns Blazing won at Lingfield a month later but, after getting a nasty knock, was never the same horse and he too retired in September 2005, while Mark Howard never made it as a jockey and within 18 months became a milkman – how very odd is all that?

CHAPTER 38

CLOSE CALL

–May 2004 had been earmarked as an extremely lucky month for us, almost as if it were written in the stars. Two weeks after the Nottingham day of glory, we were on our way to Brighton to see Hard to Catch run on probably his favourite track. Alongside him in this race was Guns Blazing, it was the first time that we had ever had two horses in the same race, H in Karen's colours and Guns in mine. A very difficult decision as to who to bet in the race was made easier by deciding to bet them both, H was 5/1 and Guns 11/2. We had decided to travel back home after racing because it was a work day in the morning and Brighton was only an hour and a half away from home with a good run.

Brighton is a sort of a switchback course, with a big downhill run to the bend and then a sharp incline into the final furlong, connections always describe it as an easy trip but I've always disagreed because firstly, you have to handle the big undulation and secondly, you need a very strong finish and, indeed, I have witnessed many Brighton races where everything changes in the last half furlong.

On this day Hard to Catch was completely outpaced in the first couple of furlongs, not really handling the dip, while Guns Blazing was in the van disputing the lead. Mark Savage, another one of our favourite riders and who was usually retained by the trainer Ron Harris, was on board H while, the hero of Nottingham, Mark Howard was on Guns' back. As they met the rising ground, Mark Savage drove H around the field to challenge and steamed past the lot of them to win, going away, by one and a half lengths while, Guns Blazing came in sixth, though not beaten by much. In the winner's enclosure, and yet again at Brighton, Karen collected her latest silverware, she and her colours were getting pretty famous by now.

After basking in a bit of glory for a couple of hours, we got back on the road to drive home in the Z3, with its flashy number ROS5'5. This car had everything on it and was graced by two really wide super tyres on the back. It was the 2.8 version and was, as they say, quite speedy. It was in this car that I had touched 140mph with the roof down when I took Doris, my elderly next door neighbour, to Tring on a freezing cold Boxing Day.

I have had a couple of cars, the Porsche 944 and the BMW Z3 that don't really lend themselves to hanging about, although I definitely was not an "over the top" fast driver. However, going back to that night's trip home from Brighton, in relatively light traffic, we were making our way up the M23 towards the M25 turnoff towards Stansted when I overtook a police car travelling in the middle lane and doing about 65mph. Because of this police car all the drivers, including me, were on their best behaviour and my overtaking speed was probably barely 70mph. As I returned to the middle lane, probably only 20 seconds later, I struck some debris in the road which, in a millisecond, resulted in my nearside back tyre being completely shredded. Effectively with no tyre on the back wheel, the bare hub dropped down and struck the carriageway and, as it did so, it jammed into the tarmac and sent the Z3 into a crazy tailspin. As the car rotated, seemingly endlessly and in what seemed super slow motion, I remember noticing just how bright dashboard lights were and, as we turned to face the oncoming traffic several times, you could see the headlights of the approaching vehicles. The Z3 was a very small car which a big lorry would simply have driven over and obliterated - oh for that tank of a Porsche! I can clearly recall saying to Karen, as we spun round and round, "I'm really, really sorry."

We both knew that we were in deadly serious difficulty but the bonus for us was that the police car which we had just overtaken had, by its presence, made sure that everyone was keeping to the speed limit and, therefore, would have a chance of avoiding us. Instinctive driving skills, if I had any, kicked in as I tried to control the incident. At least I was a very experienced driver, even now I do 75,000 miles a year.

Somehow, I really don't know how, we managed to come to a stop on the hard shoulder, facing the right way. We ended up stationary, just below one of the raised police viewing points on the motorway. The incident probably lasted less than 10 seconds, but events seem to take an hour to unfold, such is one's perception of time. As we took in many deep breaths of relief in our now, motionless vehicle, the police car pulled in behind us to check on our condition. After making sure that we were alright, which by some miracle we were, the copper quipped to me, "Buy a lottery ticket mate!"

With that, unbelievably, they drove away leaving us to get on with changing the wheel. We were very lucky that the refuge point was quite a width and, the fact that it was the nearside rear tyre that had gone, made it a relatively safe operation for me to change the wheel. So, after a successful hunt for the jack, we managed to put on the spare, one of those ridiculous half width monstrosities, but then we were faced with the problem of what to do with the hub of the original back wheel, this was still decorated with shreds of the burst tyre and was too big to go in the boot. There was nothing for it but to put the race trophy in the boot and travel home with the wheel on Karen's lap in the passenger seat. It certainly was not the easiest of things for me to do to drive home after this accident, but the piddly little spare limited our speed to 40mph and that was a good thing. For sure it was a big plus that I was able to get into a nice big van and drive it at work next day, that definitely helped boost my shattered confidence.

So it was that the luck that had been ordained for us for May 2004 continued and, this time, it worked for us by saving our lives.

CHAPTER 39

PARTIES

The enigma that was Kumakawa was back at Damien's. He continued his career, only deeming to run well when he was ridden by an apprentice. Give him an experienced or top jockey and he just wasn't interested. He won twice at Southwell in 2005, February and November, but his claim to fame in that year was that he became the racehorse that had run the record number of times in any calendar year - 30 times, some feat! It was an amazing fact that Kuma was such a low rated horse that he should have struggled to get into any race at all. Indeed, his rating dropped to 30 at one stage and, when you consider that a rating of 45 is about as bad as it can get for a racehorse, you can see the difficulty that he should have encountered getting into races, let alone winning them. There are so few horses of that class that our solution was to enter him for every single race that he was eligible for and, incredibly, time and time again so many horses would drop out that the result was that Kuma would get into almost every race he was entered for. It certainly gave Karen and I the chance to do a lot of driving and experience a lot of Premier Inns, as well as some really funny experiences.

On one occasion, it was Mother's Day, we travelled to Brighton to see Kuma run, taking with us Karen's two grown-up sons for a nice picnic and a pleasant day out. Just as we got there and parked on the downs, would you believe a sea mist swirled in from nowhere, coming out of a clear blue sky so that you couldn't see your hand in front of your face. The meeting was abandoned and the weather was so bad that we couldn't even eat our picnic outside the car and we just came home.

Kuma had one more win in his locker for us though and in February 2006 he got into a class 6 handicap at Southwell over his favourite mile course. On board was an apprentice, Tolly Dean, so everything was set fair in his favour. The race meeting was mid-week which meant that neither Karen nor Damien could make it and so I travelled up, not unusually, alone. Southwell is a really nice racecourse; it has a really great restaurant and there is a magnificent view of the whole track. I had a lovely lunch and waited excitedly, with my usual hundred pounds, to see what price I could get on the main man today. He was a miserly 22/1 but that would do. Amidst a very sparse mid-week attendance, my incredibly loud ex-teachers voice could be heard echoing around the track with a shout of "Go on my cocker", a colloquialism that I had picked up in my greyhound days.

Kuma looked as if he was in the mood and decided that he would run at the back of the field, and who was the jockey to tell him otherwise. As he came into the long Southwell finishing straight, he made up his mind to apply the afterburners, took off and just left everything behind him. Things went exactly to "his plan" and he won as he liked and indeed, when he wanted to, Kumakawa could be a really fantastic horse and, on that day, he certainly was.

Again, the special bit was yet to come because, as I picked up my £2,300 winnings from yet another unlucky bookmaker, I was approached by a radio reporter. Uncannily, the flagship 5 o'clock evening news programme broadcast by BBC Radio 4 was doing a story on all-weather horse racing and the reporter was actually at Southwell. He took me for a cup of tea and I spoke to him about all the ins and outs of being a racehorse owner - if you were a genuine horse lover that is - the distances involved in the travelling and the dedication that you need to show to visit your horse every week to watch them at work in training.

It was plain to see that the unbridled joy of seeing your own horse win did not have to be explained to him, but I did tell him that, although winning was lovely, winning is hard and there are many losing bets and one hell of a lot of money to pay out in fees. At every race meeting there is usually at least 70 or more horses and only 6 of them can win, depending on the number of races. However, it is all about the glory when it comes down to it and it definitely is not possible to put into words the joy that you feel when your horse wins.

I had many years of just enjoying the racing, never expecting to win, but Karen and I and started winning lots of races and Kuma was the love of our lives, we called him a rogue and he is the most special horse you could ever wish to meet. I really think that reporter understood what I was trying to impart. Driving home from Southwell that evening, with my trophy standing proud on the dashboard, I received a phone call, hands free of course, from my bank manager at HSBC, the one who was in charge of the RP account. The company was forever embroiled in cash flow problems, and I feared the worst.

"What are you doing racing?" he said, "and betting money no doubt! I've just been listening to your interview on Radio 4 and it's all about you winning £2,300 on Kumakawa. I will of course expect to see that money in the account tomorrow!"

He was, of course, winding me up big time and, at the same time, having a major effect on my mental health but it just shows you that nothing is ever a secret especially if you've got a mouth on a stick, as Jessica used to refer to me, later fully endorsed by the marvellous and wonderful Karen.

CHAPTER 40

WINNING

Our good friend Mike Murphy, who had recently retired as an amateur jockey and from his career in The City, was setting up his own yard as a trainer in Westoning. He had taken his horses home from Damien's Yard and we had half-retired Kumakawa to holiday at Mike's yard as well.

Kumakawa briefly went to Nick Littmoden's yard, transferring from his stop off point at Mike's, in February 2007 and ran a few more races until June 2007 when, clearly, he had lost interest totally in the sport. We thought the world of Kuma and so we had to find him what we were absolutely certain was a fantastic home.

Nick Littmoden used his contacts to find him probably the most wonderful home we could ever have envisaged and, with our great gratitude, he moved in with Helen McCarthy, a gifted scientist who absolutely adores animals. His destination was near Cardiff in South Wales, another coincidence considering my background, to a marriage made in heaven. He has since become a legend on the retired racehorse circuit, he has retrained to do a bit of dressage and some show jumping but is as much of a rogue as he ever was and he even has his own calendar these days. We are so delighted that he has found such a wonderful home and I am truly amazed at how very emotional I feel about him even now as I write his story. He really is an astounding horse and one lovely outcome is that Helen finally sorted out the unsightly and probably painful problem of that injury he sustained while running down Reading Highroad during his sojourn at Eric Wheeler's. Kuma, at 22, is keeping his remarkable story going strong.

We had joined Trevor Black's yard in 2000 when Misty Magic moved from the yard of Peter Harris and when Trevor retired, his son Damien took over the reins. We met some great people when we were with Damien, Ron and Millie Bright, Mike and Denise Murphy, John and Jane Lloyd and also an IT consultant named Mike Perkins. Mike's star horse was a mare called Love You Too who had won some top-class races but was now, all too often, refusing to race and not coming out of the stalls. So it was that Mike decided to breed from her, a very expensive operation, especially as

Love You Too was covered by the famous stallion, Averti. In fact, the foal Love You Too would give birth to would be the last offspring sired by Averti, who passed away not long after covering that mare. When Love You Too was carrying the foal, for some reason Mike suddenly decided to uproot everything and emigrate to Australia. Everything went with him apart from the pregnant mare Love You Too who would have been very expensive to get to Australia and, anyway, she probably would not have been allowed to fly while in foal. So it was that Love You Too remained at a stud in Elsenham until the foal was born safe and well. He was a beautiful little colt. At that time, I didn't really know the ins and outs of what was going on with Love You Too and her baby, I was unaware that the colt was going to the sales, let alone what it might be worth and sell for. It was only from what I had picked up in the yard that I knew that the stallion involved was Averti.

Out of the blue I got a phone call from Damien Black telling me that, at the sales, the foal of Love You Too had failed to sell. Consequently, Damien said, Mike Perkins was now very keen for the foal to be moved on. As Damien put it, this was a golden opportunity to get what could be a very good horse for a knockdown price. He told me that he had agreed to pay Mike Perkins £2,000 for the animal and that I could have a half share in it for £1,000. Certainly, it was an amazing opportunity, considering what we had paid for other horses.

On my way to meet Damien at Elsenham stud, where the foal was born and was based, I collected £1,000 in cash from the bank to pay him for my share. It was May 2004 and having bought the little fellow, my next job was to get a decent photograph of him as this was going to be Karen's Christmas present. Hopefully, she would think it was really special especially as, unusually for me, I would manage to keep the whole thing a secret from her for seven months.

We had booked a spectacularly upmarket manor Hotel for Christmas that year, 2004, at Sopwell House, a place to stay which was like being on a luxury cruise on land, with breakfast, elevenses, lunch, tea and dinner to keep you going, and then a supper before bed just in case you were hungry. It was very formal and there was quite a lot of the evening dress involved. In fact, it was rather like being in an episode of Poirot. Just down the road was St Albans Cathedral and, part of the stay included a trip there for the

Christmas Eve service and Carol Concert, a truly magnificent experience, really memorable.

Christmas Day at the hotel was a bit like Ross and Karen versus food and our clothing seemed to have shrunk more every time we tried to put it on. At Christmas lunch, full of romantic overtones, I presented Karen with the photograph of her new foal and she was both stunned and overjoyed at the same time. I think that this must be the best present I have ever given anyone ever. It really was a tangible moment of total love.

Following the food exertions of Christmas day, we were in desperate need of air and exercise on Boxing Day. Damien's yard was only a few miles away and so we drove down the road and spent a lovely morning with the horses. It was on the way back to Sopwell House that a newsflash interrupted the music playing on the car radio announcing the terrible events that were taking place due to the tsunami that had hit so many countries from East Africa to Thailand.

Karen was immediately consumed by worry and concern because her eldest son, Mark, had left for a holiday in Phuket, Thailand a few days before we went to Sopwell House. She really was in a bad state of upset and panic for the few days. However, we discovered that Mark had been delayed on his journey so that, fortunately, he was safe. The relief for us both was palpable. Over the future years, Mark was to persist in causing Karen continuous worry because his worldwide travels always seemed to coincide with natural disasters. He was in Prague during the terrible floods there, he was in Berlin during the terrorist market attack with the lorry and, to cap it all, was on the flight just one before flight MH17 was shot down. You really need to be somewhere else if Mark is around.

CHAPTER 41

LORD THEO

After I'd bought into this little horse, he was kept at Elsenham Stud for the first eighteen months of his life before he was ready to move to Damien's yard, but from the date of the purchase, of course, I had paid Damien his monthly invoice detailing all the vet fees and upkeep costs. The next difficult job, which Damien had kindly allowed us to undertake, was to find the foal a name which, in essence, sounds easy but in actual fact is very difficult because so many names are restricted in horseracing. The first name we came up with was Theophilus, after my wonderful grandfather who died before I was born but, as there was a stallion in 1901 with that name, we could not use it. We decided upon Theo for short, but again that name was unavailable and we had to find a name to go in front or behind Theo to get it accepted. We came up with Lord Theo because he was a very regal looking animal and came from the aristocratic line of Averti, with "Be my Chief" also in his lineage, so Lord Theo it was.

When Theo was at Elsenham stud, which we would visit every weekend to see him, he had some sort of set to with another horse in the field and received a heavy kick to the chest. This was a pretty nasty blow and gave him a zigzag scar on his chest for life and possibly, we think, caused an internal injury which was not apparent and may have had more far-reaching effects in the future. The time passed quickly at Elsenham and it seemed that in just a fleeting moment he was ready to transfer to the racing yard, ready to start his race training. Here he met up with his new work rider who would be responsible for his every need and for his training.

As usual we visited him every weekend to monitor his progress and his work rider let us know that he thought he was extremely promising. At this time, Damien had some really good horses and some quite wealthy owners and didn't really show that much interest in Theo's early progress. One of these horses was called Bertoliver, a horse that went on to win the Epsom Dash as well as some other big races and, when Damien decided to take some young horses to Kempton Park to get some racecourse experience, Theo accompanied Bertoliver to that track along with a couple of other horses. At this outing to gain racecourse experience was going to take up a whole morning, Damien was unable to spare the time to come and see how the horses got on and it turned out that, apart from the work riders, Karen and I were the only ones there. We were both delighted as Theo put in an incredibly impressive performance, so much so, in fact, that his rider told us that the horse could be something quite special. Our own eyes had confirmed that assessment.

He was now primed and ready for his first race, and a 5 furlong sprint on the turf at Lingfield was selected for his debut. At that time, in big fields on the turf course at Lingfield, the runners generally split into two groups, one each side of the track with the far side, high drawn, numbers having an advantage. Theo was drawn low on the near side of the track and made matters worse for himself by almost falling out of the stalls. He finished very strongly and quickly though and his position was 10th of 17, although he was recorded in the form figures as having come 2nd in the group on the near side. Karen and I were pleased and excited by his run, but Damien was not at all impressed by his performance. Following the debriefing after the Lingfield race we had a much more positive view of Theo's ability than did Damien, while James Millman, who rode him, also told us that we had a very good horse indeed.

This was a time when quite a few of our other horses were coming to the end of their careers, retiring and being found homes. Kumakawa hadn't long to go, Hard to Catch, Supreme Salutation and Guns Blazing were all coming up to retirement and, so it was, that we decided to approach Damien with a view to buying out his half share of Lord Theo, thus making us the full 100% owners of the horse. There is no doubt that having sole ownership of a racehorse is by far the best way to go, if you can afford it. Partnerships and shares are all very well but when the animal is wholly yours you have, or should have, the complete say over his racing career.

Damien was keen to sell, he hadn't been that bothered about the progress Theo was making and he calculated his price by saying that he wanted his original £1,000 purchase price back, plus all the upkeep fees he had paid when the horse was a foal and any training fees that his half share had incurred during the period since the horse moved from Elsenham to the racing yard. He came to the figure of £10,000, so £9,000 for 2 years half fees. We were very happy to accept the deal, which actually valued Theo at £20,000. Damien, however, did not want money to pay the bill, he wanted goods.

CHAPTER 42

SMALL PRINT

Damien had just acquired a very large building which he was converting into a mansion for himself and his new wife. As an electrical wholesaler, I was in a position to supply electrical goods for the development and we had supplied basic first fix gear in the past in a normal business relationship, never bothering with PODs or signatures. To settle the deal for his half of Lord Theo, Damien required for his new property three extremely large chandeliers for which he had been quoted around £15,000 by the chandelier company he had chosen to use. He surmised that, as an electrical wholesaler, I would obviously get these items at a better price than him and he proposed that he would except those three chandeliers in lieu of payment of the £10,000 for Lord Theo. Chandeliers were not something that we had ever sold before and so the first job was to open an account with the Chandelier Company. That achieved, we did manage to get a better price than £15,000 which he had been quoted for the chandeliers and that was £7,000+VAT, which meant an outlay of £8,400 to buy Lord Theo, a result. Basically, Karen and I bought the chandeliers and gave them as a present to Damien who reciprocated by giving us his share of Lord Theo. As these were very unusual items for us to purchase and as they were of an extremely delicate nature, we decided not to get involved with the logistics of the operation and had the chandeliers delivered directly to site by the supplier, who then forwarded to us the POD (proof of delivery). This turned out to be a very, very important document for us, as it was the only POD that we had ever received from Damien and it was a vital one.

On the conclusion of this arrangement, Damien informed us that he had transferred his 50% share in Lord Theo into Karen's name and so she was now the 100% owner of the horse, enabling him to run exclusively in her colours but, more importantly, ensuring that all prize money was paid into her account at Wetherby's bank and all fees and other expenses related to horseracing for Lord Theo were taken from that account. All of horseracing's administration and infrastructure revolves round Wetherby's Bank.

Our relationship with Damien remained solid and completely unchanged in the course of this transaction and it was a normal business deal between good friends. While all this was going on, Theo was entered for the second race of his career at Wolverhampton on the 26th June 2006 and, before this race took place, his transfer to us had been completed and so the new Wetherby's Lord Theo account had begun to have transactions flowing through it. We were over the moon when Theo came 3rd of 11 in this 6-furlong maiden race and his run confirmed our optimism for his future success. After this second very encouraging performance, we really needed to find a good quality race for Lord Theo and, over the years, we had become quite knowledgeable about choosing races and race entries in general.

When we were in Damien's racing office as usual the following Saturday, we noticed that the trainer had entered Bertoliver in a good class 6 furlong maiden race at Windsor on 17th July 2006 and we thought that this would be a perfect chance for Theo as well. It was not unusual for a trainer to run more than one horse in a race, particularly a maiden race, and Karen and I approached him to ask him to enter Lord Theo into the same race, bearing in mind that there was no guarantee that either horse would get into the race.

Damien was adamant in his view the Lord Theo was not good enough to go to Windsor and certainly not in the same class as Bertoliver, but it was his tetchy and belligerent attitude that surprised and disappointed us. He was quite clear that Lord Theo would not be entered in the Windsor race. We weren't having that and, for once, we stood our ground, ground which started to crumble and undermine the foundations of our friendship.

Damien was extremely unhappy when we used our new position as owners of the horse to exert pressure on him to demand that he entered Lord Theo where we wanted him to run. We were at a loss to know what this row was all about and why it had come about, considering neither horse was guaranteed to get in the race.

There is an old saying about Windsor racecourse which is "If you can win a Windsor maiden, then you have a really good horse," and that is what spurred us on to get him into that race. As it happened both horses were declared to run and we were lucky enough to have James Millman as our jockey for Lord Theo.

Mike Murphy, owner of Bucks on that Super Yankee day at Nottingham, was now a trainer in his own right. At this particular time, he had been recovering from a serious illness and had been undergoing, eventually, successful chemotherapy treatment. We asked him and his wife Denise to join us at Windsor for probably the biggest race so far in our horseracing adventure.

Damien had been more than a bit miffed that we had got in the race as well as Bertoliver. We certainly got the cold shoulder before racing on that Monday night as Damien ignored us completely and spent all his time with the owners of Bertoliver.

This would have been perfectly fine with us but, as the horses circled the parade ring, instead of both sets of owners and jockeys standing with the trainer, we were left alone to "give instructions" to James Millman, while Damien was alongside Bertoliver's connections giving instructions to their jockey on the opposite side of the arena. The whole thing was very strange indeed.

As we positioned ourselves in the stands for a good view of the race, Lord Theo was a 10/1 chance with Bertoliver one of the favourites at 7/2. When the stalls opened Theo broke quickly and got into pole position on the nearside rail. As the horses hurtled down the track, he held his position until, at the 2 furlong marker, most of the field, including the fancied Bertoliver, came to challenge strongly, throwing everything they had at Lord Theo. He would not be denied! He stuck his neck out and just kept on and kept on until the brilliant James Millman had driven him on to win the race at 10/1 and sent us into heaven.

By now we'd won our fair share of races but never with a horse that we had had from birth, and never in such a high-class race. Bertoliver also ran very well that day and actually came in fourth. We couldn't quite believe Damien's attitude after the race and, as we collected the trophy with Mike and Denise by our side, Damien was nowhere near us and not interested in sharing our celebrations.

We had no congratulations from Damien that night and it was all so strange because we had been with him in his yard and had success there for more than six years and, indeed, spent time on holiday with him. Windsor races are held on a Monday night and we could not wait to get to the yard on the following Saturday, as we always did, to continue basking in the excitement of Theo's success. James Millman was the first to congratulate us when we arrived and further confirmed his view that Theo could be a really special horse while we were delighted to reciprocate the congratulations to him for such a tremendous ride on the Monday night.

Damien was extremely muted in his welcome, however, and after all the owners had watched the horses working as usual, we moved to his office, ostensibly to consider where Theo's next run was to be. What we got was the presentation of an allegedly new training agreement, new being the operative word here because we had never ever had a written training agreement before. We were advised that we needed to sign this document immediately without even being allowed to read it first. Fortunately, Karen is the ultimate stickler for detail and said that, as we were going shopping that day, we would have to take the document home in order to read it before confirming it with a signature. We did indeed pop down the road to do some shopping but, after we parked up, we read through the document to find that, seemingly, it listed not only standard payment terms but, on extra careful scrutiny, at the very bottom of the paperwork, in extremely small print was this clause "As a condition of the sale of Lord Theo, this horse must remain in the Damien Black yard for its lifetime".

To say that we were stunned would be an understatement and there and then we decided that we would have to end our association with that yard. That afternoon we spoke to our good friends John and Jane Lloyd, two of the many great friends we met while spending many happy years at the Black yard, happy years which ultimately seemed to count for nothing.

CHAPTER 43

DISAGREEMENTS

John and Jane had also had a disagreement with Damien about their horse Kindlelight Debut and had transferred their filly to the yard of Nick Littmoden at Newmarket. They suggested that we contact Nick with a view to transferring Lord Theo to his yard, a Windsor winner definitely would not be a difficult horse to place, after all. Nick was delighted to be chosen and suggested that the following Saturday he would bring his horse box to the yard and wait down the road while we told Damien that we were taking Theo away and severing our contact with the yard. On that next Saturday we went straight to Damien's office and told him of our decision.

All hell broke loose and Damien was apoplectic with rage. The insults he hurled at Karen were nothing short of disgusting and, to say that he called me rotten, would be a gross understatement.

How and why had it come to this? We were absolutely in the dark. He told us that we did not own the horse and had never owned it.

He screamed at me the never to be forgotten words, "I am a multi-millionaire, I've got money, I've got power, I will destroy you, your business and you will never see this horse again".

He ordered that Lord Theo be locked in his box and demanded that we left his property forthwith. I called the police and when they duly arrived, because no bill of sale or any paperwork at all which could prove that we owned Lord Theo seemed to exist, the officers informed us that there was nothing that they could do to enable the horse to be removed and then told me that we would have to leave the property.

I then contacted the Racing Post, racing's bible, so that they would cover the story but when their reporter arrived, he could simply report and, although we made the headlines next morning, the paper could not be of any assistance to us in resolving our problem. The horsebox, driven by Nick's head lad, Chris, had no option but to return to Newmarket empty and it was us who were escorted from Damien's yard by the police, while Lord Theo languished in his locked stable.

With a tirade of horrendous abuse ringing in our ears, as we departed the property, I assured Damien that I would sue him for the horse adding the words which, even today, I remember vividly "You may be a multi-millionaire with lots of money and lots of power, but you have never, ever come up against anyone like me". He had at least been given fair warning.

Lord Theo was locked up, we left the property and drove home to consider our next plan of action. We needed a solicitor and someone with expert knowledge in this field. We looked to Newmarket and found the legal firm Edmondson Hall, whose top man was Justin Wadham, husband of the racehorse trainer Lucy Wadham. I made an appointment to see Mr Wadham and, when I met him, I ran through with him the problems we were having with Mr Black. The solicitor bluntly gave it to me straight, informing me that cases concerning the ownership of horses were extremely difficult to resolve and that this case was not easy. It would be an extremely expensive undertaking, which was the likely reason why, cases such as this, rarely worked out satisfactorily. He told me that his charges normally would be set at around £200 per hour or part thereof, with extra charges being made for letters etc. However, to my eternal gratitude, Mr Wadham decided that he would actually charge me at a rate per minute, which suddenly meant that I could afford to pursue the case.

The initial problem was the lack of a bill of sale and it turned out that, the fact that the horse was registered in Karen's name at the British Horseracing Board and, the fact that it raced in her colours and all administration was done via Wetherby's Bank did not in essence prove ownership of the animal. This seemed like an amazing anomaly to me, especially as the Wetherby's bank system was up and running for Lord Theo in Karen's name. Payment of the initial £1,000 pounds in cash for a half share in the horse and the £10,000 subsequent buyout via the chandeliers would also be problematic and difficult to prove. The Racing Post had, after that Saturday morning altercation, run the story under the headline "The Chandelier horse" but this was not definitive evidence either and would be classed as hearsay.

We needed concrete evidence of any kind to somehow prove that we had paid for and secured 100% ownership of Lord Theo. This is where the POD from the Chandelier Company proving that some sort of deal was concluded before the Wolverhampton race became very important while, following Damien's registration of the horse in Karen's name at 100%, he had made a catastrophic mistake and had invoiced us, only days before presenting that new agreement on that fateful Saturday morning, for 100% of the fees involved in that months' charges for Lord Theo.

It was our very first bill since our share changed from 50% to 100%, we hadn't had time to pay it yet, but nevertheless it was a 100% charge in black and white and a crucial piece of paperwork. Damien was now furious and spitting blood that this bill had been posted to us and, immediately, attempted to cancel it, without success as we simply ignored his demands.

Legal advice was to get this bill paid as soon as possible and this is how we managed it. We thought it best that Karen carried out the operation to minimise the possible confrontation if I was involved and she got the cash ready for the sting. We enlisted the help of a friend of her son David, Brett, a professional cage fighter with a fearsome reputation, not that Damien would have heard of him, but he did have the patently serious demeanour of a very nasty piece of work. Unannounced, Karen turned up at Damien's office that morning with the very imposing Brett as her strong and silent bodyguard. She presented Damien's assistant, David Gray, with the cash that settled that outstanding invoice. The stable team did its utmost to refuse the money, first ignoring the money, then pushing it back across the table, but the silent and threatening presence of Brett speeded the conclusion of the business and the pair left with the invoice stamped "PAID".

Justin Wadham felt that this was a massive step forward in the evidence gathering process as this paperwork was, without doubt, unequivocal evidence that the horse was 100% owned by Karen. The absence of a bill of sale was still problematic and Damien was in no way budging from his position, suggesting that Theo had been "lent" to Karen and that's why she had to pay his bills. It just shows you how easy it is to manipulate justice. Shortly after this Lord Theo was listed in the Doncaster sales, with the popular racing disclaimer that "the horse was being sold to resolve a dispute in partnership arrangements", with Damien maintaining that he at worst was a 50% shareholder in the horse and best the full owner of him. I contacted the sales but was told that we had no power to stop the auction but our solicitor obtained an injunction to put a stop to the sale, at the same time obtaining for us visitation rights to see Lord Theo at the yard at reasonable intervals.

In the meantime, we arranged it so that Hard to Catch and Kumakawa moved to our friend Mike Murphy's new yard at Westoning. After this first injunction, another was needed to follow and succeed as Damien tried to impose relentless pressure. We visited the yard and viewed Lord Theo on the walker, he was locked in his stable for all but one hour of every day, during which escape, he spent time on the walker. I set my phone to record any conversations that we had but complete silence was the rule and no evidence was forthcoming. Luckily for us the same work rider was still responsible for looking after Theo. He was very upset at the turn of events and promised faithfully to keep in touch with us with reports on Theo's well-being, and we will be forever grateful to him for keeping his word during this nightmare period.

As the case dragged on, I managed to collect all kinds of damning evidence against Damien and we were buoyed by the support we received from all the friends and owners at his yard, most of whom drifted away during and after this upset. It was when Mr Wadham managed to stop the second attempt to sell Lord Theo out from under us that he discovered that Damien had engaged a very top solicitor to take over his case.

The dispute had now been going on from July 2006 to January 2007 and Damien's new solicitor, not the nicest of opponents, managed to pin down a court date to resolve the matter once and for all. Documents from both sides had to be exchanged and I had a great deal of evidence to present, evidence that I was extremely confident about and covering many avenues. My Classics background had made sure that I was meticulous in my evidence gathering.

However, a document emerged from Damien's submission which was of vital importance to underline the ownership issue and also the inconsistences and clear lack of truth in Damien's assertions, particularly in view of our evidence of paying that first hundred percent invoice. This damning document was a fax to the British Horseracing Board, signed by Damien and dated and timed to a particular Friday at 5 pm which transferred the ownership of his half share of the Lord Theo to Karen.

Why he had included this in his evidence, I have no idea, but it was a schoolboy error. Damien's submission was that his assistant David Gray had faxed this document to the British Horseracing Board at this time by mistake and that it was done by David Gray when he was alone at the office and without Mr Black's permission.

Uncannily, you might say, because of my "renowned photographic memory" the time and the date on that fax rang a lot of bells with me and it beamed into my head that Damien had had a winner at Newmarket in the last race on that date, and that race was run at 5 o'clock. I did my research via Racetech, the company responsible for racecourse coverage in the UK, and I found evidence that, when Mr Black received his trophy at Newmarket for winning that race, David Gray was standing beside him, so how could he have been in the office alone, sending that fax without permission?

This error meant that Mr Black had severely undermined his own case and I communicated my views to his solicitor's office. The court case was now pending and, the day before the trial, I received a phone call from the solicitor in which he said, "Mr Hartshorn, soon you will lose this case and, not only will you never see this horse again, but I will be suing you for a quarter of a million pounds worth of damages caused to Mr Black."

"Sir," I replied, "I have got no money, so you can sue me for anything you like, but one thing is for certain, after this case Damien Black will never train another horse in this country."

That ended our conversation. 15 minutes later the phone rang, it was the solicitor and he said simply, "Send a horsebox to collect the horse."

The case did not get to court, we had won. We had our horse back. It is impossible to describe how Karen and I felt. We had been under so much stress for so long. I think we just collapsed from the joy and exhaustion of the whole episode. Justice had prevailed.

Our friend Mike Murphy was kind enough to send his horsebox to the Black yard and collected a very boisterous Theo. As he spent a few days with Mike, it was clear how much pent-up energy Theo had stored up while locked in his box, he was jumping 6 feet into the air on a long rein and was obviously very excitable.

Nick Littmoden collected the horse from Mike and we changed our base to Newmarket. Lord Theo absolutely, loved his new home as did we and, considering the length of the layoff and that he had been in his box for so many hours, he started to train really well. After 275 days break from his win at Windsor, on his debut for Nick Littmoden he came 15th of 18 in a hot handicap at Newmarket, before travelling up to Warwick on the 7th May 2007 to take part in the race for the John Smith's Cup, a race which would happen in front of all our friends and supporters from Damien's yard who had all come up to Warwick to watch the race and support us.

CHAPTER 44

GOLDEN PIGS AND SUPER CATS

Nick's yard was based in Hamilton Road Newmarket, an idyllic spot from which the yard backed onto the actual Rowley mile race course. As well as a training run which runs parallel to the main A11 in Newmarket, there is another training gallop which runs parallel to The Rowley Mile itself. Theo absolutely loved this track and was a sight to behold as he put his imprisonment behind him and got stuck into his work. That debut Newmarket rehearsal race set him up nicely for his trip to Warwick and it was almost three years to the day since those incredible events at Nottingham, which saw the triumph of the Super Yankee. As was the norm at the time, Karen and I decided to travel up to Warwick for the weekend as the race was part of the May bank holiday meeting. The plan was to travel up on the Saturday and stay over for two nights at the Premier Inn at Warwick, visit Warwick castle on the Sunday before going racing on the Monday. We were in for a fun start to the long weekend a bit of a laugh when we booked into our hotel though.

Karen and I are not married - something that would prove to be invaluable in 2014 - and surprise, surprise because of that we have different surnames. When we booked into the hotel, as a joke, I casually remarked to the receptionist "Give us a call if her husband comes looking for her, as we don't want any trouble."

The receptionist turned as white as a sheet and we thought she was having heart failure before she realised that I was having her on. She then told us that, on the previous weekend, an older gentleman with a young "wife" booked into the hotel in a perfectly unassuming manner before going upstairs to their room. Within half an hour a very irate woman, namely the actual wife, had arrived and furiously demanded to know which room her husband was occupying, threatening to storm round every room in the hotel until she found the right one. Faced with little option the receptionist gave the lady the information she needed and, armed with that knowledge, she disappeared upstairs. Minutes later, a naked man flew down the stairs, at some considerable pace, and sprinted into the car park to make his escape, with his wife giving chase close behind him. The receptionist added that she, with another staff member, ran upstairs to check that everything was okay in the room that had been allocated to the, now departed, man.

What they witnessed, she said, would live in their memories forever. The young lady he had arrived with was handcuffed securely to the bed by means of some very attractive fluffy restraints and thus it was that the receptionist was very concerned about the prospect of another incident like that repeating itself, although, in all honesty, in our case it probably would involve Karen handcuffing me to the bed in order to keep me out of mischief.

We had a great Sunday at Warwick castle which is, undoubtedly, one of the best places in the country to visit and certainly got us in the right mood to enjoy a day at Warwick races on the bank holiday Monday. It was yet another beautiful day weather wise as we built up to the race. All our friends and supporters had turned up as promised and it was all set up to be a great day, whatever the result of the race.

I managed to get my usual bet on at 11/1, although Theo went off at 10/1. James Doyle, Nick's rising star, who is now at the very top of the racing tree, was the jockey and, indeed, he would go on to ride this horse many times. Theo was drawn in the favourable number 1 stall and, at this time in his career, he liked to race prominently. He flashed out of the stalls and took up a position on the rail from which he could dictate the running. Leading all the way, as he rounded the bend and entered the last furlong, he found more when James asked him and won by a neck, to the euphoria of his massed supporters on the rails. The scenes were amazing and all the emotion flooded out as our entourage took the opportunity to celebrate not only the win but also the fact that we had triumphed in that eight-month battle to keep Lord Theo.

The wonderful photographs we have of all of us receiving the John Smith's cup for winning the race tell the complete story – joy, joy, joy! After this Theo went on a tour of the country running at Ripon, Ascot, Newmarket, Haydock, Leicester, Yarmouth and Beverley where, when we had travelled over 150 miles and he was red hot favourite, he copied his mother and wouldn't come out of the stalls.

During this barren spell after the Warwick race, Nick had severe doubts about Theo's overall well-being. Sometimes, he would appear to cut out in his races and just not be able to go the pace and, suddenly he had changed from being a front runner to a horse that preferred to come from behind. All in all, he just did not seem to be himself and Nick suspected that it may be some sort of heart problem and we began the process of taking him to several top vets of it to see if we could get to the bottom of it. During these examinations he did training runs with all kinds of electrical gadgets on him and he also went on the horse treadmill with many cameras and monitors fixed all over his body, but nothing conclusive was ever found and it was just a case of that he would run well when he felt 100% and below par when he didn't.

Nonetheless, 2007 was a really cracking year for us. Not only was it the Chinese Year of the Pig but also the Chinese Year of the Golden Pig. We were informed by Ricky, the owner of our often-frequented Chinese restaurant, the Stortford Garden, that the Year of the Golden Pig occurs only once every 60 years. As this was my 60th birthday year he added that is without doubt why I was very special indeed.

The Dragon dance and display that was performed for Chinese New Year at Ricky's restaurant, turned out to be done in honour of me and, the greatest gift that came out of those lucky wishes was the discovery of another super cat a few weeks later.

Collecting supplies, as I often did, at one of our lighting suppliers, Emco in Hertford, I was assailed by the tiniest of tabby kittens. She was absolutely beautiful and very cheeky. When I asked the staff in the warehouse about her, they said that she had just turned up out of nowhere, a couple of days previously, and appeared to be either a stray or have been abandoned. The chap in charge of the warehouse at Emco was a guy named Gareth Tucker, amazingly now a work colleague of mine at Ware, and I asked him if I could take the cat home. I was sure that Jurgen would be very happy to get a new friend. Gareth went upstairs to ask the boss if that would be okay, but she was a bit iffy about the idea and called the cat league first, to make sure that the cat hadn't been reported missing and also to get their permission for me to take her home.

Because of this I had to leave the tiny kitten there, keeping my fingers crossed that permission would be granted for me to take her. About ten days later, I got a call from the cat league to inform me that no one seemed to know anything about the kitten and no one wanted her. They told me that it was their policy to neuter female cats and this they had done. If we were prepared to allow their representative to come to the house to vet our suitability as owners then, if we passed their test, we could keep the kitten but she would cost us £40. The inspector duly arrived and we passed the test, the kitten would be allowed to move in.

Jurgen welcomed this minute new friend with open paws and, as soon as she was through the door, she tore all around and all over the house, upstairs, downstairs, checking out every room.

We gave her the very special name, Megan, and she brought, and still brings 13 years later, real joy to our lives. Megan had a sweet relationship with the fantastic Jurgen, but he sadly passed away in 2009, leaving a gaping void in our lives. A devastating loss to us both and to all of our neighbours, particularly Frank, now 93, who has been our faithful and true cat sitter for over 20 years.

Megan obviously needed company and she attracted into the garden another stray ginger cat, much bigger than her but very timid. Karen had been worried about this cat for some time and in one instance she got him treatment at the vet for a badly injured back leg. Then we also had him neutered because, as a full Tom, he was always causing big trouble with the other cats in the area.

We found out later that he used to live in the first house along our road but that his owners had moved and abandoned him. After Jurgen died, we finally persuaded the ginger tom, with Megan's help, to enter the house to take his food and we were delighted that he soon adjusted to our surroundings. He too is still with us today, weighing in at 5kg compared to, the still tiny, Megan's 2kg. With my attachment to Tottenham and historical precedent, we named him Luca after our player Luca Modrić, a player who Tottenham thoughtlessly then transferred causing us to toy with the idea of changing his name before we decided to stick with it.

Also, in 2007, I had my official 60th party, on the actual weekend of my birthday, at the Bedford Lodge Hotel Newmarket, another superb night which was a celebration of that whole Year of The Golden Pig. I'm not a great one for my own birthdays but this was special, as we were surrounded by about a dozen really great friends that we had made from our association with horseracing. The same crew that had been so brilliant during our recent struggles with Damien - Ron and Millie Bright, Mike and Denise Murphy, John and Jane Lloyd, John and Mary Waterfall plus Nick and Emma Littmoden and their head lad Chris - friends who would, in the years not too far down the line, prove what real friends are.

In 2008, Great Leys Racecourse, now called Chelmsford City, had just opened and there was a race there which gave us a great opportunity to have a run and not travel quite as far as usual. Lord Theo had shown himself to be very versatile, running over various distances ranging from 6 furlongs up to 12 furlongs, and this was a 10-furlong race.

As we got him ready to run, something about his demeanour told us that he seemed to be his old self. He was very much on his toes and back to becoming a real handful when the jockey mounted him in the paddock. In this race, he absolutely stormed out of the stalls to grab the lead, which he then held comfortably all the way round, without it ever looking like anything might catch him. It was quite a performance to lead all the way over that 1 mile 2 furlongs and we knew he was back on song and feeling good.

So it was that we were off to Lingfield on the 24th November for another 1 mile 2 furlongs spin with James Doyle riding. He seemed so very well that I really fancied his chances on this day and, of course, without mentioning it to Karen, I took odds of 12/1 on a £500 bet for me to win me £6,000. As he went off at 17/2 that was a great price. Theo was clearly in the mood and as at Great Leys, flew clear from the start and with a couple of furlongs to go he was eight lengths out in front and did not look like stopping. Ridiculously, with 50 yards to go, for some reason never to be discovered, James Doyle decided to look at himself in the big screen situated next to the finishing line. As he seemed intent on admiring his riding and hairstyle, he lost momentum and consequently lost the race on the line by a short head, which is millimetres. Disbelief and fury don't even come close to describing it, and some unpleasant expletives were clearly audible as the horses entered the trophy area.

Robbed by the jockey is the correct description. That day, it was reported that the At the Races TV channel had more than 1000 emails of complaint concerning James Doyle and that ride. Once again, we were in the headlines of the racing post the following day, but no action was taken against the jockey, would you believe that the Stewards had gone home early from Lingfield that day because ours was the last race and they wanted to beat the traffic.

All horseraces run in this country have a written description which goes into the form book, and even the official written description confirmed that Doyle had accepted that he looked at the screen but had stated that he had not lost momentum. There are times, unfortunately, you do wonder if racing is, indeed, a fair and honest sport. So, we lost the prize money, the bet was down the pan, just move on and get on with it.

CHAPTER 45

NUMBER PLATES AND ASCOT

During our time with the horses Karen and I had a bit of a game with our number plates. While still a teacher, I purchased the registration number 923 RH for my car and, I must say, that this did not in endear me to many of my teacher colleagues, as a bit of envy did seem to set in. Nevertheless, it gave me a taste for number plates which, after I had added R10 SSO, I carried forward to the times of the horses.

The first acquisition was the plate M2 STY which we put on Karen's old Vauxhall estate in the days of Misty Magic. This led to our first "pull" by the police when she raced at Salisbury. The nice West Country police officers were not too happy about the fact that we had closed the gap between the numbers and the letters to produce M2STY, but we got away with a warning. We then bought the number G11 NSB which, when we had cleverly used a screw to produce a U, spelt out GUNS B for Guns Blazing.

Then we decided to go that route with Lord Theo and we bought the number plate L2 HEO as we thought that the 2 could be read as a T so, L 2HEO. Then a random person meeting us in a race course car park and knowing that we were connected to the horse Lord Theo suggested to us "Why don't you change the number 2 to a 3 and then you will have Lord THREE O (L 3HEO) and that is exactly what we did.

Just after we changed our registration number over, we were on the gallops, running parallel to the A11 road, at Newmarket one Saturday morning, when a reporter from the Racing Post, who was there to check out the horses training, noticed the car number plate as it was parked on the roadside. Quite fascinated, he interviewed us about it and the story really tickled his fancy. Next day the story appeared in the racing post and featured the number plate in the headline, with the explanation in the article underneath.

Theo continued to run quite well and we set off for Pontefract in July 2009, to race at a course which he'd never been to before. This was going to turn into the day from hell.

Pontefract is a pretty country course where the finishing line is situated parallel to the car park, which is on the far side of the track itself, at a slightly lower level than the course but which actually borders the track. Unusually, Theo was running in a visor that day and, as he came down the walkway from the parade ring to the track, unable to see and unaware of what was going on around him, a very large trumpet shaped loudspeaker blared out from behind him, announcing the runners.

Lord Theo panicked and became completely disorientated. He bolted onto the track, throwing his jockey to the floor, before hitting the running rail on the far side of the course. The running rail catapulted into the car park and struck a car as it cartwheeled its way down. Lord Theo then took off round the track at high-speed in one of the longest runs ever by a loose horse before being caught. In fact, I don't think you could say he was caught more like he completely ran out of energy. It all lasted about 20 minutes and he was so exhausted that the horse ambulance had to be sent to collect him because he had become completely dehydrated after, probably, galloping about 3 miles. When he was finally returned to the stable yard at the track, he consumed about 10 buckets of water before some wag was heard to say, "You need to enter that horse in the Grand National mate, he'd get the 4 miles easily."

It was then that Nick Littmoden could not conceal his disappointment with the situation and asked us, almost apologetically, if we thought we should consider moving the horse on because he wasn't showing his true ability consistently enough and a change of scenery might be good for him. Later, the three of us often joked about this, commenting that we swore blind that Theo had heard this remark and, because he was so happy at Newmarket, he decided to turn over a new leaf. Which he did immediately.

Theo came out of the Pontefract debacle with not a trace of distress and in fact he was absolutely as right as rain. Incredible really. We had no worries or apprehension when Nick decided to go for a 1 mile 2 furlongs handicap at Newmarket where, basically, Theo could walk out of his stable and onto the track. We were lucky enough for Nick to book the champion jockey, Ryan Moore, to ride him at this meeting, one of those Friday night jollies featuring a rock band and meaning that the course was crammed with revellers, half of whom didn't care about the racing. It's always a buzz to be seen in the Parade Ring at the July course, and friends loved being invited to join in. We met up with a lot of people we knew in the Owners and Trainers area before racing that night. John and Jane Lloyd were there and we invited them to join us in the Ring.

After meeting Ryan Moore, he mounted up and we all moved up to the high viewing area facing the track head-on on the July course. This location gave us all a fantastic view of Theo tracking the field before Ryan Moore brought him out in the last furlong to pass everything and win going away by more than 3 lengths - he definitely wouldn't be going anywhere now, not that he ever was anyway!

We decided to avoid having to climb over many couples involved in passionate activities in the car park on that Friday night and so didn't watch the group. On the drive home we received a call of congratulations from another owner in our yard, a man called Dave Curran. We didn't know Dave all that well, but we knew he was a very successful telecoms businessman who loved and also bred horses. He had recently purchased a sprinter called Group Therapy at a pretty good price because the horse had suffered a serious injury while racing. However, he felt that Nick could get the horse right and, indeed, Nick having successfully achieved that objective, Group Therapy was running in the 5 furlongs sprint race at the big Shergar Cup meeting at Ascot the following day, Saturday.

We couldn't quite believe it when he continued the conversation by asking us if we would like to go and represent him as owners for the day at the Ascot Meeting because he had an important business commitment that he could not get out of. He knew that Karen and I always liked to dress in our colours and thought it might be a good idea if we would do the same when we represented him at Ascot - his colours were orange, by the way, not easiest to match up at short notice.

We snapped his hand off of course and Karen put her foot down to get home as fast as possible in order to have time to try and sort out some orange gear ready for the next day. This was a very big deal, a huge televised meeting on the BBC and we were owners, not in the usual sense, but VIP owners with superb cuisine and a wonderful reception laid on for us.

Into the paddock we went, with Karen festooned in a great orange dress that she, somehow, had found at the back of the wardrobe, and with me in a black suit with an orange shirt decorated with a new, and then very unusual silk multicoloured striped tie, which I had purchased from an exclusive tie supplier in Halstead.

We thoroughly enjoyed our VIP reception when we arrived at the course, it really was a different world and even this was surpassed as we mingled with the very rich and famous in the Parade Ring, or they mingled with us, should I say. As the horses travelled down to the start, we took up our position in the main stand at Ascot and it was absolutely packed.

Group Therapy was backed in from 25/1 to 10/1 on the off, undoubtedly Dave Curran's money although he wasn't there. I got our usual £100 bet on at the biggest price, we had our last night's winnings from Theo to build on of course! The excitement reached fever pitch as the stalls banged open and, after a level break, the horses spread right across the course with Group Therapy travelling really well down the centre. Spectacularly he took the lead at the furlong marker and went clear to win well.

Very well versed in such operations, we raced down to the finishing line, getting there in time for Karen to grab the reins and lead the horse under the archway and along the concourse to the winner's enclosure. I, of course, followed behind her at a respectful distance. Now we were walking directly towards the TV cameras and we had made it onto BBC 1 for the whole world to see just how good looking were.

The presentation of the trophy, was to be given to us by Sheikh Mohammad himself no less, the biggest name in racing. What could we say to him or what would he say to us? His first words to me were, "where did you get that tie?"

He then presented us with a monstrously big trophy and I gave him the details of the tie shop in Halstead where, sometime later I was told that the Sheikh became a regular customer (as the owner presented me with a free tie in thanks).

Clearly, we were in the big time, leading the horse in and getting the huge trophy live on BBC1. At the first match of the new season at Tottenham Hotspur a couple of weeks later, all my neighbouring supporters - that had sat next to me for years - were talking about was the fact that they had seen me on BBC1.

"Oh, just a small £200,000 race," I said. "Helps us pay a few bills I suppose."

This was another experience that doesn't happen to that many people.

CHAPTER 46

BETTER AND BETTER

The following Saturday was another big 17 runner 1 mile 2 furlongs handicap at Newmarket and we invited just about everyone we knew for a massive picnic in the car park before racing. There were about 30 of us altogether, with racing colleagues and friends, particularly our great friend John Costello and his wife Debbie. John worked at Marshall Tufflex and had been our main source of help when we moved KR, our electrical wholesale business, from the Latin Bush Business Centre to Harold Close industrial area at The Pinnacles in Harlow. Indeed, John had continued the tradition in the Hartshorn family where we always had at least one great friend who came from Ireland. John certainly was that and he has since returned to Dublin with his fabulous wife Debbie and their two wonderful children Adam and Ciara.

That day, as so many had, seemed to be set up for success, there was a special trophy up for grabs unusually these days, one of those that you keep for a year and then hand back, although it's up to you to get it engraved. Also, on that day, Mike Murphy had a horse running at Lingfield in the evening meeting and that's why he couldn't join us at Newmarket but it did mean that the ground was perfectly prepared for a double. To avoid having to bet at the course on the Saturday, what with the picnic, the gazebo and all those guests to entertain, I placed my £100 to win on Theo and my £100 win double on Theo and Mike's horse at Lingfield in the Corals betting shop at Sawbridgeworth on my way home from work on the Friday night. We drove up to Nick's yard early on Saturday morning and visited Theo in his stable. Karen needed to have a word with him about running especially well today, and he did seem to understand what she told him.

By 10am we had managed to get pole gazebo position in the beautifully turfed car park, literally no more than 100 yards from the track entrance. At 11 am we had the gazebo up and the picnic tables in position, as everybody started to roll into the course. John Costello and all the guys with their wives from the Marshall Tufflex warehouse, plus all our friends including one of our big KR customers, Anthony Kent, who came with his wife. This was a really lovely couple with a very successful business, but they had never been racing before and, although we were set up in our usual parking area, we were actually in the posh bit and we hadn't considered that any of our guests might not know the dress code, particularly the "no jeans rule!"

Anthony was wearing jeans, very nice jeans which probably cost more than my entire suit, but we had a feeling, later confirmed, that they might be problematic. Never mind, we all settled down to a great picnic, fantastically laid on by Karen in her chef guise, great food and lots of wine before, at about 1 o'clock, we all made our way to the entrance. We were all suited and booted with every lady looking radiant and extremely elegant but Anthony's jeans proved a major stumbling block. The bowler hatted Stewards were in extremely belligerent form and, indeed, we do expect them to stand up for the standards that make racing special. However, the ladies, in particular, used all their feminine wiles and charm to beseech them to allow Anthony into the course and, to his great credit, he actually offered either to go into town and buy some trousers or to simply wait in the car park until the meeting was over.

Fortunately, this submissive behaviour together with the unbridled female pressure melted the hearts of the gate men and the whole group of us were ushered in. On such a special day, it was great that the weather smiled beautifully upon us again and, as the tickets allowed our guests to roam free and explore the whole of the Newmarket course, I'm sure they enjoyed an experience that few of them ever thought that they would. Karen and I diverted into the Owners and Trainers area to be greeted by even more people that seemed to know us, I suppose that we had been in so many happenings that we had become quite well-known figures around the different courses, indeed the bookmakers, particularly the William Hill guys, were always pleased to see me, opposite to what it may appear, our horses definitely lost a lot more times than they won.

A better than 10% win rate would be considered very good indeed but I doubt we actually achieved that overall and, although we won some really big amounts from the betting, Karen always used to remind me, "Without the horses we would be living in a great big house with no mortgage."

She, and I, know that she was completely correct but I also know that she wouldn't change anything because you must live the dream if you can, and we were.

Time ticked by and soon Theo was in the paddock parading round the Ring. We got as many of our friends into the ring as we could, giving a lot of people the thrill of a lifetime by being in the parade ring at Newmarket and being on the tv.

When 100% well, Theo's trademark was to walk round as if he were asleep and he was renowned for his great action when walking, unlike a lot of racehorses. However, when the jockey mounted it was "watch out time" and he became like a coiled spring, unravelling at rocket speed until the jockey managed to get him from the paddock and onto the course. On the course, he went back to being the consummate professional, easing his way down to the starting stalls. To make sure that we saw his mini journey down to the start, we all dashed to the high viewing area where, only a week previously we had witnessed the horse's great winning performance. What would he do today?

I must say that he had almost as many supporters as Spurs because, as well as the 30 of us, virtually the whole stand would be cheering for him. This was a 17 runner race, he was top weight carrying 10 stone and the number 1. Unbelievably, he was 10/1 which meant £1100 for me if he won. 3 o'clock ticked up and they were off bang on time. Theo settled in the front rank as they made their way around the slight bend at the top of the course and came into the long July course straight. He was there or thereabouts, going well with Robert Havlin, another one of our favourite jockeys, deciding when to make his move. As he passed the 2 furlong pole, to the most incredible crescendo of noise from the stands, Rob shook Theo up to make his move and, almost in the blink of an eye, he shot 3 lengths clear. On he went, pulling away to win by a massive six lengths. My God, when he was well and in the mood Lord Theo was right up there with the best of horses. The adulation from the stands was amazing, and now all 30 of us rushed to the winner's enclosure, a very small area on the Newmarket July Course, to witness the trophy presentation to Karen.

The welcome that Theo got that day was the best he ever received anywhere and it was nothing short of fantastic. I don't think that the photographer at a course will ever take a picture of a winning presentation with as many people in it as the photograph that we have, and will treasure forever. The rest of the meeting disappeared in a flash and we were all back at the gazebo in the car park for more food, drink and celebrations. The event that day was almost beyond description and everyone came out of the course richer than when they went in, a very unusual state of affairs. It must have been as late as 7pm before we all started to drift away, Karen, wonderful woman as she is, doing most of the clearing up and taking the gazebo down. In all the excitement I had completely forgotten about Mike Murphy's runner in the evening meeting at Lingfield until we were driving back down the M11 towards home. On a road notorious for no telephone reception, I finally managed to get a signal on my phone so that I could access the racing results and, would you believe it, Mike's horse had won at 9/1. The shock of my audible exuberance nearly caused Karen to swerve from the outside lane to the inside lane on the motorway, the double had made £11,000 and so I had £12,100 to collect from Corals on the way home, although that meant going past home to Sawbridgeworth and then coming back, about a 6 mile detour, but well worth it. What a day, what a week, 2 wins at Newmarket, a win and a TV appearance at Ascot, I really think it could get much better than that, but it did!

I know it seems that I won a fair bit of money at quite regular intervals and that is, indeed, the case and all the amounts are exactly accurate, but when you consider that we had three horses in action together at any one time, and sometimes it was as many as five, the monthly bills could be as much as £5,000 per month. The record bill for fees for one month, and in a moment, you will realise why I remember it so clearly, was £9,664. Now you can understand those wise words of Karen which I quoted earlier, "Without the horses, we'd be living in a great big house without a mortgage." We did collect prize money for winning races, of course, Lord Theo alone won more than £50,000, but I still find it really difficult to comprehend the huge sums of money that we both generated and spent, be it in business or horseracing, especially when you consider the irony of the fact that, when I won the £43,385 at Nottingham in 2004, I paid the whole lot into the RP business account in order to cover the VAT and the Inland Revenue demands and never, myself, enjoyed a single penny of that win. Still, it is all about the glory.

CHAPTER 47

COMING TO AN END

These were our finest hours and Lord Theo's time. The pace did not slacken. The following Thursday, 20th April 2009, Nick had entered Theo for the Ladies Derby at Epsom, over the proper Epsom Derby course of 1 mile 4 furlongs. Nick's wife Emma had the ride. Theo had gone from a debut race at 5 furlongs at Lingfield to running middle distances and now up to 1 mile 4 furlongs at the country's Premier Course. Not a huge crowd at Epsom on a Thursday night and we managed to get Karen's sister, Anne, and her family to make this short trip from Dorking so that they could enjoy a first visit to a racehorse meeting. Worth remembering that Theo was in brilliant form, Emma got him nicely out of the stalls and he travelled well to the high point of the course before handling the undulations into Tattenham Corner and rounding that bend in about 5th position.

As the runners thundered into the long finishing straight, two horses were clear the field as Theo moved into fourth position, then third and then closed on the leading pair before taking second with 100 yards to go and half a length to make up. Curses! Emma dropped her whip and we lost a tiny bit of a momentum on the adverse camber and ended up losing by a neck but it was another terrific run and the excitement was coming by the bucket load.

It seemed a long old journey home on that Thursday night and genuine exhaustion, added to the slight disappointment of the race was definitely taking its toll on us - we had to work as well, remember. We soon put all that fatigue behind us when we went up to the gallops on the Saturday to watch Theo have a bit of a "train down" exercise, or so we thought. This was such an amazing time to be involved with such a superstar animal, he was so unbelievably well and we did not want the races to end, we were living the dream. When we arrived at the yard and went to pet Theo in his box before   his work, Nick told us that Sheikh Mohammed had been in touch to request a favour.

The Sheikh had recently purchased a top-class horse that he hoped to run in the upcoming main Group Races. A Group Race in racing is at the very top of the tree, it doesn't get better. This horse would have cost the earth. Regrettably, no horse in the Sheikh's yard was good enough to get near, let alone test, this animal on the gallops and he asked Nick if he would allow Lord Theo to set the pace for him over a mile and a quarter to give his horse the test that it needed. Nick told us that he had agreed to the Sheikh's request but, candidly, had warned him that Theo might not be quite what he was looking for, because of how good he was. For sure Theo was in top form at the moment but he was always, and I mean always, exceptional on the gallops. The phrase "morning glory" has its origins in the way that some horses work so much more brilliantly on the gallops in the early morning, totally eclipsing what they achieve in their performances on the track. Theo was THE morning glory horse. Over the years, we had witnessed him show amazing talent on the gallops, with nothing ever being able to live with him and, we honestly believe that, had it not been for his mysterious heart problem, which we always related back to that kick he received as a foal at the Elsenham stud, he could have been a top, top horse, remembering also that his sire, Averti, fathered some terrific horses and that Theo was the very last of his offspring.

The Sheikh brought his horse to the gallops and they set off on their 10 furlongs training run on the track parallel to the Rowley Mile. Theo set the pace and wound up the speed so that they were flying into the final 2 furlongs, all set up for the Sheikh's horse to come through and show his turn of foot and superb finishing speed. Theo had other ideas, stretching away to leave this wonder horse floundering lengths behind. There is absolutely no doubt at all that Lord Theo could have been one of the very best horses around. The Sheikh was a bit crestfallen but readily accepted that this did not show up his own horse at all, because it was up against one that was very special indeed. Theo was now ready for his third race at Newmarket in as many weeks, another 1 mile 2 furlong race with a £10,000 prize. There were some seriously good horses amongst the 11 runners. We took another large contingent of supporters, not quite as many as before, but he still had his massive group of fans in the stand.

This time, because of the rise in class of the race, Theo was one of the bottom weights, wearing number 10 and carrying 8 stone 12lbs, a full 16lbs less than the week before. Today, his form ensured that he was one of the favourites, only 4/1, and again he raced prominently from the start and, with Robert Havlin once more in control. This time he waited until the final furlong to attack, storming up that demanding and unforgiving final

Newmarket incline. Unleashed, he stormed through to lead, ran on well and won by neck - he really was at the very top of his game and very few horses win three races in a row at Newmarket! It was an absolute honour to own this horse and with him in the form of his life sweeping all before him Karen and I could simply count our blessings.

With Nick Littmoden, we took the decision to enter him in a £50,000 race over 1 mile 6 furlongs at Haydock Park, way up north. This would be the farthest he had ever run but our own eyes and glowing recommendations from the likes of Ryan Moore and Richard Hughes, another champion jockey, encouraged us to believe that he would see out the trip.

One of the main things to know about Lord Theo was that he was a "top of the ground" horse, meaning that he did not appreciate any ground with the letter S in its description, GS, good to soft was not his going and, S, soft was a definite no-no. With Haydock Park being a long way north it was decided to take the horse to stay overnight on the track and, unfortunately, after a really great spell of weather, it had turned and, up north it was a very wet week with particularly heavy rain on the Friday evening that Theo travelled. The ground at the racecourse changed to soft but, as this was the greatest value race of Theo's career and the chance may not come again. After long and agonising discussions, we made the catastrophic decision for him to take his chance. He hated every minute of the race, hated the ground and hated the whole event. We, mostly I, had clearly made the wrong call and it was a matter of great regret to me that I made an incorrect decision knowing full well that Theo would not be able to go on the ground.

The thought of the £50,000 prize was cruelly tempting and, that I could not resist the lure, was a lesson in greed that I would take forward in the future. Three performances over the next month showed how much damage that Haydock race had done to Theo's overall well-being and we made the decision to give him a six-month break.

When he came back in April 2010, he was entered in a couple of high-class races but he didn't show much form and his prices were in the 50/1 to 100/1 range so the bookmakers didn't rate his chances either. He owed us nothing so we gave him another two-month break before bringing him back in July 2010. He started to show some of the old dash and he had posted couple of 3rds and a 4th before embarking on one of those purple patches that he did seem to get into. Between 22nd December 2010, and 29th January 2011 he won three of his next five races, all over 1 mile 2 furlongs and all on the all-weather at Lingfield. In all three of his winning performances, he achieved victory by coming from last to first, and I remember vividly the words of the track commentator in one of those races when he said, "Here comes Lord Theo, he really can be such a special horse when he puts his mind to it."

After this ninth win of his career, a career in which he won £53,000 in prize money, devastatingly, he suffered a very bad attack of colic. Nick found him on his back in the stable the next day and the vet worked miracles to save his life. He recovered, but would never be the same horse again. We tried to get him going again in the summer of 2011 but it wasn't to be, he seemed to cut out midway through every race and trailed in last in his next five races. After another break and on the last Saturday of March 2012, by which time Nick had moved to a beautiful new yard further into Newmarket, Theo, the most enthusiastic of all workhorses, came out of the stable and refused to go on the gallops. Remember his mother, Love You Too, a successful sprinter, also refused to race quite a few times in the last months of her career. Theo was certainly telling us that he had had enough, it was time for him to retire and we needed to find him a really good home.

CHAPTER 48

PARTING

There are a few tales of the success we had in finding homes for our retiring horses and, like so many people in racing, we really were concerned about the horses as they retired. We always been a soft touch for poor quality racehorses who needed to be loved and looked after and, in the last period of our happy times with Damien Black, we were persuaded to take on a waif named Dennis. Damien, a great salesman, thought that Dennis could probably make the track and so, having taken him on, we gave him the fantastic name of Hurricane Dennis although as some wit remarked that "he was more of a breeze". To cut a long story short Dennis made it to Warwick racecourse via Mike Murphy's yard (he was there because of the Lord Theo legal case) and, after trailing in a long way back at the tail of the field, we asked his jockey, Liam Keniry, to be brutally honest about Denis' ability. His words were "He's a lovely natured horse but a racehorse he is not."

That was blunt enough for us and we visited a good home at a nice farm in Suffolk, a place where we were happy to leave him with people who we believed wanted to take Dennis on. Six weeks or so later, we received a shocking phone call from our friends, Ron and Millie Bright, telling us that one of their friends had noticed that Hurricane Dennis had been put in a poor-quality sale for very low-class animals. Our conscience would not allow this to happen. We headed for the sale and ended up buying Dennis back for £700. At least he was safe and, this time, we took even more care and found him a brilliant home in the borders of Scotland, a long way away, but well worth his trip.

Almost at the same time, Hard to Catch had reached his time to retire. He, too, had moved through Mike Murphy's yard to be with Nick at Newmarket. Nick put out his tentacles again and found Hard to Catch a lovely retirement home, near Dennis, on the Scottish borders at Hawick. Hawick is famous for the Hawick Common Riding Festival which commemorates the capture, in 1514, of the English flag by a local youth in the build up to the Battle of Flodden. The festival lasts for about a week with many "ride outs", sometimes featuring as many as 600 horses. After a series of build-up events, the main Rideout takes place on the Friday. Snuff is distributed at 6am and the main party take breakfast together before the ride out, led by the head rider, called the Cornet, brandishing his flag. 600 or so horses ride to an area for racing and the whole group is led into that area by the Cornet with his flag held aloft. It is a great honour to be chosen as the lead horse in such a long standing and prestigious event, where the crowds are enormous, mostly equestrians.

A dinner and Grand Ball form the climax of the whole week and is held in the Central Hall at Hawick in the evening. Imagine our pride when, Sue and her husband, Hard to Catch's new owners, told us that he had been selected to be the lead horse in the final and most important Ride out, carrying the Cornet and his flag.

Without a second thought we were in the car and on our way to Hawick for the week. It was a really lovely town, with beautiful scenery everywhere and we found a super guesthouse to stay in, on a trip that gave us the opportunity to visit Dennis in his new home as well. All good. We were up at the crack of dawn each day watching the horses, in their hundreds, making their way around the borders, an absolutely magical and unforgettable sight. Onto the final day when the horses made their way into the final race area, a sort of horseshoe shape with a makeshift straight of a couple of furlongs. We led the cheers as Hard to Catch led in the hordes of horses, with the Cornet in the saddle wielding his flag. I think H had flashbacks to his many sprint wins at Brighton as he flashed down the track like a rocket, I don't think that that flag has ever been subjected to such a gale force wind before. It was a truly heart wrenching and emotional moment for both of us and, an unbelievable honour to witness Hard to Catch being such a star.

When we were invited, as guests of honour no less, to the Grand Ball, we simply could not believe the incredible hospitality of those wonderful people. It was yet another very special and unique moment brought about because of the horses. Of course, "the all-time great placement" of a retiring racehorse was when the angel that is Helen McCarthy took on the rogue that is Kumakawa, affectionately known, as Kuma!

When it was Lord Theo's turn to call it a day, we wanted to find him somewhere really special and a place where we could regularly visit him. A lady running a small stable in Fakenham, a little town not far up from

Newmarket, often got in touch with Nick about horses about to change direction and expressed an interest in taking Theo.

We visited her stables in Fakenham to satisfy ourselves that she had a suitable place for him. She also came down to Newmarket to visit Nick, and he talked through with her what would be required in the care of Theo. Both Karen and I, and Nick, were very happy that she was suitable. Everything was fine and all the horses in her care seemed to be extremely well looked after and contented.

Although, it was heart breaking to lose Theo, he needed to be with people who knew how to look after horses and it would not be possible for him to live in a racing yard, full of working horses, the expense alone would be prohibitive. This is a major problem for people like us who fall in love with our horses and yet are unable to look after them when they retire because we simply haven't got the land or the know how to be able to do it.

When Theo went up to Fakenham, we decided to give him a couple of weeks to settle in, obviously no matter how good his new home was it would not be of the same standard as a high-quality racing yard, where the horses are treated like stars and are highly pampered. After our first visit to see him, we were delighted at how pleased he was to see us and how happy and well in himself he was. Retirement seemed to be agreeing with him.

Just a week later, when Karen and I were working with the accountant at the KR warehouse on the Saturday morning, Karen took a phone call from Fakenham. Immediately she went down the stairs and right to the back of the warehouse where, I could see that she had completely broken down in tears and was utterly distraught. Theo was dead. He died alone in his field and the lady had found him that morning when she went to give him his breakfast.

This ranked right up there with any dreadful and tragic experience I had ever suffered in my life. Karen cried for three weeks solid after that terrible day, and I was traumatized and felt that I had a hole in my heart. We think that his mysterious health problem had finally won the day, he knew he couldn't race any more, and what he had achieved was awesome. His courage, to the very end of his life, had been immense and he so deserved a long and happy retirement, but for him it wasn't to be and he left a gaping chasm in our lives.

CHAPTER 49

END OF THE RACE

When something as tragic as this happens, somehow you have to pick yourself up and carry on. Through bitter experience, Karen and I seem to have developed that gift. The foundations for our, now necessary, rehabilitation had been laid in the happier times of 2010. We had paid a second visit to our old friend from Damien's yard, Helen O'Mersa, now alongside her new husband, John, at their amazing stud and farm at Kensworth, near Dunstable. John had sold his business for many millions of pounds and we had recently attended the couple's fantastic wedding celebration when, after the ceremony, all the many guests returned to that magnificent home at Shortgrove Manor Farm.

This beautiful occasion was not only memorable because of the sheer size of the event and the incredible wedding, the scale of which I have never seen matched, but also because of the wonderful service at the lovely little church of Saint Mary, Kensworth where John, the bridegroom, had arrived on a magnificent white steed, wearing formal riding gear including top hat. It really was like being in a movie and a truly super day.

This latest visit was on an open day at the stud, where some very expensive horses were being paraded in front of potential buyers. John had followed his dream to breed horses and he had the perfect partner in the lovely Helen, an expert veterinary surgeon who sadly, within a few short years, would be incapacitated by a serious stroke. We, of course, were just interested bystanders as these horses were way out of our league, gone were the days when we could splash out thousands of pounds on horses, and it wasn't only the 2008 crash that had seen to that.

Nevertheless, unashamed of our relative poverty in this company, as we took a walk around the farm, away from the main parade area, and in a quiet corner, we stumbled upon two lovely little two-year-old horses frolicking in a paddock. We found out that they were a filly called Lily, and a gelding called Bertie. Karen was very taken with the two of them and they were very, very sweet. So, fatally, Karen asked Helen what was happening to them.

Helen told us that the two horses were not of the standard to go to the sales because, when fees and commission were paid, the stud wouldn't make any money out of them. Lily was very cheeky and Karen asked how much she would cost. The answer was £800.

Getting in on the act, I interjected "If you throw in Bertie, how much for the two of them?"

"£2,000 for the pair," she replied.

What a pair, us - not the horses that is.

There and then we called Nick and asked if he would take them on in the yard, as if he would say no to more training fees? So it was that within two days they had settled into the Littmoden yard, coincidently at a time when some of Nick's discarded Hong Kong horses became available. Each year, funded by the Hong Kong Jockey Club, Nick bought a set number of horses specially earmarked for the Hong Kong racing season. He would train them for a year before they would all be shipped off to the Hong Kong sales, where Nick received a percentage of the profit on the sales returns. It was very lucrative on most occasions but not always. Also, every now and again, horses purchased by Nick did not make the grade to be shipped to Hong Kong, in saying that, I must stress that there was a very high benchmark for these horses to make.

On this occasion an interesting bay gelding became available for sale. During our time with Nick, we met even more lovely horseracing people and one such person was a great fellow called Andrew Highfield. Andrew was extremely shy, and one of the quietest and most genuine of men you could ever wish to meet. Not only was he a brilliant guy, but he had a very unusual job in that he was a professional snooker coach. Not just an ordinary snooker coach, but the one who coached Ronnie O'Sullivan, no less. As you can imagine, Andrew is a pretty fair player himself, putting my record break of seven rather into the shade. Andrew had been a syndicate member with Nick for many years and had owned shares in several successful small syndicates.

Karen, Andrew, and I decided to take on this bay, with all three of us as named owners but with the horse to be named by Karen and myself and to run in Karen's colours. This latest horse purchase came at a time when my mother was rapidly losing her health and, indeed, she would sadly pass away within six months. However, on a visit to her house in the autumn of 2010 we engaged her in the conversation about trying to come up with a name for the new horse. As we reminisced about my mum's arrival in England from Wales in the early 1930s and her wedding to my dad in 1938, she recalled how they had managed to get that brand new top floor flat in Ladysmith Road, Tottenham, just a quarter of a mile from White Hart Lane, as their first home. Immensely proud of their Welsh heritage, they gave the flat the name Penbryn, which in welsh means "top of the hill", by the way Brynmawr, where my dad was from, means "big hill".

Following our conversation, the new bay acquired that name, Penbryn. All of a sudden, in spite of all the economic circumstances demanding frugality, we ended up with three more horses.

The filly, Lily, gorgeous but probably only with short term ability, had been sired by the stallion Monsieur Bond but, in spite of the incredible difficulty of naming horses, by using an incorrect spelling, amazingly, we were allowed to name her Miss Moneypenni, notice the "I" at the end of the spelling. Karen had a weakness for the Chronicles of Narnia stories and so Bertie became Vertumnus.

Of course, when we cheered them on at the races, we called them by their real names. Unbelievably, Miss Moneypenni was the first to strike. In her debut race, a Windsor maiden would you believe, she had come a creditable 3rd of 14 at 33/1 and then she was eighth of 12 in a good class race at Newmarket before going to Brighton on 13th July 2010. This was only a 5 runner race, but it still had to be won and Lily duly won it picking up a £3,000 prize, no less, by doing so.

Nick always doubted that she would train on after her two-year-old career and, although she showed a bit in her next few races, this was clearly not the career for her and we found her a lovely home in one of our local stables which did a lot with disabled riders. Vertumnus, the more expensive of the two, at £1,200 was, it was becoming apparent, completely devoid of any racing talent whatsoever. In 10 runs, from 2010 to 2011, he finished almost last on every occasion. However, another one of those days was about to unfold at Wolverhampton, on 25th November 2011, the day before my sisters 70th birthday.

Virtually everything that possibly could go wrong up to the race time of 5.25pm, did go wrong. We were in the first race that evening and I left work at 10 am to drive up to Wolverhampton, giving myself plenty of time for the journey around the notorious M6. Vertumnus must have left Nick's yard around the same time as that as a precaution because the horses need to be booked in at the racecourse a minimum of two hours before they race. So, on that day, both myself and Vertumnus arrived at the track in good time. Karen had a meeting in London, and her plan was to try and catch the race in a bookmaker's shop after her meeting.

The enormous fly in the ointment came when there was a huge road traffic accident on the M6 approaching Birmingham. Nick was coming up by car a bit later than the horse, as indeed was our jockey, whose name escapes me, but we always put a top jockey up on Bertie.

On the M6, the traffic jams were horrendous and, by 4.30pm, it became abundantly clear that neither Nick nor the jockey would make it to the racecourse in time. To exacerbate matters, phone reception was not good that day at the track and, basically, I got a text from Nick telling me to try and get a replacement jockey, not something that even I, with all my multitudinous experiences in racing, had ever had to do before. I went to the weighing room to see what I had to do and, indeed, to see if there were any jockeys at all available, bearing in mind that a lot of the other jockeys would also have been affected by the accident and the traffic on the M6. The only person I could come up with was a young lad of 16 named Jack Duern, who just happened to be at the track with his father and his uncle. Jack had done a bit of work riding for some trainers around the Wolverhampton area and wanted to be a race jockey, but he had never ridden on a racecourse, let alone in a race.

Time was very short, the only thing that mattered was that Jack was available and willing to give it a go. In our favour was the fact that Vertumnus was so bad that he was bottom weight, carrying 8stone 5lbs, and that would be reduced further by the 7lbs claim that Jack Duern would receive as a low-grade apprentice.

Although Vertumnus now was carrying only 7stone 12lbs, I think we still needed to put some lead in the saddle because Jack was such very tiny 16year old, almost in the Megan class. His father and uncle were beside themselves with gratitude and I felt like Aladdin's Genie in giving him the ride, even though he was on board, probably, the worst horse in the race, miserly priced, by the tight bookmakers, at 25/1.

As Jack and I got together in the parade ring, I think we were both shaking, him from nerves and me from the stress of sorting everything out. No further communication was forthcoming from Nick and so now, having booked the jockey, was the time for me to give him instructions on how to ride the race.

"Stay on board and let him do what he wants," were my commands, thinking that, if we got round, it would be an achievement. The race was a 6 furlong sprint, the normal trip for Bertie, and he was drawn in stall 5 - which was, at least, quite favourable when you consider that a high draw at Wolverhampton, over 6 furlongs, is almost a death knell before you start. I have a preferred viewing spot at nearly every flat racecourse in the country and I took up my regular position at Wolverhampton, in the stand right on the winning line. This was the perfect position to see both the start and the finish of the race. True to form, Vertumnus missed the kick and, at the end of the first furlong, he had lost his position completely and slipped back to the back of the field, with Jack Duern hanging on for dear life in the saddle, not easy in all that buffeting in a very rough race. At least Vertumnus, for once, appeared to be trying to race and, as the field swept into the long turn heading towards the finishing straight, poor Vertumnus was shuffled out six horses wide and ended up entering the 2 furlong final straight in last position, so wide in fact that he was almost touching the nearside rail, a track's width away from the rest of the field battling on the other side of the track. He had no chance whatsoever.

What happened next is impossible to explain let alone believe. Vertumnus took off like Lewis Hamilton from pole position and flew down the outside, totally alone, grabbing the race to win in the last stride. Even I was lost for words, I did not cheer, I did not make a sound, I just stood there in stunned disbelief. How had he won? All that mattered was that he had, and Jack Duern, the 16-year-old from nowhere had won on his first ride on a racecourse. His dad and uncle were made up with joy and I could not dislodge them from my company and indeed, wherever our paths crossed in the future, I had that recurring problem and that extended, after this, to Jack's mother as well.

The story did not end there though. As I was invited to step up to receive the trophy, bing bong, and with that sound a racecourse steward came up to inform me that there was a stewards' enquiry into the improved running of the horse. I had bet my usual £100 on Vertumnus at 25/1, so I had rather cleaned out one of the bookmakers at the track, a venue where anyone is lucky to get even a £20 bet on. No longer one to mince my words, and having been on the wrong end of a couple of stewards' enquiries in my time, the one with James Doyle at Lingfield and another involving Frankie Dettori at Epsom to name but two, I decided to go into the stewards' room with all guns blazing, so as to speak. Luckily, Karen who is far more reticent and polite than me was, of course, not there and it turned out that she had spent the race in a bookmakers' shop at Liverpool Street station, the most popular, and possibly only, woman ever to go in there, because when the punters found that she owned Vertumnus, they all backed him and cleaned up. As I entered the stewards' room, I was confronted by five stewards, three men and two women and as you can imagine, even at Wolverhampton, tweed suits and hats were the order of the day.

I did not wait a single second for them to address me but took the wind completely out of their sales by attacking and saying, "How come that, in the last 10 races, when Vertumnus has come last every time, even though I expected him to win all those races and bet £100 on him each time, there has never been a stewards enquiry, but now that he has fulfilled my expectations and won a race, there is one. How can that be right?"

To be honest, the stewards were in a state of shock and did not seem to know what to say or do. Finally, one of them muttered something about the horse showing an unexplainable improved performance but it was down to a quirky animal, which actually was the case. That was about it, the result stood and I collected the trophy, standing alone on the podium, it was probably witnessed by about three of the 20 people who are at the course at the time. After all this was done and dusted, I got a call from Nick, who had turned round and gone home, and from the super popular Karen, still doing the conga in the bookies at Liverpool Street.

Another one of my life's incredible coincidences was that Jack Duern went on to become Damien Black's apprentice jockey and he has seen some great success at that yard. It is indeed a strange world. Poor Vertumnus ran 4 more times without success, finishing 20 lengths or more behind the winner in each race, he clearly wasn't a racehorse and our decision was that, in May 2011, he went off to join a local hunt in Newmarket, which was another happy outcome.

Karen and I also had other horses not mentioned here, largely ones that we took on because no one else would but no matter, we loved our time in racing. Not only did we completely fall in love with each and every horse we had the honour of being associated with but we also met some of the most amazing people, wonderful and steadfast friends who would standby us when we needed them most. They had stood by us throughout the Lord Theo court case and they would be there for us during the most demanding time yet to come.

The last horse to take part in our adventure in horseracing, was the gorgeous and unsung hero Penbryn. We had a real soft spot for him because of his connection with my mum who had inspired his name. He started racing for us in late 2010, and in February 2011 he started a break of nine months. My mother passed away in March 2011, and combined with other horrible business problems, things were very difficult for us at that time. Penbryn was a real solid workhorse and ran regularly in "journeyman" type races until February 2014, winning 3 of his 36 races and coming 2nd another 8 times. He always gave his best and we thoroughly enjoyed supporting him at the three main all-weather courses where he was ridden regularly by top jockeys like Seb Saunders and George Baker. The financial crash had taken its toll on racing however, and now the prize money for winning at an all-weather track had fallen to as low as £1,200 for winning and you might only get £200 or £300 for coming second or third. When you brought into the calculation the cost of entry, travel, and jockey each race would cost you about £500 to enter, and so you could lose money even if you were in the first three.

Nick had suffered a serious loss of owners, very few people had the money to spend on horses anymore, and racing had returned to being more like the plaything for the rich that it used to be. It just didn't seem to be the same anymore. Unhappily and to our great dismay and sorrow, our final connection to the sport ended when Nick phoned to tell us that Penbryn had broken his leg while zooming round his paddock and, sadly, had been put down. The tears returned big-time and it represented a dismal end to a fantastic journey.

In the cold light of hindsight, it turned out to be an advantageous time for us to come out of horseracing because, within three months of Penbryn's passing, we were faced with the fight of our lives to keep KR afloat and we needed all our inner strength and willpower to physically survive.

CHAPTER 50

GOING BACK IN TIME

The difficulty for me in this story, is that I have had to get to grips with the reality that all these different things were going on at the same time and not only is it almost unfathomable how that was possible but also that is very hard for me to separate it all out into some sort of comprehensible narrative.

From 1996 to 1999 things got really busy at KR Electrical Wholesale and when Ken's former company, North Electrical, ceased trading, most of its customers moved over to us. North's owner, Paul Jessop, set up a new company and concentrated on internet sales, while still smarting from the fact that I got my Z3 car first.

As KR grew in strength, the struggles still went on at RP because, although RP still held the Boots contract, we just could not translate all that work into profit. We had to take on extra staff at KR but most of our appointments were not very wise choices and we soon moved them on.

Karen worked for an important journalist organisation called the NCTJ (the National Council for the Training of Journalists). This job held a lot of responsibility for her and she often had to go to meetings away from the workplace. However, when she was at Latton Bush we often met up at those fateful rubbish bins and it was here, when one particular evening we saw a feral cat scavenging a living in a small fenced off area near the bins. After taking him little snacks for a couple of days, we thought that it might be best to rescue him and so we borrowed a cat trap, laced it with pilchards, and we completed the kitty nap. We brought him over to my house where Karen was spending a lot more time with me, although she always had to return home because of her dog Pepa.

Karen's being at my house put next door neighbour Doris' nose massively out of joint and, because Doris had a key to the front door, necessary to look after Jurgen, she would often deliberately come into the house unannounced, when sometimes Karen and I would be snuggled up watching the TV. This was just to be obstreperous and deliberately mischievous. We learned just to ignore these interruptions, pretend they weren't happening and just carried on snuggling.

The new cat visitor was pretty aggressive and, although we had him in a large cage in the lounge, there was no doubt that Jurgen was also a bit put out and scared. When we took the rescue cat to the vet, they discovered that he was a full tomcat and, therefore were not really surprised that he was so wild and aggressive. After we had him neutered, he became a lot more amenable but we decided that it was not fair to upset Jurgen so one of Karen's workmates at the NCTJ took him on and named him Breezer, after the most popular drink of the moment.

It was around this time in 2001, that Jurgen was about to become a national celebrity. In my square, the house situated on the top corner, next door but one to me was rented out to aircrew from nearby Stansted Airport which was just up the road. One of these aircrew was a flight steward with the name of Brian Dowling (who became the winner of the Big Brother TV show in 2001). Jurgen was a popular visitor to all the houses in our square and it turned out that he was spending quite a lot of time in Brian's house and so it was that he became a celebrity item on the Big Brother Programme as Brian would speak about him constantly. It was amazing how so many people talked about him, but nice to think that at least one of us made it to the big time.

By now, I thought that I had converted Karen into a football fan and we travelled far and wide watching Spurs play. Indeed, we went to the embarrassing 2-1 defeat to Arsenal in the 2001 FA Cup semi-final at Old Trafford when, after the game, as we traipsed back to our hotel, thousands of Arsenal fans, half of whom probably knew us, were giving us very severe stick as they drove by.

Yet probably the funniest thing on one of Karen's football excursions occurred when we went to an away match at Aston Villa and Karen asked me this poignant question, "Why is it that most of the Spurs fans spend all their time looking and shouting at the Aston Villa fans, and seem to ignore the match altogether?"

I must admit that even I could not answer that one. Meanwhile, amusingly at KR, we received a visit from a teacher who worked at St Marks School and, even though my last contact with the school was some 14 years previous, I really did have the collywobbles about what was about to happen. It transpired that St Marks was hosting an event for local businesses, hoping that they would come to the school and give their pupils a chance to see what was on offer in the jobs market for Harlow

School leavers. The teacher who came along was Derek Bonich, one of my former colleagues at the school, but not only a former colleague but also a person who I actually taught when he was a pupil. I must say that he was a bit stunned to see that it was me in the office and I felt obliged to tell him that I was actually banned from St Marks. I then wondered whether this banning order was a very closed shop management decision at St Marks because Derek was completely unaware of it and, therefore, he could see no reason why St Marks shouldn't extend an invitation to KR to attend the function.

I accepted the invitation with glee. I have to be brutally honest and confirm that I did derive enormous pleasure when I parked the Z3, ROS5'5, in pole position in the school car park, then slowly entered the school to visit to the KR stand as I was being eyeballed by a lot of curious pupils. There was still a lot of staff there who knew me and, I have to say, I got a real feeling of empowerment during that visit.

By 2004 Karen's dog, Pepa, had sadly passed away. He and Jurgen hadn't hit it off at all, and although Karen was probably right, as usual, when she said that they would have adjusted, with Jurgen no doubt in charge, I wasn't so sure. That is what made it impractical for us to live together. Now, however, it was possible for Karen to move in almost full time at my house, although we spent time living at hers on other occasions as it was sensible that both homes appeared occupied.

It was almost immediately after moving in, after enjoying those wonderful years following Tottenham Hotspur, that Karen told me, without mercy, that she hated football. There was no alternative but for me to accept that notification and she hasn't been to a game since. Well, that's not quite true now because, early this year, 2020, I took her to see a match at Spurs' new Stadium, "for the experience". We drew 1-1 in an awful match with Sheffield United and she couldn't find any reason to change her mind

Karen's Nissan was a great car and still carrying the number plate M2STY and there was no way that she wanted to get rid of it. Nevertheless, we purchased a nice Mazda MX5 in British racing green for her and, to set it off, we got the registration number that was nearest to the spelling of Karen that we could find, it being K666 REN. We tried to slope the sixes so they would make an A but, in the end, we kept them as they were because the 666 was a devilish protection that seemed quite apt. Our neighbours in the square at Bishops Stortford were, of course, absolutely thrilled with us living there now because, in our busy little square, we would need to park five cars, M2STY, R10SSO, K666REN, 923 RH and ROS5'5, so there was not much room for anyone else to park. Sadly, the Porsche was now more than 16 years old, two-and-a half tons of exquisite machine but, as it was not being driven much now, the bodywork was deteriorating and actually rusting as it stood on the driveway. So, I sold this brilliant car to a local fireman, whose hobby was restoring Porsches and it went to a very good home - without its number plate, I hasten to add, which I put on retention.

CHAPTER 51

WORK LIFE

By now Ken, at work, had a new woman in his life. Things got very serious very quickly and it wasn't long before wedding bells sounded and, indeed, I was the best man. The new Mrs Roberts eventually ended up doing three mornings a week for KR. In no time they had two children, a boy and a girl, making a grand total of four for Ken. Also, Karen had joined KR to all but replace me in charge of administration as RP's problems necessitated my constant attention. By late 2004 moving into 2005, it was abundantly clear that RP had to be put out of its misery as no amount of money seemed to get even close to putting things right. It was blatantly obvious that the £191,000 bad debt from 1991 was insurmountable and I suppose we, or perhaps that should be I, worked miracles to keep a lost cause running.

In all honesty, all the mortgages and credit card debt had gobbled up hundreds of thousands of pounds worth of interest and basically paid my and Patrick's wages. Even the £43,000 that I had won on the horses at Nottingham barely made a dent in our debts and that is why, in hindsight, we should have packed it all in in 1991. It would have been far better if we had we had started again. Disappointingly, this was something I didn't learn enough from and, indeed, I was to repeat my misjudgements in 2011 although, this time around, it was probably a more understandable error that I made.

RP needed around £200,000 to pay off its overdraft and loans with HSBC, to make sure that the Inland Revenue, VAT and rent was up-to-date, and also pay up suppliers, which intrinsically meant paying KR. My director's loan account with RP stood at around £750,000 in the accounts and this was confirmed because, not only had it been testified to and been signed off by Brian Dobby, the accountant, but also courtesy of my recent Inland Revenue investigation. Tragically, this debt would need to be written off but the company would close down without a single black mark against it in any domain. Indeed, Patrick would be able to carry on doing consultancy work for Boots from home, while I would now only have the problems at KR to contend with. All these matters were completely dependent on me accessing the £200,000 to eradicate the debts. Of course, after meetings in the presence of HSBC management and Brian Dobby, it was agreed that it should not be me alone who was to take a massive financial hit. At the same time, the sums involved were so very large that it was unrealistic to expect Patrick to sign up to £475,000 worth of indebtedness to me and so I had to arrive at some sort of sensible and half decent compromise. An agreement consisting of three declarations by Patrick was drawn up to the effect that, he would owe me and have to pay me £100,000, with an initial payment rate of £300 per month, increasing if his work for Boots turned out to be lucrative. I had to make sure that I presented Patrick with a receipt for any money he paid over to me. Our explanation to Boots was that I was leaving RP to concentrate on KR, while Patrick was setting up a new company dedicated to advising Boots. If all the arrangements went as planned there would be no black marks against RP, Patrick would be able to maintain a good income from Boots and so this was seen as fair and equitable by all present.

For me it meant that I would at least get half of what I was about to assimilate, and looking at it in a cold light of day much of the directors' loan account was actually money that I created from credit card funds, although there were re-mortgages and horse winnings mixed in there and that was, actually, my own real money that I had paid in.

Whatever the cost, I needed my life and my independence back. C'est la vie - it seems like I collected, spent and lost money constantly almost as a whim and, as I am re-assessing everything as I write this. I think that I probably amassed £1 million and spent it again at least three times, if not four, over the years. The solution to raising the necessary £200,000 was the sale of my mother's house, which was still, theoretically, owned in 50% shares by myself and my mother.

Although now in her 80s, mum was still very sharp and on-the-ball and she was quite aware that I put forward nearly all the money to buy the house in the first place (when I returned from the USA), and she also knew that I had given her a lump sum in 1977, when my father died, as well as always making sure that she was financially secure thereafter. The situation I found myself in did not have any effect on her position because, it would be Karen who would be buying the house, and so mum wouldn't notice any change at all in either her living arrangements or her financial position. The two of us, mother and I, therefore, met with the solicitors and the house was transferred entirely into my name. Now I was able to sell it and get the RP dissolution under way. Karen paid £165,000 for the house at Churchfield, all of which bypassed me and went directly to HSBC's RP account along with the other £35,000 that I had managed to collect from Credit cards etc. So, the house was sold, the money to clear RP's debts was lodged with HSBC and the paperwork signed by Patrick Simmons was absolutely watertight. He would have to start paying me back the following month. Finally, I was free of RP and had my life and my independence back.

So it was that Karen owned two houses in Harlow, her own one and my mothers. As I have mentioned, Karen is an angel, although sometimes in wolf's clothing to me, with a huge caring heart. She was really amazing with my mother and always ensured everything was right and provided her with a very loving environment. When my mum was away on one of the many cruises she went on with my sister, Karen arranged for a new heating system to be installed in the house, as it had only ever had one fireplace, and also for the house to be rewired because it still had the 1951 wiring installed. I now had only KR to concentrate on and could get really stuck into the horses.

KR Electrical Wholesale was becoming quite a successful operation and a little classroom unit wasn't sufficiently big enough to hold all our stock. We still had the RP stores at Burnt Mill to use and indeed, it was only a few years earlier, when Burnt Mill wanted to become an Academy that we paid the school another £20,000 to help them to be able to do so, with the concrete agreement that RP, now in the person of me, could retain use of that facility for ever. We were certainly very generous to Burnt Mill School, I wonder if they remember that? Indeed, a fair bit of gear is still there, obsolete now I expect, I haven't been to see it for a couple of years.

After serious discussions between everybody at KR, we decided to buy a warehouse to ease our storage problems and it would be bought in the names of Ken, his wife, and Karen and was a leasehold property about a mile away from our business centre. This was the start of a relationship breakdown between the two couples, although for a couple of years the warehouse was a very necessary and successful asset. Up to the last quarter of 2005 all went relatively smoothly, the only fascinating part being an entrance by myself and quite a few of our customers into the American stock market. At the same time, we purchased a couple of corporate seats at White Hart Lane but, even though we offered them free to customers, as incentives, would you believe that most of them only wanted to go to the half-dozen "big games" at the stadium. Man. Utd and Arsenal games were fine, but Sunderland and Wigan didn't seem to cut it. From the business point of view, the seats were in fact a flop and we usually had to send family members to take them up. Concerning the dabble on the American stock market, Steve Cutchey, the owner of an IT company at the business centre, got a tip about a start-up company in the United States which was pioneering iris recognition technology. Shares in the company were priced at around $0.10 and a few of us, with Steve and I in the van of activity, started to buy them up. The company was called Upgrade and the shares really did take off. I believe I still have a printout of an upgrade share chart showing just how high they went; over $20 I do believe.

With RP out of my hair, and credit cards still to fall back on I ended up investing quite a few thousand pounds in the Upgrade project. Steve Cutchey did the same and one of KR's main customers invested one year's profit from his firm in the stock. Upgrade shares soared in price and we were all worth a great deal of money, but once more greed took over from our common sense and basic business acumen. Overnight the shares were suspended following an American led class action suit against the company and, pop, all our investments were dead and well and truly cremated. I can honestly say that I really have learnt to be very philosophical when it comes to money and losing it - I suppose it's a little bit to do with the gambling mentality, but that mentality does help you pick yourself up and keep going.

CHAPTER 52

CREDIT CRUNCH

At the very end of 2005, completely out of the blue, I received a visit from a man named Tony Carter, completely unsolicited.

I had never heard of him or knew what he was about. He simply arrived at the unit and asked for Ross Hartshorn, introducing himself and saying that he would like a meeting with me in private, if that was possible. I wondered what an earth this could be about, what could I have possibly done now that I didn't know about? At our private meeting, Tony Carter informed me that he was a debt advisor and he was part of a new phenomenon, credit advice companies, which was taking off in the country following the explosion of personal debt and anticipating the crash of 2008. As I have mentioned before I had now amassed the usage of 89 credit cards and this gave me a combined credit limit of in excess of £1,000,000.

Tony explained that he had been representing his firm at a financial conference in Bournemouth, where he lived and where he had travelled from that morning, when one of the lecturers had used a businessman named Ross, as an example of how some directors were using huge amounts of unsecured credit to run their companies. Tony said that he met up with the lecturer afterwards, and the gentleman explained that he was an ex-colleague of our accountant Brian Dobby when the latter was working at Barnes Roffe, and that my machinations with credit cards had become a legendary topic of interest at that company.

This made him think that these financial shenanigans would make a great subject for a lecture at one of these conferences. He had only used my Christian name in that context, and didn't mention the name of the company, so everything was above board and no securities were breached. However, he did have my full name and details in his records and once he had extracted these from him, Tony used his impressive initiative to come and see whether he could be of assistance to me.

I had never really considered if and how I could bring my financial wizardry to an end but it was an amazingly timely intervention by Tony Carter, because coming to an end it certainly was.

Under the system I used, things would be okay and work as long as you had one empty and serviceable card, with 89 on the go I don't think there were any left for me to collect and my room for manoeuvre was severely curtailed.

I agreed with Tony, that I realised I would run out of rope pretty quickly and that his almost psychic visit could help me exit from the credit card strategy. He told me that it would take probably two years to defeat the problem and that the going would be long and extremely hard. He said that we would do very well, indeed, to avoid either county court judgements or bankruptcy or both. Almost casually, he dropped in that, for providing his service and advice, there would be a charge of £20,000, (2% of a £1M debt) which he hoped that I would pay with a credit card and, therefore, lose it as a debt. Unfortunately for me, I had nothing available on the cards and had to pay the £20,000 over 3 months as we earned it in profits. This visit and advice actually put everything into a nutshell for me and concentrated my mind on the fact that things had to change. For over 20 years I'd been paying all these cards bang on time and never having a single problem, I was now proceeding, head long, into the nightmare scenario.

Fully on board with Tony Carter's offer of assistance, the first thing he told me to do was to change my telephone numbers so that I could not be hounded on the phone. He then apprehended all the credit cards so that they could not be used again, and it was almost like having withdrawal symptoms for giving up smoking or drugs, I suppose.

I was to stop paying any credit card bills and just sit back and wait for the flack to come in. I think the minimum credit limit I had on any one card was £5,000 and many of them were set at £15,000 or £20,000 limits. He then told me that I should own nothing, in other words I would have to liquidate any assets because, what he was aiming for was a full and final IVA, which meant an insolvency agreement that was done and dusted all in one go, with no long-term payments to follow.

At this time Tony did ask me, "If there is only one thing you can save, what would it be?" He was completely taken aback and visibly shocked when I replied, "The horse, Lord Theo".

He told me that this was a first, as all his clients always said either the house or the car. Funnily enough, as I realised afterwards of course, I did not own Lord Theo, Karen did. One of the most important things that we had to do early in the process was to transfer the business into Karen's name, before any real arguments about what I possessed began. This was done quite straightforwardly by the accountant Brian Dobby who now, after 25 years of being in the thick of all the financial chicanery at both RP and KR, was getting somewhat jumpy. He was very concerned that anything dodgy would, shall we say, reflect on him, together with the lack of minutes from all those "board meetings" that had apparently taken place over those years. Tony had written to all the credit card companies to explain the situation and tried to intercept all the phone calls about repayments, while I received a torrent of threatening letters, some extremely nasty and worrying, but amazingly I had no calls from debt collectors at the front door. For the first six months the demands poured in for the full outstanding amounts, but in the year following that, it was quite amazing how the companies were prepared to settle for half or less than half of the debt. The main aim was to collect together as much money as possible to offer in an insolvency meeting with the creditors. This would come 18 months or two years into the process and we needed an amenable insolvency practitioner to deal with the matter and, of course, Tony Carter knew exactly the right one, a very able lady named Fiona Monson.

In order to prevent the house from being completely liquidated I had to re-mortgage it yet again and, this time, up to 95% of value figure. By doing this, it would mean the house would not be worth selling, as all the equity would already be in the fund, as any money that I raised had to be paid directly into Tony's clients account so that nothing could be diverted away from the creditors. The more transparently this was done, the more likely that the creditors would be satisfied with the efforts made to pay. The Z3 had to be liquidated as well, of course. To the rescue came our important client, he had been a valued customer and friend since the inception of KR Electrical Wholesale in 1996 and had featured in the Upgrade adventure on the American stock market and was also another Spurs' season ticket holder. Very generously, he bought the Z3 from me at book price and this was a massive boost to the funds in Tony's clients' account. While all this was going on throughout 2006 and into 2007 Ken Roberts was becoming more and more unsettled. His wife believed, and convinced him, that he was the only reason why KR was doing alright and that he needed to have greater rewards and control. At the time that we transferred KR into Karen's name to help with the credit card problem, we offered Ken a 50%

share in the business for no outlay, naming him and Karen as directors. Brian Dobby drew up the papers after Ken agreed to the deal, but when it came to the time for signing them at the bank, he completely lost his bottle, said he couldn't cope with the pressure and decided to remain employed as manager.

This whole episode further soured our relationship and I did feel a bit concerned at the role of Brian Dobby in this fiasco. During this year Ken and his wife had purchased a couple of buy to let flats, something that proves that he must have been on a very good salary, and Brian Dobby had become his accountant which, in my view, initiated a conflict of interest. While all this was going on, it was apparent that, although I knew the warehouse was essential, it also caused a lot of logistical problems, because we were trying to operate one business from two sites. At that time, a large warehouse, with upstairs offices and a downstairs trade counter, became available for lease at Harold Close in the Pinnacles Industrial Estate in Harlow. Ken was totally against this move, but because he had not become a director and, therefore, had no effective say in the business, we decided that we would take it on. Relationships were at an all-time low. We needed to sell the warehouse to make leasing a new, bigger one viable, so we moved quickly to sell and got a buyer immediately. With that in hand all partnerships were dissolved and when all the money was in the right accounts, we were unfettered again and able to complete the negotiations for the move to Harold Close.

It was now that Ken used his obvious ability and customer connections as a strong bargaining chip and affirmed that he would only stay with KR for the payment of a £35,000 a year salary with another £10,000 being paid to his wife. I should have had the guts to refuse, especially as this was far in excess of what Karen and I earned between us, but there was an awful lot going on, I was under a great deal of pressure and it was the easy option to just fall in behind the blackmail.

The move from the premises at the Latton Bush Centre and the warehouse up the road was a massive undertaking, and we chose to do it over the four-day Easter holiday in 2007. In spite of his now monumental salary, Ken, of course, was unavailable to help. Wonderfully, I had the super assistance of John Costello, along with Dan and Doug my sensational friends from Marshall Tufflex, one of our suppliers. Not only did they provide the lorry to move all the gear, but also absolutely amazing logistical expertise, so much so that, the three of them, myself and Karen completed the whole move over those four days, and there was no doubt that Ken was well pissed off that we managed to do it. The super guys and friends from Marshall Tufflex gave their help for nothing more than a drink, they were nothing short of a miracle-workers, and we hope they enjoyed the extra rewards we gave them on their trips to Newmarket to support Lord Theo.

CHAPTER 53

FALLING

At this time, I thought it was absolutely right and proper to let it be known to all customers of KR that, in fact, it was me who owned the company and not Ken. It now turned out to be very convenient that K stood for the name Karen, and R for the name Ross, so everyone could realise how the company "had actually got its name". Obviously, now we realised that we needed good, knowledgeable extra staff cover to stop Ken holding us over a barrel, especially as he had turned very morose and entitled, conveniently forgetting that I had rescued him from a desperate situation 10 years previously.

So it was, we took on James, an experienced wholesaler pinched from WF Electrical down the road. He was followed into KR in the next few months by Alan, Colin and Joe. Our turnover shot up to over £1 million and we, as a company, were really going places. For the next 3 years everything was going great guns, Ken's power had dissipated, though he was still manager, we were all working on an equal footing and we paid the guys the best wages in the sector. But time would seriously call into question my ability to select decent, and honest staff.

On the Tony Carter/ IVA front pressure was mounting to get the money into place ready for Fiona Monson, our insolvency practitioner, to organise a creditors meeting. The re-mortgage of my house had landed me with a monthly mortgage payment of £1867 until I was 76 years old, which would be the year 2023, but together with the sale of the car and other liquidations it meant that we paid around £200,000 into Tony Carter's client account. He had done brilliantly throughout the 18 months and we had amazingly avoided any CCJs and all talk of bankruptcy was forgotten. I had learned to ignore all the threats from the card companies and their debt agencies and it was quite incredible that some of these were now willing to settle for as little as 10p in the pound, very far removed from their initial demands. As the convening of creditors loomed, Fiona informed me that, for a full and final IVA to go through, 75% of the creditors by value, had to accept the offer, and that she would be able give seven days' notice of the date of the convention. All the outstanding credit cards and loans that I held at this juncture in time totalled around £800,000.

I thought I had done well to limit the borrowing to as low as that before being instructed to cease the payments. For sure, I felt badly about owing that kind of money but, on careful calculation, I worked out that, over the 15 year "credit card operation period", I had paid the banks over £1million in interest, and that gave me a great deal of solace and eased my conscience. The £200,000 we had managed to gather in Tony's client account meant that I was offering 25p in the pound to the creditors to settle the debts. Fiona's meeting took place, the vote happened and 81% by value accepted the offer. The IVA went through smoothly as a full and final settlement and I was finally relieved of all that misery. The paperwork was concluded early in 2008, almost 2 years to the day from when Tony Carter had mystically approached me. His forecast, and solution was bang on. Notice of the debts did remain on my credit report for six years but, to be honest, that time flew by like the rest of my life.

At the end of 2007, my mother and sister went on one of their cruises. Out of the blue, I got a call from my sister, from the ship, to tell me that our mother had suffered an accident. Apparently, the seas in the Bay of Biscay had been particularly rough and a large surge of water hit the ship and caused my mother to be thrown from her seat at the dining table, sending her head first into a side wall. The result of this accident was that she had a nasty stroke, was partially paralysed and could not speak.

My sister informed me that they were being taken ashore at the next port, which happened to be in Spain. There, the two of them spent the next six weeks in hospital, mum receiving medical care, my sister by her side. My mother received excellent care and made good progress over the six-week period so that she regained most of her mobility and her ability to talk. However, at 87 years old, this was a very traumatic event in her life and it resulted in the long-term decline in her health, both mental and physical. Although a walking frame was now a sensible aid for her to use, she absolutely refused it and, at the same time, insisted that my sister took her out on shopping trips, as before, as if her mobility was normal. Mum particularly liked to visit garden centres but, sometimes, the uneven flooring was problematic. It was barely a year later when, at a garden centre in Harlow and, frustratingly, only an arm's length away from my sister, she had a nasty fall and broke her hip. She was blue lighted to hospital and they carried out a hip replacement there and then. Sadly, the writing was on the wall. That hospital visit led to many others, usually the cause being water infections, which seemed to be self-perpetuating and gave her hallucinations which progressed to the onset of dementia. KR, in the meantime, replete with staff, continued to flourish while Karen and I were enjoying great success and fun with the horses.

There is no doubt that Ken became a totally different person after his second marriage. He seemed to resent the success and interests of the two of us, in spite of probably being the best paid employee at any electrical wholesaler in the country. He believed that Karen and I were minted and spending all the wealth, as he saw it, created for us by his efforts alone. He saw only his sales contacts as the yardstick by which the business could be judged, looking past all the administrative, logistical and financial problems that needed to be dealt with every day. His relationship with the accountant Brian Dobby, who I had replaced after 25 years of association when we moved to Harold Close, didn't seem quite right to me, although I could not put my finger as to why.

CHAPTER 54

CUTTING OUT THE DEAD WOOD

Then, in 2008 another lightning bolt to deal with, when my sister approached me with a personal problem. Apparently, she had been so impressed with my credit card manipulation that she thought that, if money was that easy to come by, then she would have a go at it herself. The problem with my sister was that she didn't really consider paying the cards back as one of the necessities involved in the operation. So, all that new furniture in the house every year, all those upgrades of televisions, growing in size until one almost filled their entire lounge, and all those clothes and cruises had stacked up quite a substantial debt.

I contacted Tony Carter and he advised that, clearly, although there was no way for Avron to be able to pay him a fee, his services were not really needed because her case was relatively simple as it involved no assets. He advised her that she should seek a decent insolvency practitioner immediately and ask to file for bankruptcy. She lived in a council house, had no savings account and had a small car, necessary for her mobility and owned in her husband's name anyway. Fortunately, when she had taken her pension from Harlow Council a few years previously, she had invested her lump sum payment of £10,000 with KR, very lucky on two counts, first, because she would have blown it by now and, second, it would be confiscated under the terms of the bankruptcy. Otherwise known as "Mr Generous", I paid her £100 cash per month for the loan of the money, which remained intact. Looking back, when people lent me cash to help me out, I think I actually become one of the world's great philanthropists!

I accompanied Avron to a meeting with an insolvency practitioner in Sawbridgeworth. He was very efficient and, following a couple of searching and fraught interviews on the phone with creditors representatives, she was declared bankrupt. It was certainly a load of her shoulders and, of course, we didn't tell my mother anything about it at all.

At our house in Bishops Stortford, which Karen was gradually tailoring to her own tastes, with changes to decor in the bathroom and kitchen, attention moved to the back garden. Here my forest of conifers had grown to become exceptionally tall, the group in front of the patio doors were higher than the house and completely blocked the view to the garden. Behind them, the trees on Doris' fence had always been a bit of a bone of contention between us, and Doris had scythed down her side of the branches until the conifers were completely leafless and brown on her side.

We now requisitioned Avron's husband, Alan, a dab hand at gardening, to help us remove the offending conifers, all 20 or so of them - he was the key man if we were going to remove the roots. When we had cut down all the conifers so that only the roots remained, the enormous amount of foliage covered the garden, which was about 2000 square feet, to a depth greater than the height of our 6 feet high fence. Hundreds of logs and countless, fully leaved branches. How on earth could we dispose of it all? The only solution was to approach the council and hire one of their huge bin lorries, the ones that have the compactors on the back and all the rubbish is loaded from the bins at the back of the vehicle. The cost of the hire was £500, but it was well worth it, especially when it turned out that this huge bin lorry was only just big enough consume all the foliage in one go.

It took Alan a couple of weeks to dig the roots out and, at last, Karen had a garden that she could see and develop into a Chelsea-like masterpiece.

As KR continued to grow and its turnover increased, we were approached by CBRE, our landlord, who informed us that the warehouse next door to ours was being vacated.

This was another investment that Karen and I had to fund but we believed, implicitly, that we were a strong company, moving forward and looking to expand into new branches. Again, much to the disgust of Ken, we made the decision to grasp the opportunity of the second warehouse with both hands. It was very difficult for us to work out exactly where Ken was coming from. He had worked with me for 15 years having been rescued from the depths of despair. He had always earned good money, enough to have a much bigger house than us, not that we cared, plus he had 2 or 3 buy-to-let properties and had turned down the chance to be a half owner in the company for nothing. What more could we have offered him or done for him? He saw us as lazy, horsey freeloaders – totally misguided and mistaken I'm afraid.

Then, out of the blue, I was called upon to make an urgent delivery to a customer, a regular occurrence, but my van wouldn't start. Automatically and very casually I told Ken that I would have to take his van because mine wouldn't start, and the absolute panic that ensued was unfathomable. Rushing headlong down the stairs to his van, he removed from it a couple of boxes of paperwork, which he put into his wife's car, along with quite a few bits and pieces of stock. Had he not done that, I would have thought absolutely nothing of it and would not so much have glanced at what was in the van. Because he acted so strangely, it made me think quite hard.

Ken didn't actually do any deliveries, and his paperwork was always done at work, so what was going on?

CHAPTER 55

BETRAYAL AND DEATH

Pressure was coming at Karen and me from all sides and it became obvious that we needed a break, something to look forward to. Albeit, my mother was going in and out of hospital all the time, she refused to leave her home permanently, and we had to arrange for four lots of carers a day to look after her. In the summer of 2010, after talking things over with my sister, we agreed with her that it would be good for Karen and I to get away over the Christmas and New Year period. This was the only time that, sensibly, we could leave the company, because it was the time of year when everything shut down and, with luck, no stress would be generated. We earmarked a cruise around the Caribbean and, during the rest of 2010, we set about getting the resources to pay for it. Ken just thought that we would dip into our "Ken supplied" bottomless wallet but, very unfortunately, that was not the case. Amongst her so many talents, Karen was a genius with Tesco Clubcard points. We started paying as many as suppliers, as would accept it, with her (and I stress 'her' because credit cards no longer had a place in my lifestyle) Tesco credit card. Bearing in mind that we could spend in excess of £60,000 a month on stock.

Some months we could pay for as much as half of those accounts with the card and, at a rate of 1point for every £2 spent, it wasn't long before we had thousands of points, especially when you added them to our own shopping and fuel payments. In fact, the Tesco points paid for the cruise in its entirety and, it made us feel really good that we were flying to Miami for a Caribbean adventure that actually cost us nothing. In truth, we were years ahead of our time in this clever financial wizardry because nowadays, the Inland Revenue class this sort of "payment" as a "benefit in kind" and it would be taxable.

In early December 2010, about 3 weeks before we flew to Miami, we came to the conclusion as a family that our mother needed residential care and she was taken into a local care home. By this time, she was not recognising either me or my sister and, quite honestly, it was very upsetting to visit her – for all of us. I found it particularly difficult because I just could not identify with the person she had become.

Again, as a family, we thought it best that Karen and I should still go on holiday, as our health and wellbeing were also very important. However, even getting away for that Christmas break was not going to be straightforward in any way, shape or form.

It was the Christmas period when there was that unbelievable snowfall and, simply for us to get from our house in Bishops Stortford to the railway Station, barely a mile away, was like going to the North Pole. No wheeled transport of any kind was running because of the appalling road conditions and we had to drag our cases, on foot, to the station where one train was replacing three, and we could hardly breathe as we joined the other sardines in the carriages. Even that train broke down in Harlow station and we all had to pile onto another one, a manoeuvre that would have been fun even without all the suitcases. When we got to Liverpool Street Station there were no onward services and we had to try and sort out how to get to our hotel at Heathrow by bus from there, mindful that our flight was at dawn the next morning. This was another Arctic expedition in itself, and in all it took us over nine hours and God knows how many buses to get from home to the hotel. As we signed in at reception, an announcement was broadcast which told us that all flights from Heathrow would be cancelled until further notice, at which point we realised that it was most unlikely that we would make the flight that connected to our cruise ship.

We decided to stay awake all night in case there were any changes to the flight patterns, and we well pleased that we had when, at 2:30am, there was another announcement that, three flights were to be allowed to take off from Heathrow before it closed at 7am and, joy upon joy, ours was one of them. Frantically we grabbed our bags and, by some pre-ordained miracle, managed to get on a bus to our terminal. When we checked in for our flight, we were told that the schedules had changed again and we would be on the one and only flight leaving Heathrow that day. Our usual lucky stars were there to be counted yet again. From that moment on, the travel and the whole holiday was a dream come true. We were desperately in need of this break, the weather was perfect and we had a fantastic time, experiencing so many things that I didn't think I'd ever do, such as snorkelling in the wide-open ocean and careering down slides from the boats into the open sea. We enjoyed an absolutely stunning New Year's

Eve Party at sea, with all the streamers and bands, like you see on the old newsreels. This cruise certainly did the trick and we returned with fresh vigour and determination to make the company even more of that success in 2011.

Over the years, we had spent a great deal of time in Newmarket, we had really got to know the town, its layout and all its ins and outs, we loved the area and it was in the midst of the horseracing culture that we had almost become addicted to. Thinking out of the box, there was no electrical wholesaler in the area, and it was quite a vast area we were looking at. So, Karen and I not only scouted out an industrial area where we could perhaps open a new branch, but we also found a lovely house, close to Tattersall's sales, which suited us down to the ground.

Invigorated though we were, when we got back from the cruise, we discovered that mum was not doing very well at all and our focus, both mine and Karen's, had to be totally on her. The business was fine and in good hands, or so we thought. As we moved into February, one of our contractor customers, took me to one side in the warehouse and told me that he was uncomfortable about the rumours he had heard about Ken who, probably with James, was going to split from KR and set up their own business, confident that all the customers would follow. Although this man was one of the first to defect when it did happen, at least he had had the common decency to give me the heads up. I was really shaken, what a nasty and ruthless time to attack us.

Then another bit of gossip reached us about a new unit being prepared in the industrial estate nearby. Very late that night I paid a visit to that site and was able to lift a material cover over the new signage, which read Electrical Wholesale. My next move was to check Companies House for information, and the result of my investigations found that a new Electrical Wholesale company had been set up by Brian Dobby, on behalf of Ken and James in December 2010, now more than two months ago and when Karen and I were about to depart on our cruise. I know I was a little off the ball and we were a bit distracted but we certainly weren't expecting an assassination attempt, especially such an unfeeling one at such a diabolically difficult time for us in our personal circumstances.

Tragically my mother passed away on the 5th of March 2011 just short of her 92nd birthday. Nothing seemed fair anymore. The funeral had to be organised and my mother had elected to be cremated and then interred alongside my father in his grave. Incredibly she had been completely organised in sorting out what she wanted done, from the music to not having flowers. She left each family member a letter and the whole day was very moving. I had great difficulty giving my little eulogy and I believe I broke down completely. She would have wanted me to fight for our way of life and that is what we picked ourselves up to do.

CHAPTER 56

PIRANHAS

Karen and I kept silent about what we knew about the new company and you could cut the atmosphere with a knife at KR. Then, from nowhere, James snapped and suddenly gave in his notice. Asked why, he said he just needed a change, nothing else. James, breaking under strain, actually blew Ken's plan out of the water. He had wanted the full killer blow of a joint resignation by both of them at the same time. As a result, Ken's hand was forced and he had to reveal his cards a couple of weeks earlier than he had wanted to.

Drawing on the steel taken from my father's genes, I bit the bullet and forced them both to work their one month's notice period. This was a living nightmare at the workplace, but I can survive in the most evil of conditions with the best of them, and I made the days as unpleasant as possible. I went to the solicitors to enquire about the legality of setting up a similar company so close, and about ex-staff stealing intellectual property from their former company with immediate effect. I also wanted to check on the involvement of our ex-accountant Brian Dobby, who was surely operating under a conflict of interests.

The solicitor advised that, although I would probably win the case, Ken and James would have no money and so damages would not be forthcoming and, in the event of a formal hearing, the customers were more likely see me as the bad guy, as opposed to them. There was no option but to let the matter ride and get down to trying to keep hold of the customer base. However, I did report Brian Dobby to the financial authorities, untrustworthy and two faced being the description I think I used, and I was told by that authority that he received a warning as to his future behaviour.

At the end of their notice period, Ken's final nasty words to me, as he left the premises, were the same words as his old boss at North used at KR on our first day "You'll be finished in weeks."

Hand on heart, the next 3 years would be tough, but he was definitely wrong!

As we thought back to RPs Problems in 1991, when we probably should have shut up shop, under these new circumstances, Karen and I did wonder if that would that be the right thing to do for KR.

Firstly, we realised that would mean abject surrender before a battle, let alone a war, and second, why would we assume that we would lose our customer base? Ours was a great business which always looked after customers, indeed, in many cases, giving them the credit in their early days which enabled their businesses not only to be set up but also to survive and thrive. Surely there would be an element of loyalty.

Our other three members of staff swore on the Bible that they knew nothing whatsoever about this coup. How did we know if they were telling the truth? They all needed their jobs and Ken and James certainly couldn't take them on as a start-up company, even though this had been a long time in the making.

Again, we had no option but to carry on as we were, we also needed staff to run the business, and we decided that the only way that we could survive was to press on with what we had and forget that the other two existed. Unfortunately, when I thought about closing the business it always seemed to be all about winding it up, I did not give a thought the genuine alternative of selling it on. If I had sold to a strong competitor, this undoubtedly would have put all kinds of pressure on the new opposition.

Over the following year, we were very pleased that our sales held up well but both our company and Ken's were in the uncomfortable position of trying to undercut each other and the customers knew that they were in a position of strength. In a comparison between the two wholesalers, our weakness was the cost of our overheads. Now, with two warehouses, rent and rates were a massive burden, plus insurances, five vans and all the other fixed costs. Ken had a small starter unit, low rent and business rates exemption for a year. Business was tough.

Towards the end of the year cash flow became a major, major problem. Now, the way that we had planned to raise capital to fund our expansion had to be adapted to raise funds simply to keep our company afloat, and some unpleasant facts had to be faced.

With the passing of my mother, the house at Churchfield had to be used as an asset not as an investment. We were forced to sell it and put the cash into the running of KR. We still had £7,000 to £8,000 a month in wages and HMRC costs and that's without the rent and rates, while customer payments also could not be relied on as they played fast and loose with both companies. We had always been with HSBC but now Lloyds Bank came calling, very strongly pushing their invoice financing solution for business finance, as opposed to overdraft and loan facilities. One of the last interactions between KR and HSBC was another pleasant story with a good ending.

It really was quite unbelievable, but true, that our account manager at HSBC, at that time, was another of my former pupils at St Marks, Mrs Bernie Young, one of a large family of sisters that I used to teach at the school, all terrific girls. Bernie phoned and asked me if it would be possible for us to take on her 15-year-old son, unpaid, for Saturday morning work, so that he could get some experience in a work environment. He wanted to become an electrician and had applied to Harlow College to join the electrician's course and she felt that working at an electrical wholesaler would enable him to familiarise himself with every day electrical products. His name was Matt Young and he had the massive advantage of coming from a family of Spurs supporters, and so there was no question of us refusing him the job.

We were really pleased when he came to work with us, we did pay him because he was a smashing lad with a good attitude and he carried on working with us throughout the school holidays, and on his day release from college, after his application was successful. Matt was an asset to KR when he was with us, was successful at Harlow College, passed his electrical training course, and has since moved on into lighting design, earning a job for a well-known electrical company. We have continued to keep in touch with Matt, and Karen and I went to his 21st birthday party. I even managed to get him two fantastic seats at Spurs' Champions League Final in Madrid which, of course, we lost to Liverpool.

We made the decision to go with Lloyds and, never having done invoice financing before, it certainly wasn't all that it was cracked up to be. We also found it very difficult to communicate with Lloyds because, believe it or not, our account manager had been released by the bank to serve as a "Games Maker" at the 2012 London Olympics and we didn't see or hear from him for months and months!

At this time, by chance, I discovered that I had an £88,000 pension pot and I really didn't know where it came from. Misguidedly propelled by the belief that we could get the company right back on a very profitable trajectory, and the stupidity of the surety that everybody in the company shared the same desire to succeed, I moved that pension into a KR electrical pension scheme. We seemed to be a very strong bait for banks and devious financial advisors, both only interested in fleecing people and not investing in them and were totally blind to the fact that that we were actually being attacked by piranhas.

This time we were "guided "by a firm of financial advisors called Clifton, who proceeded to earn more than £20,000 from my pension just to set up the new one with a borrow back facility. We were given the absolute guarantee that this pension would be fully protected in law to become the priority creditor should any financial difficulties be experienced by the company in the future.

CHAPTER 57

LOOKING FLASH

In 2012, Mr O'Shea, the wonderful headmaster of St Marks and the man who hired me way back in 1971 with those amazing words "See you Monday", had sadly passed away at his home in Abergavenny. Shortly before that, my friend and ex-colleague, Kelvin Evans, the former PE teacher at St Marks who turned property developer in Spain, had also died very suddenly. He had been a couple of years younger than me. St Marks was holding a large memorial service for Mr O'Shea and added in Kelvin to the memoriam. This was an event that I desperately wanted to attend, it was a service that meant a lot, and held a special significance for me. Yet, attendance was by a special invitation only and I knew, very well, that there were still factions at the school to whom I was persona non grata.

I felt immense pride when I received an invitation from Mr O'Shea's children, signed by Stella, the very same young girl who sat in my first class at St Marks. She insisted that I should attend the service as their special guest. The receipt of that letter is a moment that I will treasure forever.

The memorial service for the two men was very moving and done extremely well. This was my second invited visit to St Marks as a "banned individual" and it was of great importance me that the O'Shea family wanted me there and also realised that I needed to be there for them and their father.

.oOo.

Patrick Simmons was supposed to be paying me my £300 a month from the debt that he owed me from when we terminated RP. During The first few months of the arrangement, he had stuck to the agreement but, after a few months the payments dropped off and I would only receive a payment now and again and only if I chased it very hard. Stupidly I let things ride and allowed Patrick to string me along, believing that things would sort themselves out. At this point I decided that it was time to take on Patrick Simmons full throttle, and really put the pressure on him to pay his debt to me.

After numerous phone calls between us, when he continually promised to pay but did nothing, I informed him that I would be taking him to court. This, of course, was water off a duck's back to Mr Simmons as his likely thought was that I wouldn't win and, if I did, that he still wouldn't pay.

My friend from racing, John Lloyd, had always sung the praises of his solicitor, apparently a dab hand at getting people off driving convictions and avoiding CCJ's, as well as winning them. It seemed as if he would be the man for the job.

I had a massive dossier of evidence and the agreement signed by Patrick Simmons, but the essence of the case depended on those three separate sheets of paper, intrinsically linked, with the last page, unequivocally signed, dated and witnessed, able to land the killer blow. I was absolutely certain that I had Patrick bang to rights.

At a meeting with the solicitor, I went through my evidence with him line by line, particularly underscoring the importance of the three separate sheets of paper and pointedly drawing his attention to the final page, which had the insurance of being signed by Patrick Simmons and witnessed by the bank and the accountant. We got a court date at Colchester Crown Court but it was nine months away, so another nine months without payment and a £2,000 bill to pay to the solicitor, basically for me telling him what to do. Anyway, as a sort of celebration for getting this far in the Patrick Simmons saga, Karen and I treated ourselves to a Sunday lunch at the Chef & Brewer, down the road from our house, using Tesco vouchers to pay as usual. At that time, I still carried with me cash, something that hasn't been the case for quite a few years now, and I did this mainly for the reason that I would always have funds to bet with if the right opportunity presented itself, that culture being so ingrained into my soul. I was always extremely aware of which horses were running and where, but our own mega participation in horseracing had scaled down somewhat and we only had Penbryn active then.

At that time, it was still quite unusual for flat-racing to take place on a Sunday but, on this particular day, Newmarket was racing and I knew that Nick had a couple of runners and that he fancied both of them. Karen, long used to my idiosyncratic behaviour, accepted the fact that I would probably want to back them and to pop into the betting shop on the way to the pub. I did exactly that and placed £100 win double on the two horses. Surprisingly for me, both the horses' names escape me, but I do know the prices, one was 10/1 and the other 8/1. We continued on to The Coach and Horses to enjoy lunch, courtesy of our Tesco vouchers, not giving a thought to the racing. It was only when we emerged from our meal at about 3.30pm, that, as we came out of the pub, I remembered the bet and looked at my phone to see the results.

It was another one of those days, both horses had come in and we had £9,900 to collect from Ladbrokes in Bishops Stortford Town Centre. We were probably a bit over excited with this win and, for some reason, with that cash burning a hole in our pockets we decided to go up the road and look around the BMW garage where I had bought the Z3 all those years previously. We had shrunk from the magnificence of owning 5 cars a few years ago to having the Nissan L 3HEO and the van I used for work, all the other number plates being on retention by now. It truly was fate because, as we arrived at Sewell's garage, they were giving a basic clean to a BMW M3 convertible, finished in a customised pearl paint job, a colour that had a different hue from each direction that you looked at it. This car had been used in a part exchange for a new BMW only an hour before. Logic and common sense disappeared from our thought processes and, for a change, it was the two of us who decided to spend the money on the car. After all, we always seemed to put everything into the company and, this time, we didn't really have time, or bother to have time, to think. There and then we did the deal with the garage, spending exactly what we won on the car, we were happy and so were they, as they moved that vehicle within 2 hours, so it was a good result all round. ROS 55 came out of retirement and we looked flash again for a little while, and it certainly raised two fingers to everybody who thought we were finished.

CHAPTER 58

PAPER CUTS

By the time the court case against Patrick Simmons came up in Colchester Crown Court, the ensuing nine months used up more than £60,000 in wages, £15,000 in VAT and revenue payments, and £30,000 in rent and business rates and, together with £2,000 fees for my solicitor. In total it was £107,000. It just shows you what sorts of sums of money we were having to find.

My great friend and football compatriot, John Williams, not only bought my season ticket at Spurs for the next two years but also lent us money to help us get through, he was a loyal friend and customer who believed strongly in the company. Reality meant that we could not keep the M3, it had to be sold and the money went into KR as per usual. Karen's loan account in the company now stood at £411,000.

Karen was a rich woman on paper and it was all real money that had gone into that loan account. House, warehouse, car and flat sales, there was nothing in there that had been raised or secured from third parties, just real hard-earned cash.

When we were at Colchester Crown Court awaiting the case, Patrick Simmons, who I hadn't seen in person for at least five years was sitting opposite me and looked extremely concerned and tense. My solicitor had taken on a jobbing barrister for me and I only met him when he arrived at the court. We adjourned to a small side office in order to discuss the case and, it struck me again, how ridiculous it was that barristers don't seem to look at any paperwork until they arrive at the court, which is really annoying and upsetting for any client I believe.

The first words out of this man's mouth were, "Patrick Simmons has hired a star barrister, he's on about £600 an hour and, looking at our case I don't think we have much of a chance."

I am afraid that I could not contain my anger and annoyance, and I think my attitude took my barrister completely out of his comfort zone.

"Show me your paperwork," I demanded. "This case is watertight, absolutely rock solid."

He opened his file and we sifted through his evidence together, along with the guidance supplied by my learned solicitor. It became immediately obvious that the three most important sheets of paper, the key piece of evidence, were missing from his instructions. Either my solicitor had not properly examined all the paperwork that, meticulously, I had gone through with him, or he had discarded it. Whichever it was, this certainly proved to me that he was not worth his fee and diminished my faith in our legal system. Sadly, now I really do believe that the majority of the solicitors do not give a damn about their clients and just want their money and an easy life. The only solicitor I will exempt from this blanket criticism is the one that I got on my trip to Chancery Lane in 1991 but then again, he was a classicist like me.

It certainly wasn't a case of luck that ensured that I had the full file of documents, copies of which I had submitted to my solicitor, with me. I extracted from it the three key pieces of my evidence, completely inter linked, crystal clear and all signed and dated by Patrick Simmons in the presence of witnesses. As soon as he read and confirmed these documents, my barrister's opinion and attitude changed completely.

He knew, as did I, that this evidence was, without doubt, the smoking gun which I always knew it would be, but the immediate problem was that all documents, in all court cases, have to be exchanged between the two parties' solicitors before the trial, and my solicitor had not submitted this evidence to Patrick Simmons' representatives.

Straightaway my barrister had to let the other barrister have sight of the new evidence, and this extremely expensive man was a very unhappy bunny indeed. He informed my barrister that, if we presented this new evidence to the judge, he would seek an adjournment to the case because proper procedure had not been followed, but I was adamant that we would, indeed, present the evidence anyway and instructed my barrister to do so.

The two groups of adversaries sat on opposite sides of the courtroom, as my barrister addressed the judge, "If it pleases your honour, we would like to present three new pages of evidence which will totally clarify to the court what should be the outcome of this case."

"I object," was the violent interjection by the seething opposition barrister.

"I will read the pages," said the judge.

Carefully having done so, and after what seemed an interminable pause for thought, the judge asked Mr Simmons to stand and addressed him with these words.

"Is this your signature on this paperwork?"

"Yes, your honour."

The response from the judge was forthright as he addressed his remarks to both Mr Simmons and his top rated, highly paid barrister.

"You may well decide to seek an adjournment but, if you return to court in the future, you will have no chance of winning this case. The matter is effectively over, and I find for the plaintiff."

We had won! It was a total vindication for me, a lovely scalp for my barrister, and tail between the legs time for the other one. I knew in my heart of hearts that I would win, indeed, could not lose, this case and it was only right that I did just that. However, winning the case and being awarded the money doesn't in reality actually get you anything or, in fact, guarantee that you will ever actually receive anything - which must be a terrible weakness in the system.

The award was £76,000 plus costs, but Patrick Simmons seemingly ignored the verdict and I would have to seek other means to extract the money from him. I needed to think, yet again, very carefully about a strategy that would be successful in gaining the ultimate victory.

CHAPTER 59

SELLING UP

2014 stacked out with problem after problem, trade was slowing down and it was almost a repeat of the circumstances that surrounded of the 2008 crash as customers seemed to have lots of jobs cancelled or lost contracts and we were faced with an unprecedented number of returns of goods. With invoice financing only designed to advance you money against net invoicing, the credits we had to raise were causing us major headaches in being able to access money. The allowance was there in the bank, but the lack of net value in our sales meant that we could not get enough of it. At that point in time, we were in a position that most firms would probably love to be in, we had no purchase account in excess of 60 days, we owed no Inland Revenue and our next VAT return would, without doubt, produce a credit to us. Rent was up-to-date but was over £12,000 a quarter for the two warehouses and it would be due on the 31st March. I know pressure well, but this was pressure squared and both myself and Karen were now fast reaching the end of our tethers, with very few corners left to explore. Trying to think ahead, I contacted CBRE, our landlords, and informed them that it was highly likely that I would be seven days late in paying our rent. We had been their tenants for seven years, leased two big warehouses and had never caused them a single problem, but it was on 1st April this year that a new Government policy, restricting the possible actions that could be taken against business tenants by landlords, was about to come into force. It was being widely reported in the media that landlords were very spooked at the prospect of tenants, legally, being able to get as much as an extra month's grace on their rent, but it still came as a bolt from the blue when, sent by the understanding and wonderful landlord CBRE, a very unpleasant bailiff arrived at our office to collect our rent. It was 31st March 2014.

There had been no communication from CBRE in response to my initial contact, then no warning, no announcement, just a nasty heavy turning up to put the fear of God into everybody. I have to be frank, the complete shock of this visit, knowing instantly that the consequences would be severe, shook me to my very core. It was such a traumatic event even for someone like me, who had experienced more than my share of troublesome incidents, that I was totally unprepared for my delayed reaction to the situation. We could not raise the entire £12,000 due rent, but we scrabbled around and collected every penny we had from personal and company accounts, cleaning them out entirely and were allowed to pay off half the rent, gaining a seven-day extension before we had to pay the remainder. Where do you go from there, when you have no resources left of any kind and you have drained every well to the dregs.

So far I had learnt to handle any severe stress that came my way, but this was beyond me. I was not even close.

The Easter holiday was coming on the 20th April followed by a couple of bank holidays in May. We would have two weeks only to find some invoicing, whose financing would probably only pay for the outstanding rent. In summary, it would be another six weeks before our invoicing could get back to normal and the cash flow revived. I could see there was no way out, no light, just a fast-narrowing tunnel. The fast-moving events had taken a heavy toll on my mental wellbeing and one sudden last straw had mercilessly broken the camel's back. This last savage blow had affected my powers of thought so much that I had been tipped over the edge of sanity and could visualise no possible exit from this black tunnel of total despair. Everything was gone, my self-respect, my inner strength, all my hopes and dreams. The stark realisation that my whole life had been for nothing was the overriding thought that drove me to the conclusion that everything needed to end. My brain had short-circuited and my thoughts and actions were dictated by instinct alone. I had completely by-passed the symptoms of depression and my mind was a numb, non-functioning entity.

I got into the van and started to drive, where to, I had no clue, with what purpose I didn't know. Just drive, to what end-point? As I approached the M11 something inside me clicked and, fortunately, that inner voice told me to telephone my doctor, Doctor Trask, the male half of our husband-and-wife practice. My phone call went through to his wife, the other Dr Trask, and it was quite incredible how quickly she assessed and comprehended my situation, which was a very dangerous one.

It was amazing how she put me to ease just by talking to me as I drove and I had no difficulty in telling her how I felt informing her that, in my heart, I could find absolutely no reason for trying to carry on. I am, at this moment, very emotional and tearful, as I write about and recall this day. Dr

Trask persuaded me to turn left, not right, onto the motorway and head straight for the surgery in Bishops Stortford where, she promised, she would be waiting to receive me immediately I arrived. She was good to her word and, straightaway, took me into her consulting room where she spent a good hour talking to me. The help that she gave me on that day was remarkable, and I will be forever grateful for her compassion on that morning. As a result, I was able to come out of that surgery a different person from the one that went in.

Obviously, I was still fragile but very confident now that I could carry on and get to the end game. There was, however, one terrible downside to all this - within a few short months, every life insurance policy that I held was declared null and void because now, my medical records were smitten with those damning words "suicidal thoughts". Where the fault lies for this I really don't know, although I do think it is a vitally important lesson for doctors to learn when dealing with issues of mental health. What confidence and encouragement can that give someone in desperate need of help, to ask for that help from the doctor whose advice results in the records being denigrated and changed to a highly negative position? None whatsoever.

Uncannily, finding a new inner strength and clarity of purpose, I came out of the doctors, got in the van and called my accountant. He saw the way forward as going into administration, but said that we would need an administrator, insolvency practitioner, who would be sympathetic to us and that he would be able find someone who fitted that bill. He instructed us to keep things as tight and confidential as possible, until he had managed to sort out arrangements and then added, "Have you thought of getting a buyer for the company?" In hindsight, I would have loved to hear that advice so many times before.

To purchase our stock, KR mostly dealt with suppliers direct and not with other wholesalers, although we did have accounts with the big boys like Senate and Medlocks. Medlock Electrical Distributors are the biggest privately owned wholesaler in the country and we had dealt with them for a number of years. I was aware that the owner not only was a very clever man, but also a very nice gentleman, who always had an ear very close to the ground. His name was Alan Moore.

As soon as I got through to Alan on the telephone, his instant response was, "Are you looking to sell the business?"

My answer was in the affirmative and, after that the speed of events was breath-taking. Meetings were set up between Alan Moore, his top team of about four guys, our accountants, plus me and Karen. Everything was gone through thoroughly. On offer we had a great amount of stock, had a healthy customer base and good existing premises that could be scaled down to save costs. The negatives were the amount of debt, profitability and overall viability. Far and away the largest creditor on the books was Karen, with a loan account standing at £411,000. If Medlocks should decide to purchase KR, the price paid was going to get nowhere near us getting all that money back but, at least, the deal guaranteed that most of the debts would be paid and Karen would be walking away with a small proportion of what she was owed.

Another, as we thought "plus", arising from the deal was that all five of the existing staff, including me and Karen would be kept on. We still had the honourable attitude of looking after our other three employees, and how ridiculously misguided and stupid that would look over the next few months. The receiver, selected by our accountant, was amenable to all the arrangements that were made, everything was drawn up and the deal was ready to be rubberstamped, to be sorted by just after the May bank holiday.

CHAPTER 60

THAT FIRST DAY

Somehow, Lloyds Bank got wind of what was happening and stung KR with a £350,000 charge, simply for closing our account. This £350,000, together with the money we owed to Lloyds from the invoice financing agreement, ensured that they became the biggest creditor, overtaking the amount owed to Karen and, as such, they had the power to appoint their own receiver, hostile no doubt, and thereby cancelling all previous negotiations. The original deal, brokered by our receiver, covered all their losses so they really had nothing to gain by it.

All five of the staff at KR were plunged back into limbo and we became virtually imprisoned in our warehouses, while Lloyd's new receiver and his team came into the property to analyse and check everything in KR. When we went home after that first day of the Lloyds receivers coming into our company, Karen and I sat on the tree seat encircling the willow at the bottom of the garden trying to make sense of our seemingly hopeless and rapidly worsening situation. We had no business, a hefty mortgage that would be beyond us, a house that we would probably have to forfeit and both of us would have no job. I was 67 and Karen was 61. We went to the citizens advice office and contacted the Department of Work and Pensions but surprise, surprise, we were ineligible for any help of any kind. Get a privately rented room was a suggestion, with no pets of course and we would have to lose our lovely cats Megan and Luca. I had my pension to live on and that was it between us.

We had nothing, but somehow, we did have fight still in us and we had no option but to roll up our sleeves, pick ourselves up, get on with it and above all, not give up.

It would not have been possible for the Ross who turned up at the doctors that short time ago to have dealt with all this, but this was a new Ross filled with hatred and spite and the cool approach of a gunslinger, from the old west.

As for Lloyds, their appointed receivers came to the remarkable conclusion that the business of KR was, indeed, not viable and needed to be sold. They had a secret customer waiting in the wings but they would not let us know who it was. However, we knew it was Medlocks and hoped upon hope that the deal would go through, no matter whether it was favourable or not, just to bring things to an end, give us our sanity back and perhaps even a job. Fortunately, the buyer did turn out to be Medlocks and they bought us for a tenth of the price they were willing to pay only three weeks before and, Lloyds Bank, so often in the headlines these days for all the wrong reasons, had achieved the stunning success of making sure that no one, including themselves, got anything after the receivers had taken their fees.

The receivers even kept my pension money, which I had been guaranteed would not be possible or legal to confiscate. The complete and utter vitriolic hatred of the banking system and all the bankers in it is, forever, ingrained in my persona. The Banker's Motto should read "Greed, indifference and destruction".

Medlocks, in the person of Alan Moore and his three sons, were absolutely tremendous to us. They were true to their original undertakings and kept me on as the manager of the new Harlow branch, with the three staff keeping their jobs, while Karen would go to head office at Waltham Cross to work in administration. We could breathe again, my salary meant that we could pay the mortgage and our home and cats were secure.

Lloyds, however, were not finished with us and they issued a summons against Karen demanding that the £350,000 fee that they had imposed on our company was paid immediately. As the only, and managing director, Karen was personally liable to the bank and they were being relentless and nasty in their pursuit. Tony Carter might be able to guide us on the route to salvation. We got in touch with this fountain of wisdom where debt was concerned, only to discover that he had recently moved on from the debt advisory business. His knowledge was still unmatchable, though, and now as a loyal friend, it was free as well. Only when we spoke to him, did we realise some of the positives that we had on our side, positives that we had either forgotten or not taken on board fully.

The company was solely in Karen's name, the house was in my name - Lloyds could not touch the house. The assets that Karen had been forced to sell over the years had included two houses, cashing in her premium bonds and ISA investments and even her car. The realisation of all these assets had led to her director's loan account with KR Electrical Wholesale standing at that £411,000, an investment entered into largely to secure the employment and income of her members of staff, staff who were to prove that they held her, and me, in little or no regard.

Tony Carter also told Karen that Lloyds would undoubtedly prosecute, but she was to wait until the day before the date allotted for that prosecution - by which time Lloyds would, hopefully, have spent a large sum of money on the case - and then file for bankruptcy. This they did, and that she did. By August 2014 Karen was bankrupt and the whole sorry saga of KR Electrical Wholesale was over and done with, we no longer had to move heaven and earth to look after and support staff members.

The one mega plus arising from being in complete and utter difficulty and despair is that you finally really discover who your real friends are. We could definitely count ours on our fingers. The greatest allies and loyalist friends that we had were the people that we had met and got to know through horseracing, they helped, encouraged and stood by us through thick and thin, and John Williams was a rock on which we could completely depend. This small, but wonderful, group of people will always be in our fondest thoughts and memories and we owe them a very great debt of gratitude.

CHAPTER 61

PAYBACK AND MOVING ON

I was now in exactly the right frame of mind to confront the Patrick Simmons issue once and for all. The court case had awarded me that amount of £76,000 plus £2,000 costs and now I was determined to prize it from Patrick's tightest of fists.

The costs of £2,000 I had already paid to my solicitor and he wouldn't be interested in helping me retrieve them and so, I decided to write that £2,000 off and concentrate on the main amount, to avoid complications. Patrick is married to Jessica's sister, Mary, and by now they had a grown-up son at University. I knew for certain that Patrick would have kept from Mary, all the financial dealings at RP and certainly the court case at Colchester, while their son would definitely have no clue that his father was, to say the least, not the most trustworthy of men. I knew that Mary's mother recently had sold her house and moved in with the couple so there definitely had been an influx of cash in the household and, to be brutally honest, I didn't care where that cash came from. I further was aware that Mary was a teacher and therefore that I could intercept her, on her own, as she arrived at her school.

The strategy was to tell Mary the story behind Patrick's indebtedness to me and also the result of the court case in Colchester that said debt had led to. My sister was kind enough to escort me on the trip, most importantly, to serve as a reliable witness, and the appearance of both of us at the school entrance completely stunned Mary, who was obviously completely confused as to the reason why we were there.

Mary is a deeply religious and moral person; this was a religious school and she was held in high regard by the local church and also had a position of standing within that church. Her high morals alone would, I thought, be an asset to me in this quest, and my sister listened intently as I went through the history of events with a completely perplexed Mary. I did feel extremely sorry to be putting her through all this, but I had to stick to my guns and complete my mission. I had to tell her that my intention was to publicise the chain of the events, a story which would illustrate to everyone, including their son, what had actually gone on. My sister and I had done a fair and honest job and we left, gladly still on good terms, taking with us a promise from Mary that she would deal with the matter without delay. Two weeks later, I got a call from Jessica, another lady I had not seen for some 18 years, telling me that she was on her way to call into my house with my cheque for £76,000. An hour later Jessica arrived, I accepted and signed for the cheque, a few pleasantries were exchanged with Karen, who Jessica had not previously met, and myself and, as she drove away, it suddenly dawned on me that our very rocky road had become an awful lot flatter.

My first action with this money was to repay the people that I owed. I repaid Val her £15,000, Avron, now discharged from her bankruptcy, her £10,000 and John Williams the money he lent us, including covering the season tickets he had paid for as well. The remaining sum was put towards Karen's and my next project. We had felt the misery and despair at the possibility of losing the house, and so we decided to forego everything superfluous and direct all our resources into realising the value of everything that we had left, so that we could get the house paid off. Our mortgage was due to run until I was 76, in 2023, and we needed this out of the way. We sold all the number plates, except G11 NSB and R10 SSO, still on sale, for good money, in addition we sold the 30,000+ records from my disco career, and even managed to extract £20,000 from Clifton for the loss of my pension. We spent the barest minimum on food and did nothing except save. By using every penny of my wages from Medlocks and my old age pension alongside this substantial pot of money, we were able to have the mortgage cleared by 2017, six years ahead of schedule, some magnificent achievement! We were nothing, if not exceptional fighters. We had trained ourselves to live on Karen's wages from Medlocks and we trampled adversity into the ground with great pride and satisfaction.

A couple of little twists did occur, over a two-week period, a few months after I was installed as manager of the new Harlow Branch of Medlocks. Medlock's purchasing policy often encompassed ordering supplies for the whole firm, 40+ branches, at once in order to get ultra-competitive prices from suppliers. The first one of these such purchases, that involved us, occurred when we received, as our part of a huge company acquisition, an order of 2000 LED lamps, worth about £7,500. These lamps are quite small items and the order was only two or three boxes of goods. When, literally a few days later, a customer came in to buy 20 such lamps and we couldn't find a single one anywhere, none of us could understand why. The lamps had disappeared, all 2000 of them, we searched the whole warehouse and they were nowhere to be found. The only possible conclusion was that they had been stolen.

Medlock's security systems were a different ball game to anything we had at KR. For a starter, any entry into the premises was timed and the person entering was also able to be identified by the alarm system. It turned out that a staff member was entering the unit in the very early hours of the mornings for emergencies, as he described them when questioned, although no one could understand what those emergencies were. There could be very little doubt that he was responsible for the loss of these lamps and, as Medlock's policy was not to get involved in court cases or anything unpleasant, it simply was suggested that this person should leave their employment with immediate effect. I had kept him employed for three years after the betrayal of 2011, and kept his job for him at Medlocks, it makes me wonder how many kicks in the teeth he had delivered to me over the years in our employment, notwithstanding the insult and total affront he showed to Medlocks.

A short time afterwards came an event that actually changed the direction of my life yet again. At the premises in Harlow, I was coming down the stairwell of the warehouse, which was shielded from the trade counter by a wall, when one of our long-term customers was just coming in.

As he entered, unable to see me, I heard him say to another long serving member of staff who we had treated extremely well over the years, "Is Ross around?"

In a totally dismissive manner this person replied "Ross is nothing anymore."

My self-esteem was completely destroyed in an instant. I cannot describe the utter devastation and humiliation I felt in that moment and a feeling of complete worthlessness came over me. We had been to hell and back, we were right on the cusp of rebuilding our lives and this was a stake into the middle of my heart.

I didn't reach the trade counter, but turned and went back upstairs where I picked up the phone and telephoned Alan Moore. I relayed to him what this staff member had said and added, "Alan, I desperately need a job, but I'd rather live on the street than live without my self-respect."

His reply, "Leave that job, go to Ware Branch and be a driver, same contract."

All that can be said to that, is what a fantastic and generous man! My motivation and willingness to work hard will never ever slacken after that, because it is the only way that I can express my total gratitude. I moved to Ware Branch in that instant, became the driver and have been happy there ever since. Not long after that, Karen found that the office environment at Waltham Cross did not suit her and Alan Moore noticed that was the case.

Showing even more generosity, Alan gave her three month's severance pay, allowed her to leave without notice and wished her good luck as she went on her way. The treatment and support that Karen and myself have received from Medlocks has been incredible throughout and we will always be humbly in their debt.

Finally, we are both on a long flat road, without bumps. Until I was furloughed on 24th March 2020, I was still getting up at 2.30am and delivering.

Karen is now classed as a key worker and plies her trade on the checkout at Tesco's in Bishop Stortford. Our main success after all this is that we are both extremely happy and have each other.

All three members of staff whose jobs we preserved at Medlocks were dispensed with, leaving me as the only surviving member of KR on the books. I do sometimes wonder just how much we were ripped off at KR but, in the end, it's not worth getting upset about it because we are absolutely fine now, it is pointless looking backwards and brilliant looking forward.

CHAPTER 62

TO RUSSIA WITH LOVE

Karen had always wanted to visit St Petersburg, and so when a 2 for 1 offer appeared, and we could afford it, we decided to go. So, we booked a cruise on the CMV ship Columbus for September, to travel round the Baltic states, ending up at St Petersburg in Russia.

Only a few days before departure, by coincidence, my annual OAP doctor's MOT was due and so I made an appointment and popped in for my check- up. Everything was fine, but Dr Trask told me that he was unhappy with some of the reports about Naproxen, the tablets I kept on standby for any attack of gout that might afflict me, because, apparently, they affected kidney function. I very rarely took any Naproxen tablets, perhaps once a year, at the first twinge of an attack, and then one tablet was enough to stop it.

He asked me to cast aside Naproxen and use, as a stand-by, a new prescription which would have no effect on the kidneys. It made no difference to me as I so rarely used the medication and so I dropped in at the pharmacy and picked up the new tablets ready for the cruise.

As usual for us, this cruise would not be plain sailing, so as to speak, because Storm Aileen was just starting to wreak havoc on the seas. As we neared Tilbury, our port of departure, Karen received a text from CMV informing us that boarding would be delayed for eight hours. Of course, all the passengers got this text and this created a chaotic situation at Tilbury because all the cars belonging to the incoming Columbus passengers were still filling the car park, and the arrivals for the next cruise had nowhere to stop.

Lakeside, and every other Retail Park near Tilbury, was crammed full with Columbus passengers trying to kill time. Then eight hours later everyone decided to make a dash back for the car park. As a result, it turned into a huge game of mechanical musical chairs.

We managed to park and booking in/boarding the ship turned out to be the easy part. After sorting the luggage in the cabin, the very first thing that passengers are required to do on board ship is to report to the lifeboat stations for a lifeboat drill. As we waited at our station for the drill, an announcement came over the tannoy telling us all that, because we would be 10 hours late setting sail and because of the sea conditions, the ship would have to omit its first port of call, Copenhagen, and we would therefore, be at sea for the first three days of the trip. Everybody was extremely unhappy at missing out on Copenhagen because it is such a beautiful city, but the disappointment was tempered by the information that Storm Aileen would be treating us more kindly than expected and, on this occasion, the swell would only reach a height of about 4 metres which, allegedly, was not too bad.

Whether it was the stress of all the shenanigans of the delay at the port, or the anxiety caused by the thought of the possible storm and bad sea conditions, I don't know, but for the first time in months, I did feel a slight twinge of gout in my foot. On that first morning at sea, I decided to nip the gout attack in the bud by taking one of my new tablets. By lunchtime, I was feeling a little bit queasy and my ankles had swollen up. I put this down to the heavy swell and probably being sea sick. That first night at sea was the occasion of the traditional formal dinner, a function where the passengers had a nice photo opportunity while shaking hands with the Captain.

Looking resplendent in my evening suit and bow tie, we joined the queue for the restaurant and the cameraman. Here it was that I said to Karen, "I really don't think that I'm going to make this."

I all but passed out and passengers nearby assisted Karen to get me into the lift which sped me down to the lower deck where the medical centre was situated. Within minutes I was on a drip. My blood pressure reading was 220/180, which probably meant that I should be dead. I had suffered an adverse reaction to the new tablet, I was totally disorientated, had a massive headache and badly swollen ankles, added to the blood pressure problem, I really thought I was on my way out. The doctor and nurses on board were brilliant, I could have been in a top hospital anywhere, let alone on a ship. After three hours on the drip, the best dressed drip person ever I suspect, I felt so much better and with severe hunger pangs as my motivation, and with a t-shirt now replacing my jacket and bow-tie, I actually managed to make it to the restaurant for the last dregs of the second sitting where I became the least well-dressed person at the Captain's Dinner that night.

In spite of the fact that I had to go to the medical deck each morning of the cruise to be assessed and have blood pressure checks, the incident didn't detract from our enjoyment of all the ports of call and, particularly, the wonderful destination of St Petersburg. I made continuous improvement throughout the cruise and, apart from the first few days of struggling with my ankles, we had a really cracking time. The wonders of St Petersburg, the museums, the palaces, the churches, and even the incredible metro stations, were completely unforgettable. The ship was top notch as well and, as is usual on cruises, there were lots of entertainment and participation activities.

One such activity was a creative writing class. This notification in the daily ship's bulletin for the first time ever, made me think about telling my story. I went along to see if I might have any smidgeon of writing ability. The class was being instructed on constructing a novel and we were all asked to invent a basic plot with a few characters. I decided to use my initial experiences of when I was a teacher, as my plot. When the course finished, after the final lecture, one of the lady students, who had written articles published in magazines, gave me her card and asked me to get in touch with her so that I could tell her any other stories about things that had happened to me. I was quite flattered by this but, unfortunately, I mislaid her card and all thoughts of writing went out of my mind. The cruise was over, back to my early morning deliveries.

CHAPTER 63

NORTHERN LIGHTS

Strangely, the excitement of the final few years of this saga is highlighted by medical dramas. The next year, 2018, we booked and went to Majorca for our week away. Having progressed to a position where our wages were our own to spend was an amazing feeling and a really satisfying accomplishment. After my experiences with gout tablets on board ship, I threw away the new medication that I had been prescribed and held onto the few Naproxen tablets that I had left in case of emergency. Whether they impaired kidney function or not, one Naproxen tablet always did the trick for me. Coincidentally, my annual medical MOT was due again, just before our trip to Majorca. Foolishly, it turned out, I mentioned to the doctor, who knew about my experiences on board the Columbus, of course, that I had been taking the odd Naproxen tablet but had now run out.

He flatly turned down my request to be prescribed even a few more and, instead, a brand-new remedy that had been hailed as the saviour to all gout sufferers, was my prescription. I picked them up from the pharmacy and Karen duly packed them in with the luggage. Possibly caused by travel or whether it is holiday stress caused by the travel sickness I have always had to endure, I don't know, but I had the same problem with a tinge of gout and repeated the mistake of taking one of the new tablets, this time as I went to bed on that first night in Majorca.

After I got up next day, it was 11 o'clock in the morning before I knew who and where I was. I had left my bed that morning, although completely unaware of doing so, apparently in a complete blank state, not knowing that I was on holiday, not knowing who I was and not knowing anybody. Karen thought something was not right at breakfast time and it must have been terrifying for her and she told me later that she was at a complete loss as to know what to do. By the time I had returned to normality, not only had she made enquiries about an early return home but had also booked an appointment with the doctor at home, which I could attend immediately we arrived at the surgery.

Then, at about 11 o'clock, like switching on a light, my memory was back, completely normal, nothing wrong, actually on a pedalo and swimming in the ocean. I found it incredibly difficult to believe what Karen was telling me had happened. I searched the internet to look for the symptoms and, after a lot of study, I concluded that I must have suffered from something that was called "transient global amnesia", a condition caused by a reaction to certain drugs.

We carried on perfectly normally with the holiday and enjoyed a very pleasant rest, bolstered by oodles of frozen yoghurt. When we landed at Stansted, I knew that I was facing an immediate doctor's appointment. It was a case of get off the plane and go to the doctors, knowing full well that I would be back in the Medlocks van, next morning, delivering very early in London. The husband-and-wife team at my doctors are both incredible people, knowledgeable, caring and expert at what they do and I have the utmost respect for them.

On this occasion, I met with the lady doctor as I had done those few years back when I had my "suicidal thoughts" incident. Now, her immediate diagnosis was that I had had a stroke and my immediate reaction was to vehemently disagree. She insisted that it was the case, that I must have had a stroke and, that being so, I would be unable to drive again until I was cleared to do so, with that restriction starting immediately. To say that I went ballistic would be a complete understatement and, very embarrassingly, I became extremely nasty, something for which I sincerely apologised later, and I affirmed absolutely that there was nothing wrong with me and then, wickedly, reminded her that, the last time that I had come and confided in her, the result was that I lost all my life insurance policies. This time I told her she was costing me my job.

Karen, who was in the consulting room with me, became extremely upset and was blaming herself. She told me, in no uncertain terms, to calm down and accept what the doctor was saying and then, whispered in my ear just to go to work, as usual, in the morning. I obeyed her instructions and left the consulting room on good terms with the doctor, leaving Karen there to have a word. When she emerged, Karen told me that the doctor had reciprocated to my genuine concerns by promising to book me in for a brain scan as soon as possible, so that the diagnosis could either be confirmed or proved wrong. Having done quite a few deliveries early in London next morning, just after 9am Karen phoned me to tell me that that

Dr Trask had arranged a brain scan for me at Stevenage hospital at 1pm that day. Naturally she would have to drive me to Stevenage in case we were seen and the early afternoon timeslot could not be a problem as I was allegedly resting at home.

I returned, immediately, from London and off we went to Stevenage Hospital, where I only had half an hour's wait before I was in a long metal tube having a brain scan. After that was completed, I had an interview with the nurse and she went through all the circumstances surrounding my loss of memory.

Two hours later Karen and I were summoned to the chief brain-consultant's office to talk through the results of the brain scan itself. The consultant's first words to me were, "You definitely have not had a stroke", which came as an absolute relief. He went on to agree with my internet diagnosis of "transient global amnesia" brought on by a reaction to the new drug, but the real "piece de resistance" came when he showed us both the actual image of my brain. His words again, "I have never seen such a pristine brain in all my life and, if you do not live until you are 100, I will be most surprised. "It couldn't get much better than that for me but, for Karen, who has to spend the rest of her life with me banging on about my pristine brain, it was a disaster.

Since then, we've had a pretty ordinary couple of years, managing to save up enough money for us to go on another trip of a lifetime to see the Northern Lights, this time on board the CMV ship Magellan. However, Storm Dennis was about to do its worst. It was February 18th, 2020, as we prepared to leave for Tilbury. Then we got a text from Cruise Maritime, CMV, telling us that our ship, the Magellan, had been delayed by high seas and that our departure had been put back by 24 hours. We just considered this to be one of the vagaries of cruising and had a nice day's rest at home before setting off next morning.

All aboard went very efficiently and all the passengers had reached their lifeboat stations ready for the lifeboat drill when the shipboard announcement came that, because of the 24 hour delay, although our first port of call would remain as Rotterdam, we would have to miss out the next two stops in order to maintain the timetable of the rest of the itinerary.

After Rotterdam, this would mean three consecutive days at sea, sailing in the North Sea where Storm Dennis had us at his mercy. Nobody on board was happy and the mood got worse as Dennis flexed his muscles. We couldn't believe it as the waves reached 9 metres high, as high as a house, and it was hilarious watching people trying to negotiate their way around the ship. It wasn't so funny when everyone's dinner hit the deck in the restaurant and diners were catapulted off their chairs amongst the wine bottles. A large proportion of the passengers were older people and it was quite disconcerting to see the paramedics tending to injured people all over the ship.

Our cabin was next to Ship's Reception and, when we returned there after our daredevil evening meal, we were stunned to see that the whole area was flooded. The mighty waves had breached two of the port side cabin windows, the cabins right opposite ours on the starboard side, and the water had travelled all the way down the port side corridor as well as flooding Reception. Luckily, only one of the cabins breached by the waves had been occupied, but the two people in that cabin were quite badly shocked and upset.

It was remarkable how quickly the whole incident was dealt with and, considering the length and the severity of Storm Dennis, it was great that we all lived through it as an adventure rather than a disaster. The two passengers whose cabin was wrecked were allocated a plush suite for the rest of the cruise, while we had to change cabins, only the same grade unfortunately, because of the water that got into our cabin. When we finally arrived at all our ports of call, the snow levels were at record depths everywhere and temperature dropped to as low as -34 degrees. Thank goodness Karen had used the half price Mountain Warehouse sale to get us the superb boots and brilliant outdoor gear to keep us snug and warm. Our excursions were all sensational. The husky ride was oh so memorable. The dogs were fantastic and so friendly to meet. The way our 8 dogs pulled our sled was indescribable, the speed, energy and joy of the whole adventure was simply bewildering.

We followed that with the James Bond-like experience of each driving a snowmobile over the frozen wastes. It was really surprising how much strength it took to control these vehicles and, even after about 40 minutes, both of us were exhausted. During the cruise, we even got a few glimpses of the Northern Lights, not brilliant ones, but good enough to say that we'd seen something.

CHAPTER 64

RIGHT TIME, WRITE PLACE

However, one significant result of this cruise was actually what I am doing now. On the Columbus cruise to St Petersburg, I had enjoyed the creative writing activity so on this trip to see the Northern Lights, I was interested when I heard about another creative writing class that was taking place.

I didn't go to enlist on this course but, half way through trip, a little while before the day's gathering had begun, I went to the area where it was held to see if any of the tutors were around. It turned out that this cruise's educators were from the Scottish publisher "The Wee Book Company" and, by chance, on the day I called into the group, I met the founder of that company, Susan Cohen. I explained to her that I thought that some of the events that I had experienced in my life might be quite entertaining when presented in the written word. When I informed Susan of what had happened on the Columbus, two years previously, she asked for an example of such a tale and I mentioned my record number of credit cards, 89.

This seemed to generate some interest and her words to me were, "The only person who can write your story is you."

She then, kindly, offered me the following advice that when I got home from the cruise, I should get into the habit of writing for, perhaps, an hour a day and then, when I had compiled about 100 pages of happenings, I should send them to her and it might be possible to get someone to have a look at them, perhaps with a chance of a story being published, but she stressed again "The only person who can write your story is you."

When I returned from the cruise on the 4th March, the Covid 19 crisis was unfolding. I, of course, was back delivering at 2.30am the following morning and one of my jobs, on this first day back, was a delivery to a very big site at Canary Wharf. There were loads of lorries in front of me in the queue to get on site and my waiting time was going to be an hour at least. As a top-notch delivery driver, I always have paper and pen with me and, fatefully, I decided that I would use that time to do some writing.

I made a start by listing the years from 1947, when I was born, to 1960 and then filled in, opposite those years, notes of things that I remembered happening during those periods. I repeated this each day, whenever I had to wait around to make a delivery. The list of years expanded until the 1990s and the writing, or initial preparations, became a routine, as Susan had, sort of, suggested it might.

Things were going very well, the driving was as straightforward as usual, but people were becoming extremely worried about the Coronavirus. Then, out of the blue, when I had finished my deliveries and returned to the Medlocks branch in Ware, the manager, Andy Brown, called me into the office for a chat. It was 24th March, another day of reckoning. Medlocks had decided to implement Government guidelines and lay off any employee over 70 years of age. As a 72year-old I was, sadly, not exempt but, because of sick pay and holiday pay, I would be entitled to 3 full week's pay before moving on to statutory sick pay for the remainder of my enforced 12 weeks off. My Covid19 resolution was to write my book.

In spite of quite a few lows and struggles, I really believe that I have been very lucky. The latest stroke came on Wednesday 4th April with news from Andy Brown that Medlocks had decided to furlough me for the duration of my time off. 80% pay for book writing time, not at all bad. It took me exactly 4 weeks to write the book in long hand and, at that time, it comprised about 105,000 words. It then took me two weeks, because I wouldn't know where to start as a copy typist, to read it onto my phone and then E-mail the "Notes" to my computer. It then took me two more weeks to put the punctuation back into the text and edit the story, you wouldn't believe the hilarious gobbledygook that appeared on my computer via my dictation. The book is now complete and the entire exercise has taken 58 days to complete. Published or not, I am delighted that I've done it. Karen is about to print it off right now and my brain will allow me to sleep at night again.

On the 24 October, Medlocks ended my furlough period and continued my employment, probably making me one of the oldest people not to be made redundant during these terrible times. Absolutely great!

I am coming up to 73 years old and Karen is coming up to 68. We have been together for over 20 incredible years and poor Karen has had the rough end of a very long stick but, do you know, I honestly think that neither of us would change a thing that we have done or what has befallen us because life is actually what makes you the person you are. After all I ended up with the real jewel in the crown - Karen!

I hope that you have found this book to be readable and have managed to extract some enjoyment from it, as you followed the highs and lows of this, as I think anyway, very unordinary life.

.oOo.

Two significant events have happened since the completion of my story on 20th May. On the 24th October, firstly, Medlocks ended my furlough period and continued my employment, probably making me one of the oldest people not to be made redundant during these terrible times. Absolutely great!

Then, very sadly, on 6 November, my sister Avron passed away after a very difficult final few months, leaving her son Fraser and husband of 60 years, Alan, completely devastated. I am finding it difficult to deal with the loss of Avron, especially with the realisation that I am now the only surviving member of our family.

Furlough allowed me to explore my writing credentials up to the end of May and then, until late October, I practised being retired, doing lots of jobs round the house and making the most of our fantastic summer in the garden. I actually achieved my best tan since my days on the beaches of Atlantic City in the 70s. However, when I got the call from Medlocks asking me if I wanted to return to work, joy just seemed to course through my veins. Retirement is definitely not for me and it is clear that work and purpose is what makes me tick.

The excruciating pain of Avron's death only two weeks later was a hammer blow to us all and it was utterly surreal when we attended her funeral on 25th November, the day before her 79th birthday, bearing in mind her trepidation about the 26th of any month, remember my father was born, married and died on the 9th, Avron had be born and married on the 26th. I am so pleased that she managed to read my book before she died, a matter of great comfort to me.

I hope that there are a few messages and lessons that can be taken from all that has happened to me. The key message, I think, is one of optimism. Never lose hope. Always believe that something good will happen round the corner. When I studied the Roman poet Lucretius at university, who would believe the subconscious effect his work would have on me.

Lucretius was a supporter of the teachings of the Greek philosopher Epicurus, who advocated a way of life called Epicureanism. This philosophy can be summed up by the phrase "live for today" and I think that it is fair to say that my life has followed that path – jump in with both feet, give it 100% and reap the rewards or pay the price.

Certainly, it is impossible to avoid mistakes, but my advice is to try and recognise those mistakes early and take action sooner rather than later, something which I have failed to do on all too many occasions. Wondering about how things might have turned out is just about ok, but wishing that they had, is a mistake. Life is all about moving forward, fantasy can lead you down the dark path of despair. Life is now!

I have been led up and down the garden path in all aspects of my life, be it teaching, romance, horses or business, but I have always come out the other end with optimism and the belief that everything will turn out right. I have had my heart broken once and severely damaged on several other occasions. Unwittingly, and somewhat surprisingly to me, I appear to have damaged a few hearts myself. Each and every one of these events has had a profound effect on both me and my life. Each caused a change of direction, attitude and outlook, giving me the impetus to do things that I would never have dreamed of taking on. Without doubt the sadness stays in the back of your mind forever but, at the same time, you know that you have enjoyed new moments of great joy and happiness.

None of us can turn back the clock so please take serious time to consider any devastating change in a relationship - regret is not an emotion to be cherished. Epicurus and his advocate, Lucretius, definitely got it right – live for the day and make every moment count.

Or, in the iconic phrase of my sister, Avron, "Life is not a rehearsal".

Printed in Great Britain
by Amazon